The Caballeros of
Ruby, Texas

by

Cynthia Leal Massey

Panther Creek Press

Spring, Texas

Published by Panther Creek Press
SAN 253-8520
116 Tree Crest
P.O. Box 130233
Panther Creek Station
Spring, TX 77393-0233

Cover photograph supplied by the Author
Author's photograph by Mike Peters
Cover design by Pamela Copus
Sonic Media, Inc., Plano, TX

Manufactured in the United States of America
Printed and bound by Data Duplicators, Inc.,
Houston, TX

The author wishes to acknowledge the following copyright holders for permission to quote
from song lyrics:

"You Belong to My Heart" by Agustín Lara & Ray Gilbert
Published by Peer International Corporation & Ipanema Music Corp.

Solamente Una Vez by Agustín Lara
Copyright © 1941 by Promotora Hispano Americana de Musica, S.A.
Administered by Peer International Corporation
Copyright Renewed
Used by Permission
All Rights Reserved

1 2 3 4 5 6 7 8 9

Library of Congress Cataloguing in Publication Data

Massey, Cynthia Leal

    Caballeros of ruby, texas, the

I. Title   II. Fiction   III. Mexican-American Studies

ISBN 0-9718361-1-6

Acknowledgments

I'd like to thank the following for their gracious support: Louis Draper, retired Edinburg farmer, shared a lifetime of knowledge concerning farming life in the Rio Grande Valley during the forties and fifties. Israel "Buddy" Silva, Jr., Chief of Juvenile Probation for Hidalgo County, and Dionicio Villarreal, Laura Villarreal, and Tommy Villarreal of Nicho's Produce in Edinburg, connected me with several key individuals, including Shan Rankin, director of Hidalgo Co. Historical Museum, and David Mycue, Curator of Archives & Collections; J. D. Salinas, III, Hidalgo Co. Clerk, and his assistants; Ninfa Ochoa and Rene Sandoval, Hidalgo Co. Tax Accessor Collector's Office; Robert Vargas, Port Director, Immigration; Sylvia Salazar, B & P Bridge Co., Progreso International Bridge; Dario Garcia, retired Justice of the Peace, Hidalgo County.

Heartfelt thanks to Angie López, Supervising Librarian at the Soledad Community Library in Monterey County, California, for setting up interviews and answering myriad questions about life in Soledad during the fifties. Angie is an angel, God's resounding yes to the question, "Should I be writing this story?" Thanks also to Roger and Connie Quintanilla, and Aurora Vallejo Alvarado of Soledad for spending an extraordinary afternoon with me sharing their life stories, and to John Fratis of the California Correctional Peace Officers Association for responding to my questions concerning prison life in the fifties.

Thanks also to Sister Jane Coles, Congregation of Divine Providence, San Antonio; Dr. John Anema; and Major Steve Cina, USAF Regional Forensic Pathologist for the Military for answers to a few vital questions.

Heartfelt thanks to my dear friend, Donna Navarro, who accompanied me on my research trip to California, and who read several drafts providing thoughtful, perceptive criticism. Thanks to Wayne Ude, Writer's Digest School, for his insightful criticism of my preliminary outline and first fifty pages. His encouragement and comments were invaluable.

Special thanks to my family and friends for their continued support, particularly: Mirtala Villarreal of McAllen and Elida Silva of Edinburg for caring for my children and allowing me use of their homes while I did research in the Valley; my husband, David, and my children, Michael and Meghan; the Castillo, Leal, and Massey clans; my students and colleagues at San Antonio College; the Third Monday group, especially Paige Ramsey-Palmer, for reading and critiquing a preliminary draft.

Finally, I would like to thank publisher Guida Jackson for seeing merit in this manuscript and for being such an asset to Texas writers.

Cynthia Leal Massey
Helotes, Texas

*This novel is dedicated
to my mom, Irma,
and to my aunts,
Tala, Getty, Queenie, Mireya,
Cristela, and Mary*

Part I

Isabel
The Eldest Daughter

1948-1953

Chapter 1

When Father returned home early from his annual contracting trip to Mississippi that summer of 1948, I knew something was wrong. He had come home early before, sometimes even at the end of August if the cotton season was poor, a result of weather or pest infestation or competition from other crews. That summer, he returned home at the peak of cotton season, the beginning of July, a full three months before we expected him.

I was lounging on the front porch swing noisily fanning myself with my *True Confession* magazine, peeved at Terre's comment that I shouldn't be reading such trash, when I heard the squeal of tires. I saw a cloud of dust following Father's green Ford pickup as it rolled down the bumpy street toward our house.

"Really, Isa," my sister lectured, "if you must read someone's confession, read St. Augustine and edify your spirit." She lifted the college theology textbook from her lap pointing at the chapter on St. Augustine's *Confessions*.

I scowled at her, ignoring her ridiculous comment. "It's Papá," I said, setting my magazine down. I reached for my flats and slipped them on.

My sister, who was sitting on one of our two white Adirondack chairs, glanced at the street. "I wonder what he's doing here," she said, her face scrunched in a mixture of disdain and curiosity. "I'll go get Mamá." She set the bulky textbook on the arm of her chair, then rose, smoothed out the skirt of her red polka dot dress, and promptly disappeared into the house.

As the screen door slammed, Father pulled into our earthen driveway, the ground packed smooth under the tires, a knoll of grass swiping up the middle of the drive. I rearranged my sundress straps and rushed down the porch steps to greet him just as the five o'clock train whistle sounded at the Vanburg Packing Shed. The rumble of iron against iron began to grow until I could feel the earth tremble. We lived on the north side of the Southern Pacific railroad tracks, the Mexican side of Ruby, a small town in the lower Río Grande Valley of Texas, and though the clamor of trains was as familiar to me as my mother's voice, that day I felt as if it were heralding a warning.

"Papacito!" I cried as he opened the door and lumbered out of the truck, his boots bearing down on the sparse grass next to the driveway. Father was half an inch shy of six feet tall, gray at the temples, with short, dark hair combed away from his face. He wore a white, short-sleeved shirt and khaki pants with an expensive leather belt that stretched around a large expanse of stomach. The extra weight he had gained through the years did not detract from his appearance, but instead contributed to his formidable presence. He grasped me in his arms, and I hugged him, breathing in the musky cigarette odor that lingered on his clothes, mingled with the pungent aroma of jasmine that grew alongside the house by my bedroom window.

He pulled away from me, putting his hands on my shoulders. His thick eyebrows arched over expressive chocolate eyes narrowed in appraisal, "Isa, you are a sight for sore eyes, *hija*."

I smiled, gratified by his remark, but I also wondered why he seemed so wistful. Otherwise, he hadn't changed much since Christmas break when Terre and I had traveled home after our first semester at college.

The screen door slammed four times in progression as Raul, Eloise, Lupita, and Marta ran out of the house followed by Terre and Mother. Marta, in a pinafore, jumped up and down in front of father. "Papacito, what did you bring me?" She clapped her hands together, squealing with delight.

"Marta!" Raul admonished. "*Cállate*. Papa just got here. Greet him like a proper young lady."

I couldn't help smiling at my younger brother's stern expression. Raul was all of fourteen, but as the only son in a Mexican-American family of five girls, he wielded a considerable amount of power.

Marta gave Raul just a hint of a grimace, then turned to Father. "Welcome home, Papacito." She glanced up at him, her auburn curls framing an angelic six-year-old face.

Father's face brightened as he gazed at my youngest sister. He bent down and lifted her in the air. "Have you been good, *hija*?"

"Of course I have, Papacito." She giggled as she settled against him, her arms around his thick neck.

"She got into my watercolors and got red paint all over the back porch," said Eloise, her chin thrust out.

"She didn't mean to," said Lupita. "It was just an accident." Even then, at the age of nine and two years younger than Ellie, Lupita was the peacemaker in the family.

"That's enough!" Mother's dark eyes flashed. "Your father's tired from his long trip. He doesn't need to hear your complaints. Give him a proper greeting, then all of you go inside. Ellie, Lupita, finish helping Doña Cuca with dinner, and set a place for your father."

The girls groaned, but not loud enough for Mother to hear—she would have smacked their heads—then they each hugged Father, kissing him on the cheek before running back into the house. Raul offered his hand. Papá shook it for a moment, then pulled his son close to him in a bear hug. He then turned to Terre, who was standing next to me. "*Hija.*" He held out his arms. Terre gave him a dutiful peck on the cheek, then stepped back. Father's face clouded over and his eyes narrowed, but he remained silent. A year younger than me, my nineteen-year-old sister had a grudge against Father, something that had been going on for a number of years. It bothered me that she took things to heart that really had nothing to do with her, but that was Terre for you—always getting involved when things would have been better left alone.

Father glanced at Mother. She wore her thick auburn hair in a bun and looked quite pretty in a green, mid-calf-length dress. She was small in stature, a bit thickened in the waist. Her features were delicate, like the face of a porcelain doll, and looking at her you would never guess how fierce and determined she could be. She gave Father a perfunctory kiss and he squeezed her arm. He didn't believe in public displays of affection between husbands and wives. I think that it must have been difficult for them both, his comings and goings. Father was gone every year during the harvest season, sometimes for six months at a time. After he returned, and they had just become accustomed to each other, he would have to leave.

Father told Raul to get his suitcase and a package from the pickup. As I followed Father, Mother and Terre into the house, it struck me that Father hadn't said anything to Raul about taking care of the plants. Father always brought back plants from where ever he worked, a baby magnolia tree and camellias from Mississippi, fruit trees and flowering shrubs from North Texas. As a result, the gardens surrounding our house were lush with exotic shrubs, flowers, and trees. We feasted on fruits from our papaya, guayaba, and fig trees, and delighted in the heady aroma of honeysuckle, magnolia, gardenia, jasmine, roses—whatever happened to be in season.

I dismissed this deviation from my Father's routine, attributing it to an oversight, and thought about what might be in the mysterious package he had mentioned. He always brought us the most wonderful gifts. One year, when we were still in elementary school, he had surprised Terre and me with porcelain dolls. Mine had dark hair with brown eyes that opened and closed. Terre's had blond hair and blue eyes. She had taken good care of hers. It was still in a box on a shelf in our bedroom. Mine was a bit ragged, her hair a mass of tangles, her dress torn. I loved playing with her when I was little. Terre had never been much for playing with dolls.

Ellie, Lupita, and Marta were busy setting the large, mahogany table when we walked into the house. When Father was not home, we usually ate at the pea green Formica table in the kitchen. When he was home, we always ate dinner in the dining room, which was separated from the living room by two waist-high walls of bookcases filled with my father's collection of leather-bound books. The bookcases flanked a three-foot-wide opening in the center of the room, forming an entrance into the dining area. As we crossed the wood-plank floor to the table, the screen door opened and then slammed shut. Raul sauntered in carrying Father's suitcase and the package, which was wrapped in brown paper.

Father motioned to Raul for the package. "This is for Marta."

Marta squealed and ran to Father. He handed her the package. "Be careful, *hita*. It might break," he said, his eyes solemn, as she began to tear the brown paper off the package, revealing a pink jewelry box. She opened it and a ballerina popped up as the melody to *Ojos Verdes* began to play.

"Oh, Papá, it's beautiful!" Marta's eyes shone as she hugged Father.

He glanced at the rest of us, shaking his head slightly, "I'm sorry there is nothing for the rest of you."

My brother, sisters, and I glanced at each other uneasily. "That's all right, Papá," I said. "We're just glad you got home safely."

He gave me a sad smile and then took his place at the head of the table. We settled in our chairs and ate in silence, an usual occurrence for us. We were all curious about why Father had returned home so early, but we knew better than to ask. Father never discussed business at the dinner table. Actually, he never discussed business with any of his children, with the exception of Raul, and only rarely with Mother, so we just glanced at each other, expectation and dread in the air. Finally, Mother spoke, "If I had known you were coming, I would have cooked some meat."

"This is fine," he said flatly, biting into the corn-on-the-cob.

"Señora Treviño brought us a basket of fresh corn harvested from their plot. She told me it was a small token for what you did for Chuy. She also brought a watermelon."

Father nodded, but remained silent as he continued to eat. He had given the newlywed Chuy, as a wedding gift, a down payment on a small home in Ruby. It wasn't much, about thirty dollars, but in the late forties, that was a lot of money, especially for Chuy, a field worker, whose monthly wage was about twenty-seven dollars.

The quietness in which we ate was unnerving. The only sound was the clicking of our silverware against our blue stoneware plates. As I ate the fideo Eloise had helped to make—it was slightly scorched—I glanced furtively at Father. He seemed deep in thought. He ate quietly, rather than ask us questions about our activities like he usually did. Finally, he finished and excused himself, walking to the back of the house to his bedroom. We all watched him leave, then glanced at Mother.

"*Ándale*, hurry up. Finish eating and clean up." She jumped up out of her chair and followed after Father.

*****

We had one of the largest homes on the Mexican side of the tracks. The original house, what was now our dining and living room, was built in 1938 on one of four adjacent lots Father had purchased. On the back of this building and extending to a second lot, a kitchen, bathroom, two bedrooms, one an upstair room for Raul, and a covered front porch were added in the early forties. Then in the mid-forties when Father's business was doing so well because of the war, he added one more bedroom, a bathroom, and an office to the west side of the house. He also built a detached garage. The house was unusual in that the front of it was a traditional American wood-framed house with a pitched roof, but the west wing was Spanish in style, made of adobe and stucco with rounded corners, arched windows and doorways, a flat roof, and red-tinted concrete flooring.

Thinking about it now, I can see that the house was symbolic of my Father's ambivalence about his identity—his strong desire to remain a Mexican national versus his equally strong desire to nurture his entrepreneurial spirit, something that could be realized to a greater degree in the United States than in México. Whatever the reason for our house's unusual appearance, I can attest that the west wing of the house that included my parents' bedroom and bathroom and Father's office, was always much cooler in the summer than the American part of the house, a testament to its Mexican architecture.

As my sisters began to clear the table, I wandered nonchalantly to my room. Closing the door behind me, I walked to my desk, which was lined against the wall that separated my room from my parents' room, and sat down. Although the wall between our bedrooms was quite thick, I knew I would be able to hear at least part of my parents' conversation. If that is a crime, then I am guilty, but I just had to know what had happened in Mississippi to cause my father's uncharacteristic despondency.

"I have to pay them." I heard Papá's muffled voice. "What kind of a man would I be if I didn't? They have families, too. They are counting on their salaries to put food on the table."

"I knew it would come to this," my mother said. "We should go to see Don Rafael tomorrow. He can break the spell."

"What in the hell are you talking about, *mujer*?"

10

"You know that many people envy us. I believe that someone, probably Señora Loredo, has put a spell on you. One of your shirts was missing from the clothesline before you left in April. We never found it. She must have taken it to the *bruja* and had a spell cast on you."

"Are you crazy? How many times have I told you that I don't believe in that hogwash?"

"Maybe if you did believe, you wouldn't be in this mess," she retorted.

"Maybe if I had a wife with some sense, I wouldn't be in this mess," he said.

I could just picture my mother's arched eyebrow and Father's thunderous expression, his eyes blazing fire. My head begin to ache. I hated it when Father denigrated Mother, not that she didn't deserve it sometimes. I thought her primitive beliefs were embarrassing, too, especially now that I was in college. There was silence for a while, then Mother spoke. "You can blame me if it makes you feel better. It doesn't change anything. Do what you want to do. What I say doesn't matter. It never has. But I will tell you this. I believe as you do that you should honor your agreement with your workers, even if that gringo farmer did not honor his agreement with you. But can't you just pay them half of what you owe them?"

"I am a man of my word. I will pay them exactly what I owe them, or I am just as worthless as that *gringo mentiroso*."

"But that's more money than we have. We'll be bankrupt. Isabel and Terre won't be able to return to college."

"There's nothing I can do about it. My father would turn in his grave if I didn't honor my word, no matter what the cost."

I heard the door to my room open. I jumped out of the desk chair onto my bed and grabbed the magazine lying on the night stand, trying to keep the cover hidden from view as it was an old issue of *True Confession* and I wasn't in the mood for another of Terre's scoldings.

"Isabel, what are you doing?"

"Oh, nothing," I said, paging through the magazine, my lips upturned in a guilty smile. Though I appeared unaffected by what I had heard and even cheerful, I felt horrible, not so much for me as for my sister, who would be crushed if she couldn't go back to college.

Terre crossed her arms and pursed her lips, then looked toward our parents' room, from where loud, if muffled voices periodically pierced through the wall. "Tell me what's going on," she whispered, then tiptoed to her twin bed and sat down. She rested her hands on the bed and tilted her head making her chestnut-colored hair fall almost to her elbow. We both wore our hair in the Rita Hayworth style popular then, parted on the side, long, wavy, and we hoped, sexy. Rather, *I* hoped. Truthfully,

Terre didn't care whether she looked sexy or not.

I put the magazine down, relating what I had heard of our parents' conversation, careful not to mention what Father had said about our schooling.

"Of course, what Papá wants to do sounds noble," Terre said with a toss of her head. "But what about his own family? Doesn't he ever think about us? Aren't we just as important as those workers?"

"Oh, Terre, don't be like that. Papá is right. He must honor his word."

Her eyes bulged open. "His word? Hah!"

We were both startled by shouting. "So we're going to be left destitute because of your pride. I won't have it! I won't!"

"You won't have it? I am the man of this house and I will decide what goes on here. How can I hold my head up in this town if I renege on my word?"

"If you do this, I will never forgive you."

I held my hands to my ears and looked at Terre. She stared out the window, her expression deceptively placid. "Mamá," I wanted to shout, "Stop it! Can't you see what you're doing? It's not his fault!"

"Fine, so be it." I heard the screen door slam. Father left the house from his office, his boots pulverizing the ground before he got into the pickup.

"Where do you think he's going?" I rushed to the window and caught sight of the chrome fenders of the truck as it sped down our street.

"To a cantina," my sister said, her face twisted in a scowl. "Where else?"

Chapter 2

The good thing about living in a small town is that everyone knows everyone else and neighbors can be depended on to help in times of need. The bad thing about living in a small town is that everyone knows everyone else's business and certain neighbors can be depended on to inflame an already volatile situation. For us, that neighbor was Señora Sanchez.

The day after Father's abrupt return and a few hours after he had gone into town, a knock on the front door announced the arrival of Señora Sanchez, or Dora, as my mother called her. Before I could answer the door, our next door neighbor bounded into the house wearing a dress stretched so tightly around her large bosom, I was fearful that her bodice buttons would pop open. Señora Sanchez liked to show off her rather robust physique. "*Buenos días*, Isa. Is your mother in the kitchen?" She walked past me smoothing her dyed black hair, which was pulled up in a chignon.

"Yes, she is," I said, following her into our kitchen where Mother was conversing with our housemaid. Actually housemaid is not really the correct term for Doña Cuca. My father had hired the Indian woman to help Mother cook and clean. She was also frequently left in charge of us when Father and Mother traveled, so we were all quite close to her.

"Beatriz, I heard what happened. I'm so sorry." Señora Sanchez rushed to Mother and I thought she was going to throw her arms around her, but she simply touched Mother's arm when she saw the dark expression on her face.

"Dora, how good of you to visit," Mother said, her voice cool. "Please sit down, and Isa will get you some coffee." She gestured toward the Formica table.

Señora Sanchez eased her ample bottom onto the vinyl upholstered chair, looking somewhat abashed. But from experience I knew she wouldn't budge from that chair until the whole sordid story came out.

"Cuca, why don't you take a rest? Go outside and watch the girls while I talk to Dora," Mother said as I poured coffee into two china cups.

After our maid had gone, Mother pulled a chair out and sat across from Señora Sanchez. I placed the two cups of coffee on the table and excused myself.

"Isa, stay here," Mother said. "I'm sure Dora won't mind."

"Of course not," our neighbor said, sipping the coffee.

I sat down next to Mother realizing that she wanted me to stay so that I could hear what had happened to Father. I felt ashamed for having eavesdropped on her and Father and made a mental note to feign surprise at whatever she said, not realizing that much of what I was about to hear would, indeed, be a surprise, if not a shock.

"I suppose Panchito told you what happened?" Mother gazed at Dora, cocking her head to the side.

"*Sí, que lástima!*" the woman said. "I always said you can't trust gringos!"

My mother nodded, a grimace on her face as she sipped her coffee.

"I had to go into town earlier this morning," Señora Sanchez continued, eyeing Mother, "and I saw Don Miguel in that expensive black suit of his that makes him look like a politician. Anyway, I saw him go into the Ruby Land Development Company."

I gasped and looked at Mother, whose sour expression had not changed. "He has known Señor Smith and Señor Greene for many years," she said.

"Is it possible that Don Miguel is going to sell some of his land? Everyone knows that Señor Smith has been interested in purchasing the land by the church for years."

"Anything is possible. Whatever he does or does not do with the land, I assure you that my husband's work crew will be paid for the work they did this summer."

"Then Panchito will be getting his salary, after all?"

So, this was Señora Sanchez' real reason for coming to visit, I thought. She wasn't concerned about Mother; she was concerned about her husband's paycheck.

"Did you ever doubt it? You know my husband to be a man of his word."

"But it's a lot of money that he says the gringo swindled from him."

I felt the hair on the back of my neck rise as if electrified. I didn't like her inference that my father was lying about the swindle. My father was not a liar.

"Yes, it was. And we will suffer for it, *si Dios quiere*. But my husband will keep his word." Mother rose. "If you don't mind, Dora, I need to finish some work around here."

"Of course," she said as she lumbered out of her seat. "And tell Don Miguel that my family will be forever grateful for his generosity."

I stayed in the kitchen thinking about what our neighbor had said while Mother walked her to the front door. John Smith and Alan Greene owned much of the land in and around Ruby on both sides of the tracks. For years they had been pressuring my father to sell several tracts of land he owned in northwest Ruby, but Father had steadfastly refused. The acreage included a dairy farm, a citrus orchard, cultivated farmland, and a few hundred residential lots. Father said that land was the best investment a man could make and that only an act of God could persuade him to sell his property.

I recalled the day about four years before when Father Carmody had asked Father to donate some of his land to the Church. Our parish priest was a brash New Yorker who frequently offended his Mexican parishioners' sensibilities with his overbearing personality and indelicate manners. To say he was not a popular priest would be an understatement, but I had to admit, he got things done.

One day after Mass, Father Carmody followed us outside to the front of the church. Father and Mother were conversing with several friends when the priest barged into their group with not even an "excuse me," stunning them into silence. He picked out each of us Caballero children with his eyes, scrutinizing our expensive clothes, his glance resting on my father's silk tie. "God has been good to the Caballero family," he finally commented in his textbook Spanish, his arms crossed in front of him, his black cassock blowing gently around his legs.

"God helps those who help themselves, Padre." Father eyed the priest warily.

"True, how very true, my son," said the priest, although he was in his early thirties and clearly the younger of the two men. "Unfortunately, not all of God's people can help themselves as you have."

"What are you getting at, Padre?" Father crossed his arms and tilted his head to the right, never taking his gaze from the priest.

"So you're a direct man, Don Miguel. Good. Then I, too, will be direct. I understand that you own a goodly amount of land in north Ruby. The archdiocese requires a portion of it so that a new church can be built, say three acres or so?"

"And I suppose the Church expects me to donate this land?"

The priest shrugged his shoulders. "We are a poor parish, Don Miguel, you know that. Besides, think of what blessings God will bestow on a kind benefactor."

"I thought the Church did away with indulgences centuries ago, Padre," Father said darkly.

"So it has, my son, so it has. But God still looks favorably upon those who help his Church on earth."

"I'll think about it, Padre," Father said curtly, then turned to Mother and the rest of us. "*Ándale. Vámanos,*" he ordered, his voice gruff. He strode toward the car and we followed after him like a brood of ducklings.

Father did eventually donate the land to the Church, but he always felt resentful about the way Father Carmody pressured him in front of so many people. In fact, after that Sunday, Father never stepped foot in church again, except for weddings and funerals, despite my mother's pleadings.

The several hundred acres of land Father had purchased over the years represented his life's work. When he had come to Ruby from México in 1926 after his father died, he had had 50 pesos, some pieces of jewelry that his mother had given him, and a suitcase with a few changes of clothes. Nothing else. From that simple beginning, he had amassed, by 1948 standards, a fortune.

I realized after Señora Sanchez left that our lives were going to be irrevocably changed.

*****

Father returned home a few hours later and Mother accosted him at the front door. "You sold our land? You've depleted our savings! What are we going to live on?"

"*Cállate, mujer!* Do you want all our neighbors to hear?"

"They already know what you've done. Oh, they are all ranting about what a wonderful man you are. How you honor your word. Well, I know the truth. You care more about your honor than you do your own children."

"Mamá, please, leave Papá alone. He did what he had to do. We'll survive. We'll be all right," I said.

"Get out of here. All of you," she shrilled, glaring at me, Terre and my younger sisters, who had been listening to the radio in the living room. "This is between your father and me."

"No!" my father boomed. "They have the right to know what is going on."

"Very well," Mother said, her hands on her hips, "tell them everything. Tell them we have no money to send Terre and Isa back to college. Tell them you sold their inheritance!"

"Your mother, as usual, is exaggerating," Father said after Mother had finished her tirade. He walked to the blue and green plaid armchair and sat down, sinking into the pillowy cushion, his shoulders hunched over as if he were carrying a heavy weight. He ran his hands through his hair and sighed, then began to undo his tie. He wore his silk tie, his black, double-breasted Franklin Brothers' suit and his Florsheim shoes only to funerals, but I understood why he had worn that particular outfit that day.

"Things will be a little tight for a while," he continued. "But don't worry, *hijas*. Everything will work out. Unfortunately, your mother is right about college." He glanced at Terre and me, his eyes sad.

"That's all right, Father," I said.

"Yes, that's fine," Terre said, her lips quivering.

I saw the light in my sister's eyes dim as her dreams to become a teacher disintegrated with Father's announcement. As for me, let's just say that I had been an enthusiastic participant in the college social scene and not much else. Although I would miss my college friends, the dances, and the parties, my loss was insignificant compared to my sister's.

In the quiet that followed Father's pronunciation, I heard birds chirping in the trees, children laughing in the street, and the low murmur of voices from the radio, which Ellie had turned down. Mother's face was still twisted with rage, but she held her tongue, and Father's eyes were glazed over in sorrow. I felt so horribly bad for Father, who looked beaten, and so terribly angry at Mother for not being more understanding.

"Where's Raul?" Father suddenly spoke.

"He's working at the dairy, Papá." I wondered which of the properties Father had sold to the land company.

He nodded, then got up from the armchair and walked slowly to the back of the house, Mother following close at his heels.

"Well, Isa, it looks like you're the lucky one," Ellie said after our parents had disappeared into the west wing. "Papá used to look at your report cards and say, 'Poor Isa, she is not a scholar, *pobre de mi hija.*'" She posed dramatically, shaking her head, putting her hand to her cheek. "Then Mamá would say, 'She should do better. We're paying a lot of money for her to go to that private college. What is she doing over there but wasting our money!'"

"Oh, be quiet." I laughed, throwing the sofa pillow at her.

"Then Papá would look at Terre's report card and nod his head and say, 'Terre always was the smart one—look at this, A's in every subject,' and then Mamá would say, 'Terre's always been too smart for her own good. Boys don't like girls who are too smart.'"

We all laughed at the way she imitated Mamá and Papá. Ellie was good at that, mimicking people.

"I'm not any smarter than Isa," Terre said, defending me. "She just never got over what happened in first grade, and you wouldn't have either, Ellie, if you had had that witch, Mrs. Beasley, as your teacher."

"It wasn't Mrs. Beasley's fault that I couldn't speak English, Terre," I said, though in my heart, I thanked her for taking up for me.

"Maybe not. But what did she expect in a school for Mexicans?"

In 1934, the Latin American elementary school across the street from our house was a one-room building housing grades one through six. The very first lesson I learned as a first grader was that we were not to speak Spanish at all in class or during recess. That was the hardest lesson I ever learned. My family had always spoken Spanish at home, so I could understand only a little English.

As a result, I spent a disproportionate amount of time at the blackboard writing, "I will not speak Spanish on the playground, or in the classroom, or at lunch time," that is, whenever I spoke the only language I knew how to speak. It was humiliating, even though I wasn't the only child given this punishment. I ended up flunking first grade. The next year, Terre and I started first grade together and with her help (she was always a quick study), I managed to pass. I understand now that my failure wasn't because I was dumb, but because of the language barrier. Even so, what happened in first grade helped to shape my perception of myself as a mediocre student.

"It didn't seem to hamper you," I said. "You learned English pretty fast, Terre."

"That was because of you, Isa," my sister said, patting my arm. "I learned it quickly because of you."

My sisters and I sat around talking for a while longer before Mother returned to the living room barking orders that it was Terre's and my turn to help with dinner. As we followed her into the kitchen, Terre whispered in my ear, "I saw a Help Wanted sign at McGruder's Soda Fountain. I'm going to apply for a job there. I think you should look for a job, too."

"Really, Terre?" I whispered back.

She nodded, her expression grim, but determined. I had to hand it to my sister. Here she was still reeling from a huge letdown and she was already making plans for the future.

As I pulled an iron skillet out of the kitchen cabinet, I thought about what it would be like to have a job, a real job that I got paid for. I was a good typist, the best typist, in fact, who had ever graduated from Ruby High School. I could get a job in a business office somewhere in town and with the money I earned, I could help Father get back on his feet, I remember thinking.

I was so young then, and so naïve.

Chapter 3

In 1948, Ruby had a population of about two-thousand, split between Anglo and Mexican communities. Mexicans stayed on their side of the tracks unless they had a specific reason to be on the Anglo side of town, such as to work or to pay bills. Anglos often treated Mexicans, especially those with dark skin and Indian features, with a mixture of contempt and repulsion. However, my family was not a typical Mexican family. We didn't look "Mexican." My parents were primarily of Spanish ancestry so our complexions were light and our features more European than Indian. What was more, my father was respected in both the Anglo and Mexican communities, not only for his business acumen, but also because of his innate dignity and generosity.

For these reasons and because we both had completed one year of college, Terre and I had no trouble landing our first jobs on the Anglo side of town. Terre got work at McGruder's Soda Fountain selling milkshakes and soda pops to a mostly young clientele, an odd job for someone as smart as my sister, but one that she insisted suited her. I got a plum job as a clerk at the Ruby City Water Office, where I was able to put my typing skills to good use. My weekly salary was thirty dollars, while Terre's was fifteen, but with tips, she often made as much as I did.

One day in August, after I had been working at the water office for almost a month, I glanced out the six-paned front window and gasped when I saw Marcos Benavides stroll down Main Street. The early afternoon sunlight glinted off the chrome fenders of cars as they passed by him. He stood out against the whitewashed, stuccoed structures of Main Street, a dashing figure in dark pants, a white shirt and tie. Tall and slender, his stride was confident, almost jaunty. He pulled a white handkerchief from his pocket and wiped his forehead as he bounded up the street.

"Is something wrong, Miss Caballero?"

Mr. Travers, my supervisor, walked into the reception area from the back room. "No, Mr. Travers." I walked hastily to the counter, the heels of my pumps clicking on the wood floor. "I just thought I saw somebody I knew."

My supervisor raised his eyebrows and walked to the window. "Oh, there's the young man Mr. Avery told me about yesterday. Benavides is his name. He's been looking for a job around here. Too bad he didn't finish high school. He looks like a nice fellow. Um, good head of hair." He ran his hand over his own shiny bald head. "Do you know him?"

I couldn't help smiling. Mr. Travers was the only man I ever knew who judged a man by the amount of hair on his head. And Marcos did have that—a head of thick, shiny black hair. I felt myself blushing. "Oh, I've seen him around at dances and other places." Marcos was two years older than I and from Westwood, a town ten miles south of Ruby. The first time I had seen him was at a street dance between Ruby and Westwood. I was fifteen, and I thought he was the best looking boy I had ever seen. Just a few months later, I heard that he had dropped out of high school to join the Army. The last I heard, he had finish his four-year stint in the service and had moved to Chicago with his brother.

"He'll probably inquire here. Be courteous, but tell him we don't need any help." Mr. Travers walked toward the back office. "You know, I have a cousin who lives in Westwood, the southside of course. I'm sure Mr. Benavides wouldn't know her. By the way, has Mr. or Mrs. Gutiérrez been in to pay their bill?"

"No, sir."

"I'd sure hate to turn their water off, what with them having five children and all. I don't know why they even bother to live in a house with running water anyway. Everyone knows Mexi . . . I mean, everyone knows their kind don't ever take baths. But rules are rules." He shook his head and walked into his office.

I shook my head, too. I knew how he was going to finish the sentence: Méxicans don't take baths. Of course it wasn't true, but most of the Anglo townspeople based their opinions of Méxicans on their observations of the migrant workers from México. And the only reason the migrants rarely took baths was that they lived in drafty shacks of corrugated tin supplied by their stingy Anglo employers, without running water let alone bathtubs.

I glanced out the window again, but Marcos was no longer in view. I returned to my desk thinking about him, alternating between wishing he would come in and hoping he would not. I had typed three letters for Mr. Travers when the door opened.

Marcos strode into the building, which was small to begin with but which seemed to shrink even smaller in his vital presence.

When I stood up and walked to the counter, he smiled at me, showing teeth that, while not perfectly even, were glowing white.

"Can I help you?" I tried to appear calm, though I felt slightly sick at my stomach.

"Hey, I know you," he blurted out. "You're Isabel Caballero, right?"

I smiled and nodded, hoping that my lipstick still looked fresh.

He leaned against the counter. "So you work here?" He looked around the small room at the two wooden desks with Underwood typewriters perched on them, his eyes resting on a large city map hanging on the wall that showed the city water lines and canals.

"Yes." I felt so stupid. Of course I worked here. What else would I be doing standing behind the counter?

"I heard you were going to a private college up in San Antonio."

"That was last year. I, that is, my sister and I decided not to go back." I couldn't believe what I had heard. Had Marcos actually been inquiring about me?

"Really?" He smiled again. "I'm glad. Maybe I'll be seeing you around more often then."

"Maybe so," I answered, a bit perturbed by his cavalier attitude. "Now, what can I do for you?"

"Could I speak to your boss?"

"What makes you think I'm not the boss?"

My saucy remark floored him.

"I didn't say I didn't think you were the boss. That is, I've never seen a woman who was the boss in a place like this. Particularly a Mexicana. Of course, my mother pretty much runs the show at our house. Not to say my father is a pushover. But. . . ."

I burst out laughing, and Marcos' face turned crimson. When Mr. Travers emerged from the back room, Marcos frowned at me, but I noticed that his eyes were smiling.

"What's going on in here?" my boss said, not unpleasantly. "Oh, Mr. Benavides. Mr. Avery told me you'd be in. I'm sorry, but there are no openings here. Why don't you try one of the packing sheds? They're always looking for strong, young men such as yourself. You're a veteran, aren't you? You should be first in line for a job."

"Thank you for the information, sir," Marcos said stiffly. "But I was hoping that I could find work in an office or a store. As you said, I'm a veteran and was honorably discharged from the Army."

"That's certainly commendable, Mr. Benavides. But I'm afraid I have all the help I need around here." He gestured at me.

Marcos' lips turned up slightly. "Yes, I see. Thank you for your time, sir." He turned on his heels and walked to the door. Before he left, he turned around and winked at me. "I'll see you later, Isabel."

I certainly hope so, I thought, as he closed the door behind him. The rest of the day went slowly, but I made the most of it by fantasizing about Marcos when I wasn't waiting on customers. When the five o'clock train whistle sounded, I straightened up my desk, said good-bye to Mr. Travers, gathered up my umbrella and pocketbook and practically skipped to the soda fountain, where Terre would just be starting her shift.

21

*****

I slid onto a red vinyl upholstered stool at the Formica counter between two groups of high schoolers and watched as Terre went about her business. She wiped a spill off the counter, swinging her head back to get her hair out of her face. People often said that Marta resembled Mother because of her auburn hair, but actually, Terre had inherited Mother's looks. She had a pug nose, small intense eyes, and bow lips that were replicas of Mother's. However, unlike Mother, and me I might add, she was tall and slender. Not to say I was short and fat. I was short, but not fat, at least not then. Even so, when my brother saw Terre and me walking down the street together, he would call out, "Here comes the toothpick and the barrel." We laughed at his teasing, but I have to admit, it bothered me. I mean, what girl wants to be referred to as a barrel, or a toothpick, for that matter? "Chattanooga Choo-Choo" was playing on the juke-box and I started tapping my foot to the song. "Hi, Terre."

"Hi, Isa. How was your day?"

"Pretty exciting," I said.

She put a soda on the counter and leaned toward me. "What happened?"

"Marcos Benavides came into the office looking for a job."

"Marcos Benavides? From Westwood? Really? I thought he was in Chicago."

"He came back." I related what had happened.

"You're not thinking what I think you're thinking, are you, Isa?"

"What's that?" I said, avoiding her eyes.

"Marcos has a bad reputation, and he's a high school drop-out. Papá would never approve of you seeing him."

"Since when did you care about what Papá thinks?"

Terre grimaced. "That wasn't very nice, Isa. And it isn't like you. What is it about Marcos that attracts you anyway, besides his looks?"

Before I could answer, Terre was called away by a customer wanting a banana split. I watched as she peeled a banana, sliced it lengthwise and placed it in an oblong bowl. I sighed. What was it about Marcos that attracted me? Everything. His wavy hair, his tall, slender build, his confident demeanor, his smiling brown eyes, and yes, even his bad reputation. He reminded me of Rhett Butler in *Gone With the Wind*. All I knew was that I wanted to see him again, and I had a feeling that he felt the same way about me.

I finished my soda, said good-bye to Terre, and started home. I opened my umbrella over my head as I walked north on Main Street. Tans were not popular then, like they are now, and I wanted to keep my soft, white complexion just that, soft and white. I looked in the window of Carvel's

Dress Shoppe and saw a mannequin outfitted in a red dress with a full skirt and red and white striped bodice that I thought would look scrumptious on me and made a mental note to visit the store tomorrow during my lunch break. I wasn't anxious to get home—the tension there was pretty thick what with Mother haranguing Father at every turn—but my feet hurt and my stomach was growling.

I walked north over smooth, paved roads until I reached the railroad tracks. On either side of the tracks, the packing shed and canning plant docks were temporarily quiet since the five o'clock load of vegetables had already been loaded and shipped off. During harvest time, these businesses were open twenty-four hours a day, and in Ruby, the "Vegetable Capital of the World" as *Collier's* magazine called our little town, it was always harvest time. In September, corn, tomatoes, peppers, and citrus were harvested and shipped, and out in the fields, workers planted snap beans and more tomatoes. Next month, beets, cabbage, carrots, potatoes, and strawberries would be planted, and more corn, peppers, tomatoes, and citrus would be harvested. It was an endless cycle of planting, growing, harvesting, and shipping. That was how I had come to tell time, by the vegetables.

As I walked over the railroad tracks onto the unpaved road on the Mexican part of town, a dusty wind blew against my face, welcoming me to my neighborhood.

Chapter 4

Father wouldn't accept our money. I had an inkling that he wouldn't, especially after Raul, who had started working part-time at the Quiñones meat packing plant in Mercedes, told me that Father had refused to take cash from him. But it still bothered me when he refused our offering. Mother, on the other hand, had no qualms about taking our money. She couldn't take my thirty dollars or Terre's twenty out of our hands fast enough.

"*Gracias a Dios* somebody is bringing in money to help our family and not giving it away to other people," she said as we placed the crisp bills on the palm of her hand.

That evening, Father had been reading his favorite newspaper, *La Prensa*, in the plaid armchair in the living room when we presented our first week's salary to Mother. He peered up from behind the paper, his chocolate eyes boring into her. "Give them back their money, Beatriz."

"Why should I?"

"Because we are not so destitute that we must take money from our children."

Mother glared at Father, then gave us each ten dollars back. "I'll keep the rest. It's always best to have a little money in reserve, just in case."

Father continued to stare at Mother, then without a word, set the newspaper down on the side table, rose from the chair, and walked out the front door.

Mother rushed to the doorway and looked out. "There he goes to the cantina again," fumed Mother. "Why he can't stay home for one evening is beyond me." She folded the bills, placed the wad in her apron pocket, and stalked to the kitchen, a thick strand of her auburn hair falling out of her hair net. Terre and I exchanged knowing looks. At that point, I think, even Terre was feeling a little sympathy for Father. Mother just wouldn't leave him alone. She jabbed relentlessly at Father, not realizing that the more she harangued him, the more distance she was putting between them.

*****

A few weeks later, Tío Gabriel came to visit Father. Tío Gabe was Father's first cousin, his closest friend and confidante. They had grown up together in México. Tío had moved to Texas with his family—his mother, father, and half-sisters—about seven years before Father had, so when Father immigrated, Gabriel had shown him the ropes, so to speak. Tío Gabe had gray eyes, the color of a wintery sky, and was tall and lanky. He always wore a straw Stetson hat, western shirt, jeans, and cowboy boots that were so worn the heels were almost even with the soles. He owned a fifty-acre farm near Mercedes, where he grew summer cotton and winter vegetables, like many of the farmers in the region. He and Father often visited each other to discuss farming issues.

"I had no contract," I overheard Father say after I turned off the water faucet beneath his office window. I had been watering the jasmine by my bedroom windows and decided to stop after the mosquitoes came out to feast on my arms and legs.

"With no contract, it was your word against a gringo's word," Tío Gabriel muttered.

"I've always worked without a contract. A man's handshake is his word, or so I thought. When I gave that *gringo mentiroso* the bill for the work my men did for the two months they worked his farm, he laughed at me. He said that no stinkin' Mexican was worth that kind of money. Then he tore up the bill right in front of me and told me to get off his property. *Primo*, I wanted to kill him. I wanted to strangle his scrawny neck. Instead, I left his farm and went to the law. The sheriff told me I had no case. No contract. No case. No money. *Nada!*"

There was silence and I imagined that Tío Gabe had simply shaken his head in disgust. *I* certainly was disgusted, and mortified. I couldn't imagine anyone talking to my father the way that horrible gringo had.

"I've decided to sell the trucks," Father continued, referring, I guessed, to the five International flatbed trucks that he used to transport field workers on his contracting trips.

"Is that really necessary?"

"I can't go through another loss like this. I don't think I could ever trust anyone again, and that's the name of this business. You know I invest several thousand dollars in the migrants before I ever see one cent of the money from the growers. I have to pay for gas, food, shelter, medical bills, bail, for almost one-hundred workers. I've been a labor contractor for almost ten years and it's not been an easy life. Until now, it's been profitable. But if growers refuse to honor their word, then I am running a charitable organization. I can't afford to do it anymore."

I confess that I stayed to listen. That was the way I got most of my information in those days, hanging around open windows, listening through walls. We had no telephone and no television, and since we also had no air conditioners, everyone kept their windows open. People couldn't help being privy to other people's business.

"There's another reason," Father continued. "Think about it. You have always hired farm workers without contractors."

"Yes, but my spread is small and I can talk to my workers without a go-between. A contractor would take too much of my profit and you know my profit margin isn't that big."

"Well, more of the big farmers are beginning to think like you. They are hiring migrants without contractors. They want to eliminate us from the picture to save money. The workers have no loyalty. They don't care who they work for as long as they get paid. I can't say I blame them, but it has put me in a bad position. Besides that, some farmers who can afford it are buying tractors and are eliminating the need for farm workers."

"I'm looking into buying a secondhand tractor myself," Tío Gabe said.

"Is that so? Are you doing as well as that?"

"*Pues*, you know the farming business. One ill-timed rainfall or frost can wipe out an entire crop. We've been lucky so far."

"I hope our luck holds out. I'm counting on the orange harvest to get me on my feet again."

"And you kept some of the lots in Colonia Caballero, didn't you?"

"Twenty out of two-hundred," Father grunted.

As I walked to the front of the house, I wondered why Father couldn't talk about things rationally and calmly with Mother the way he did with Tío Gabe. Why were they so contrary with each other? I heard the din of radios from various houses in the neighborhood, and as I stepped up onto the front porch, I saw Señora Sanchez in her front yard yelling for her two sons to come in for supper. Tito and Nardo appeared from behind the weatherworn school building across the street and scampered home.

Despite the hungry mosquitoes, I sat on the porch swing and glanced up and down the street. On that Sunday evening, the neighborhood was settling down. Most of our neighbors were indoors getting washed up to eat, that is except for the Alvarezes who lived across the street. The Señores Alvarez and their five children, ranging in ages from four to sixteen, were leaving their house dressed in their Sunday best, the two girls and their mother in clean, if worn, dresses, the three boys and their father in black slacks, ties, and white short-sleeved shirts. They waved to me as they came out of the house, Bibles clutched in their hands. Then they turned east and marched down the dusty street to the Mexican Pentacostal church a few blocks away.

I hate to admit it, but my sisters and I used to make fun of the Alvarez family. We used to call them the Alleluias. They were an enigma: a Protestant family in a neighborhood of Catholics. When they had first moved into our neighborhood, Señora Alvarez came calling, Bible in hand, and tried to convert Mother. Mother had listened politely, but told her firmly that she was Catholic and had no intention of giving up her religion. "And furthermore," I remember her saying, "you'd better keep away from my children. They are good Catholics and I don't want them exposed to that mumbo jumbo religion of yours." That ended Señora Alvarez's attempt at converting the Caballero family. But she never held it against us. I have to say that the Alvarezes were *buena gente* and they never missed an occasion to help others in our community.

I continued to watch as the family of seven made their way past several houses, which like most of the houses in our neighborhood looked like square wooden boxes with low-pitched roofs built on neatly kept strips of land about fifty feet wide by one-hundred fifty feet deep. White picket fences surrounded some of the properties. Others had shrub hedges along their property lines. Many of the home owners had also erected shacks on the back portions of their lots and rented them out to migrant families and other Mexican nationals.

As the Alvarez family passed the home of Señora Cavacho, who ran a boarding house, I thought back to when she and Mother had been special friends. They had had a falling out a few years before and had not spoken to each other since. Terre despised Señora Cavacho, though I don't know why. What happened between Mother and Father wasn't her fault. Well, not exactly.

The Alvarez family disappeared onto the adjacent street and I glanced back across the street. The sun descended slowly behind the wood frame house. For a short while, the pitched roof of the house made the sun look as if a triangular wedge had been cut out of it. Then the golden orb disappeared and the world took on a misty gray appearance.

As I swung back and forth, a blue Chevrolet lurched onto our street in fits and stops. I watched as it made its noisy way down the packed earth road and stopped in front of our house. The young driver jumped out and ran around the front of the car to the passenger side. He opened the car door and to my utter surprise, Terre got out. The back door opened and I almost fainted when Marcos emerged, grinning. "Hi, Isabel!" He walked toward me, stopping at the porch railing. "I've been thinking about you. A lot." He stopped smiling and gave me an intense look. "Hey, I got a job. I'm working for American Fruit Growers in one of their packing sheds. Because of my military service, my boss says I'm already in line to be a supervisor."

"That's great," I said, truly happy that he found a job. In my opinion, the only thing worse than not having a boyfriend was having a boyfriend who didn't have a job.

"You'd better leave, Marcos." Terre walked onto the porch with Marcos' friend. "Thank you for the ride, Bernardo. But you'd both better

27

go. If my Father or Mother sees you, Isa and I will get in trouble." She glanced around.

They both started back to the car, but Marcos stopped and returned. "I want to see you, Isabel. Come to the dance this weekend in Westwood," he said urgently, referring to the Mexican Independence Day celebration held annually on September 16th in Westwood.

I wanted to act cool and detached, but I was so overwhelmed by his desire to see me that I blurted out, "I'll try. I really will."

He flashed a smile, then turned around, jumping into the front passenger seat. In a few minutes, the car lurched forward and disappeared down the street. I could hear it for a full five minutes, even after it turned onto the adjoining street.

I jumped out of the swing and rushed to my sister. "Terre, I can't believe you let them bring you home. Wasn't Raul supposed to pick you up?" She had spent the afternoon with Phoebe Gutiérrez, her best friend, who lived a few blocks from us.

"Yes, but I got tired of waiting for him, so I started walking home. At first I said no when Marcos asked if I wanted a ride, but he was so insistent. He said that he had to talk to you." She paused and gazed into my eyes. "Isa, I think Marcos is in love with you. You'd better be careful."

"You will go with me to the dance in Westwood, won't you?"

Her eyes narrowed. "I suppose if I don't, you'll go with Lina, and she's more boy crazy than you are. Yes, I'll go. Someone has to protect you."

I smiled, hooking my arm through Terre's as we strolled into the house.

*****

First off, let me say that I was not boy crazy. I'll admit that I had a greater appreciation for the opposite sex than Terre did, but that didn't mean I was boy crazy. As for my best friend, Carolina, it would be more appropriate to say that boys were crazy for her. She had an hourglass figure, jet black hair that hung wavy and long to the middle of her back, a porcelain complexion, and full ruby lips. I remember that in high school, all the boys, especially the Anglo ones, used to follow us around during breaks, and I can tell you, it wasn't because of me. But Lina had eyes for only one young man, Jerry Hamlin, an Anglo boy from south Ruby, with whom she was carrying on a clandestine relationship and whom she eventually married.

Anyway, the following Saturday night, Lina accompanied Terre and me to the Mexican Independence Day dance in Westwood. Father had insisted that Raul go along as a chaperone, so my brother drove us in our family car, a light green 1947 Buick. Although he was only fourteen,

Raul had been able to get a driver's license because Father owned farmland. The county judge, a good friend of Father's, had issued the driving permit, along with a court order saying that Raul could drive.

We, that is Lina and I, chattered excitedly as we drove the ten-mile route south of Ruby past towering palm trees and acres of cotton and citrus fields to the much larger town of Westwood, which in 1948 had a population of about eight-thousand people. Like Ruby, Westwood was one of the main shipping centers for the vegetable and citrus industry of the Valley, and its Mexican population lived on the north side of the railroad tracks.

As we drove into town, we saw numerous people hurrying down the sidewalks on either side of the busy main street. Raul parked in front of a small dry goods store about a block away from the corner of Emerald and Third, the intersection where the street dance was being held, and we all jumped out of the car. I heard the syncopated tempo of a Mexican rumba and moved in rhythm to the music. I loved to dance and, if I may say so, I was quite good at it though I was more a fan of American jitterbug dancing than of Mexican rumbas. We followed the flow of pedestrians, turned east on Emerald, and saw several hundred people milling around the intersection, which was blocked off with rope. Many of the celebrants were migrant workers dressed up in their finest, ready to forget even for a little while, the harsh reality of their everyday lives.

I was beginning to wonder how I would ever find Marcos in this crowd when I suddenly spotted him conversing with Bernardo in front of a pink house on the southeastern corner of Emerald and Third (I later found out that this was his parents' house). He looked so handsome in his dark slacks and pale blue button up shirt.

"I've got a plan to keep Raul occupied so that you can talk with Marcos," whispered Lina.

Raul took his role as chaperone very seriously. Trying to slip away from him so that I could talk to Marcos without being scrutinized required scheming of the highest order. Luckily, Lina Alonzo was the queen of schemers. From out of the crowd, three young girls materialized before us and Lina introduced them as her cousins. One was a pretty fourteen-year-old whose crystal green eyes fluttered demurely when she spoke to my brother. Her formfitting dress and well-developed figure kept him in such rapt attention that he didn't even notice when Marcos spied me, asked me to dance, and then spirited me away into the crowded street. Though Raul didn't notice my departure, Terre had. But I knew I didn't have anything to fear from my sister, except perhaps another lecture on the treachery of men.

Marcos took me in his arms and we began to mambo. The mambo

was a very popular dance then and the music, the brassy horn, throttling percussion, and heavy bongo beat seemed to invade Marcos' body. I was immediately aware that I was in the hands of a very accomplished dancer. I tried to keep up with him as he moved in rhythm to the beat, swaying his hips, propelling his feet in fast intricate steps. He was afire with joy and I found his delight infectious. Soon, I was laughing, moving my feet in step with his, feeling his hand on my waist like a firebrand. When the dance was over, I fell against him, tired and spent. I looked up into his merry eyes. He grinned and touched the tip of my nose with his finger. That was when I fell in love with Marcos Benavides.

So began our courtship. After that night, we met whenever we could arrange it. We went to Pedro Infante and Jorge Negrete movies in Edinburg and to soda shops in Westwood. We met at dances whenever we could. We went to Delta Lake for picnics, always properly chaperoned with one or more of my friends or sisters, of course. I simply told my mother that I was visiting or going out with Lina, and that was how I managed to see Marcos.

Looking back on it, it seems odd, our cloak and dagger courtship. But in those days, Mexican girls didn't date, at least not openly. We certainly didn't have those "just friends" relationships with the opposite sex that the girls do today. I'm still not sure to this day that I understand why, except that it had something to do with the machismo belief that women are inherently weak and unable to say no to a sweet-talking man. In a word, fathers didn't let their daughters date in the belief that they were protecting their virtue. It worked to a point. In those days, pregnancy out of wedlock was less common, though certainly not unheard of.

So, my clandestine relationship with Marcos continued and blossomed until it became obvious to both of us that we were meant for each other. There was only one problem. How was I going to convince my parents that a high school dropout, even one who could dance like Fred Astaire, was a suitable mate for the first-born daughter of one of Ruby's most prominent families?

Chapter 5

The last Saturday night in January, the temperature fell to thirty degrees. My sisters and I, wearing woolen skirts, sweaters, and heavy socks, huddled on a braided rug near the gas heater in the living room. I looked enviously at the woolen pants Raul wore. My brother's pants looked extra warm and comfortable. In those days, girls ("decent" girls my parents would say) did not wear pants. Raul was fidgeting with the knob on the RCA radio trying to find the Gene Autry show when the voice of a weather newscaster leapt out of the box.

Father set his newspaper on his lap. "Wait, *hijo*." He focused his attention on the boxy brown radio on the coffee table.

We all listened as the announcer predicted rain, and if the temperature continued to plummet, sleet. Father pushed himself out of his chair and plodded to the front window, a grim expression on his face.

All month, newspaper headlines had chronicled accounts of cold snaps, blue northers, below freezing temperatures, blizzards, freezing rains, and raging snow storms all over the state of Texas. Usually, the lower Río Grande Valley was spared such extreme weather, but if the weatherman was correct, it looked as if the Valley would not be able to escape the onslaught of freezing temperatures.

Mother glanced up from the doily she was crocheting. "What is it?" She ran her hand through her auburn hair as she sat up in her chair, which was separated from Father's by a side table and lamp.

"It's raining," Father muttered.

"I told you you should have kept the dairy instead of the citrus orchard," Mother said. "Being in agriculture is too risky. You're always at the mercy of God and the elements."

"Is that all you can say?" he retorted as he returned to his chair.

"What else am I supposed to say?"

"Nothing," he growled as he picked up the newspaper from the side table and then slapped it down again, a pensive look on his face. He looked back at Mother. "Why can't I get even a shred of compassion from you? No matter what I do, it isn't the right thing."

Mother set her needlework on her lap. "What does it matter what I say one way or the other? You want me to agree with everything you say and do whether I agree with it or not. I refuse to do that."

Terre and I rose, then Raul, Ellie, Lupita, and Marta scrambled off the floor. We excused ourselves and hastened to our bedrooms, anxious to get away from the storm gathering inside the house. Mercifully, my parents' altercation didn't last long. About fifteen minutes later, I heard Father take off in the truck. About an hour later, as I began to fall asleep I heard a rap-rap-rap on the roof. Terre and I eased out of our beds and peered out the window. Hail the size of golf balls pummeled our yard. I'm not sure how the weather could have gotten any worse, but it did.

The next morning, I woke up and immediately ran to the window, pulling open the Venetian blinds. Ice coated the grass and hung like stalactites from the shrubs and trees. A thin sheet of ice glistened on the roof top of the house next door, and icicles hung from its edges. It looked beautiful, and deadly.

Father had already gone by the time the rest of the family stirred and dressed for the nine o'clock Mass. Mother told Raul to take us to the orchard before driving us to church. We trudged out the back door to our detached garage, our feet crunching on the icy grass, and piled into the Buick. My sisters and I sat shivering in the car, watching our warm breath form puffs of smoke in the air. Raul turned the ignition several times to try to start the cold engine, until finally, the engine revved up. Mother snapped at Raul to be careful after we had rolled onto the icy road. My sisters and I held onto each other as the car slid to and fro on the way to the orchard. The whole world seemed to be iced over, and though I hate to admit it, considering what that freeze would cost us, the glistening ice hanging like conical diamonds from all the trees and rooftops was an awesome sight.

As we drove along the road that paralleled our twenty-acre orchard, we saw that ice coated all of the fourteen-hundred orange trees. Father, his accountant, and one of his foremen stood by Father's green pickup near the south side of the orchard. Raul pulled up next to the truck, and Father picked something up from the ground and walked to the car. Raul rolled the window down and Father thrust the thing into his hand, then walked away. We all peered over the back seat. In Raul's hand was half of an orange, or what used to be an orange. The pulpy fruit was nothing more than slush.

At Mother's command, Raul threw the remains of the orange out of the car and drove us to church. When Father returned home later that afternoon, he expressed hope that not all the fruit had been lost. But it was not to be. We lost the spring orange harvest and the six-thousand dollars it would have brought in.

We weren't the only ones to suffer. Virtually every grower in the lower Río Grande Valley lost fruits and vegetables, and a few lost trees. The spring tomato crop had frozen, along with the young corn. There had been some damage to the beets, broccoli, and lettuce, but these crops survived relatively unscathed as they are cold weather crops. It was a terrible winter for Valley growers, and by extension the entire Valley community.

Father became pensive after the freeze. A worried furrow developed on his forehead, and he seldom smiled.

*****

"Why don't you get up and do something, Miguel?" Mother stood before Father, her hands on her hips, a few weeks after the disastrous freeze.

Father gazed up from his book. "What am I supposed to do?"

"I don't know. You're the businessman, you tell me."

"Señor Greene wants to buy the orchard," he said simply, going back to his book.

"Really?" Mother's eyes brightened.

"Yes."

"What did he offer you?"

"Five-hundred an acre," he mumbled.

She gasped. "That's ten-thousand dollars. What are you waiting for? Grab it while you can. Who knows, the next freeze we may lose the trees and then what would we have?"

"The orchard is worth twice that amount," he snarled, slapping his book on his lap, his thick eyebrows knit together. "Ten-thousand dollars seems like a lot now, but it will be gone in no time. Those trees will keep producing year after year, guaranteeing a steady income."

"Like they did this year?" Mother arched her brows.

"You dare to talk to me in that sarcastic tone? I will not have it!" Father's expression instantly turned thunderous, but he calmed down just as quickly. "I will not sell the orchard," he said firmly, shifting his eyes back to his book. "I will provide for this family as I always have. You will just have to be content with less than before. Now leave me be."

Mother hovered over Father for a few minutes more, her hands still on her hips, then she stormed out of the room.

I had been sitting on the couch paging through a movie magazine, daydreaming about my boyfriend, Marcos, while this altercation ensued. After Mother had gone, I glanced at my father. He had aged since the summer. New creases had appeared on his forehead, and his mouth seemed to be turned down in a perpetual frown.

"Isa, what is it?"

Embarrassed that Father caught me staring at him, I stammered and said the first thing that came to my mind. "I was just thinking about the time you and the neighbors hung from the rafters to keep the roof from flying off during that terrible hurricane."

Father put his book down and gave me a curious look. "You remember

33

that, *hija*? Why, you couldn't have been more than four or five at the time."

"I was five and I remember every bit of what happened that night and the next day."

Father flashed a welcomed grin. "That was something wasn't it, *hija*? The wind from that hurricane blew so hard, I thought that we were all going to take off flying."

"I did, too, and I was so scared."

"But everything turned out all right, didn't it? Just like I promised."

I smiled. "Sí, Papá. Just like you promised."

He nodded as he picked up his book and went back to reading, the perpetual frown momentarily gone, replaced by a smile.

I wondered why I had been thinking about the hurricane. Maybe it was the contrast that caused me to dredge up that memory, the vigor of the father of the hurricane and the apathy of the father sitting before me. I closed my eyes and saw Father again, young, in his late twenties, lean, muscular, and full of life.

At the time, we lived in the house across the street from where we now lived. It was a rectangular building with two rooms that was elevated about three feet above the ground on a pier and beam construction. Father had rented the residence while he saved money to build a house on the lots he had purchased. We had lived in the little wood-framed house until I was about ten years old.

A northwest wind had blown hard and steady all day long. Terre and I played together inside, frequently running to the windows to watch the downpour of rain. The front room of the house served as a living room and bedroom (where Terre and I slept), and the back room served as a kitchen and a bedroom for my parents.

Although I was young at the time, I knew when Father began boarding up the windows and telling Mother to fill up containers with water and to get out the lanterns, that something terrible was going to happen, although I wasn't sure what. Our house was the sturdiest of all the houses in the neighborhood so Father had encouraged our neighbors to take refuge with us.

In 1933, there were just a few houses on our block, the town being barely five years old, so our neighbors consisted only of the Cavachos, Treviños, and the Mendozas. The Cavachos would one day run a boarding house, but at that time, Concha was a housewife, and her husband, Jerónimo, worked with Father at Vanburg Packing Shed. The Treviños, Maria and Hector, lived next door to the east of us, and the Mendozas, Lydia and Ignacio, lived on the other side. They had a daughter, Lisa, who was about three. Hector also worked at Vanburg Packing Shed, and

Ignacio was a field worker. This was before Father had started his contracting business.

As the night progressed and the wind howled, our gathering became festive, almost like a party. I hovered between the two rooms, determined not to miss anything. The men sat with Father around the small kitchen table in the back room, a bottle of tequila and several shot glasses between them. Jerónimo, who had a pencil thin mustache and greasy combed back hair, had known Father the longest, so their conversation with each other was easygoing. The other two men mostly just listened.

"Did you know how Miguel here got to be foreman of the packing shed?" Jerónimo sat back in his chair and gave Señor Treviño a quizzical look.

"*Pues,* I've heard stories," mumbled Hector, a heavy-set man with unruly black hair. He reminded me of a lumbering shaggy dog, big, but harmless. I noticed that he seemed to have a difficult time looking directly at people when he spoke, as if he were telling a lie. Now I realize that Señor Treviño was just shy, not to mention a little intimidated by my father.

"Well, let me tell you how it happened. And I should know because I was there." Jerónimo pointed a thumb at himself.

"That's not necessary, amigo," Father said good-naturedly as he poured another round of tequila shots. "Spare the poor man."

"I'd like to know." Hector glanced at my father.

"Me, too," agreed Ignacio, a dark-skinned *indio* who was a field worker and who mostly smiled and nodded as if everything said in this small room was gospel.

"Let me see." Jerónimo looked up at our exposed rafter ceiling. "We had been working only about two months at the packing shed—Miguel and I started on the same day, you know—when the gringo foreman, Peters, came around to our section where we were crating cabbages. He was scratching his head." Jerónimo mimicked the gringo scratching his head. "Then he said, 'Do any of you greasers, I mean, men, know how many of these crates will fit in the new reefer?' He laughed like he had made a big joke. *Pues*, Miguel walks over to him and says, 'I can tell you.' You would have thought a thunderbolt had struck Peters. 'You?' he says. 'Sure,' says Miguel.

"Next thing you know there's bets going all around, mostly against Miguel. I, of course, knowing that my friend here is an educated man, put my money on him. Anyway, Miguel tells Peters he needs to measure the boxcar first, so Peters takes him over to it and without so much as a ruler I tell you, Miguel walks down and across the boxcar, looks up for a few minutes, then jumps out of it. He pulls out the little pad of paper and pencil he always keeps in his shirt pocket and starts writing. When he finishes, he rips out a sheet of paper and hands it to Peters and says, 'This boxcar will hold two-hundred twenty-five crates of cabbages.' Peters, his eyes all bugged out, looks at Miguel and says, 'What's your name?' 'Caballero,' says Miguel. 'O.K., Mr. Caballero, let's see if you're as smart as you think you are.'

"So, one by one, we counted each crate as we put them in the boxcar and you should have seen the expression on Peter's face when about half an hour later, we had loaded exactly two-hundred twenty-five crates in that boxcar!" Jerónimo grinned in admiration.

"Just simple math," Father interjected with a wave of his hand. "And the fact that my father once owned a produce company in México didn't hurt." He grinned. "You see, he shipped several tons of produce by rail during harvest seasons. I became very familiar with the capacity load for rail cars since I helped out at the company part time while I was in school."

"Next thing you know, Peters is out of a job and the big boss himself asks Miguel if he would take over as foreman of the packing shed," Jerónimo said.

Both Hector and Ignacio looked at my father, their eyes opened wide, a look that not only indicated amazement, but profound respect. Then they laughed—big, hearty belly laughs. "A toast to Don Miguel!" Señor Treviño bellowed out, to everyone's astonishment. "Anyone who can put one over on a gringo deserves and gets my highest respect!"

That was the first time I heard my father referred to as don, which was a title of respect not attributed to many, and certainly not to one as young as my father.

Father nodded, his eyes indicating agreement and, along with his friends, he gulped down a third shot of tequila.

"Where did you get your schooling, Don Miguel?" Señor Treviño continued, his shyness gone.

"I studied with the Brothers of the Sacred Heart in Monterrey, then I continued on to the state university. Unfortunately, my college career was cut short when my father passed away," Father said matter-of-factly.

"I only went to the third grade myself," said Señor Treviño, a note of regret in his voice.

"Education is important, but it is not the only thing," Father said consolingly. "I have known many men of integrity who had little education. What counts is common sense. A man with a good education, but no sense, may as well have no education at all."

With that comment, my father secured his position as someone who was *muy educado*, not just educated, but wise and well-mannered, and from that day forward, both Hector and Ignacio began to call him Don Miguel, and soon after, everyone was addressing my father in this manner.

While the men were downing tequila in the kitchen during the storm, the women were clustered on the small sofa and two upholstered armchairs in the living area. My mother had made a pot of coffee and that's what the women were drinking, except for Concha, Jerónimo's wife. Concha was a heavy-set woman with a boisterous laugh. She enjoyed telling jokes that at the age of five I didn't understand, but which made the women flinch with embarrassment and the men laugh heartily. Even Father had laughed, though he later told Mother that he'd better never catch her acting the way that Concha did. When Father had first pulled out the bottle of tequila and poured out shots for the men, Concha went right over, poured herself a shot and gulped it down. She returned to the living area, her plump face flushed. "Ay, *comadre*, that went down nice and warm!"

Mother laughed at her friend's comment while she served me, Terre, and Lisa cups of frothy hot chocolate. Later, when we all had to relieve ourselves, mother was angry at herself for giving us so much liquid when she remembered that our outhouse had fallen over during the storm. She brought out the ceramic chamber pot that we used when we were sick in bed, and we had to use this portable toilet behind a makeshift partition near the back door.

After the excitement of having so many people in our little house wore off, I lay on my bed in the front room with Terre and Lisa, a sad-eyed *morenita*, whose mother sang like an angel, and who that night, sang a ballad to help us fall asleep.

A deafening roar woke us up a few hours later and we all started crying. Mother gathered Terre and me next to her on the bed, and I saw that the lanterns were on, pitching an eerie light in the room. I felt rain drops on my head, looked up and saw the roof vibrating and rain flowing in through cracks between the roof boards. Father shouted at the men and the next thing I knew they were hanging from the rafters, trying to keep the roof from blowing off. The four men must have weighed a lot. Even so, for a few minutes, I thought that the roof would fly off taking my Father and our neighbors with it. I started crying, begging Father to get down. But he couldn't hear me over the shattering glass and thunderous explosions coming from outside.

I remember how safe I felt pressed against Mother's warm body, even amidst the storm. After what seemed an eternity (three hours, I found out later), the wind stopped howling, and the room went still. Finally, Father came to us. "Are you all right?" He looked at Mother, concern etched on his face as he ran his hand over her head and down her back over her long, coppery hair.

"Sí, we're fine." She gave him a wistful smile.

He looked at me and put out his arms. I jumped into them. "It's only a lull in the storm," he said as I snuggled against him. "All we can do is wait." He walked to one of the upholstered armchairs and sat down, cradling me in his arms, while I sobbed into his chest. "Now, Isa," he whispered in my ear. "Everything will be all right. I promise, *hija*. You must be brave." The wait would have been torturous had it not been for Father's soothing presence.

About two hours later, the wind started up again, this time from the opposite direction, and soon it was tearing away at one-hundred miles per hour (I found this out later when Father read the newspaper account to us). For the next five hours, the winds howled and the rain poured, and Father and his friends spent much of the time hanging on the rafters. Finally, at about midmorning, the howling ceased. Everyone stood silently for a few minutes, then Father strode to the front door and opened it. A rush of wind blew into the room, sprinkling those of us by the door with water.

"*Oyen*, come and see," he said, his chocolate eyes wide open, marveling at the sight.

I eased my way next to him. Water lapped at the bottom of the doorway. Down the rushing river of our street bobbed tires, splintered wood, building remnants, signs, mangled tree limbs, shingles, a bloated goat, and fruit of all types, mangos, figs, oranges. The destruction of the hurricane was truly a sight to behold.

Almost a full week passed before the water completely subsided leaving our little street a giant mud-pile, which Father refused to let us play in. He said that we could get diseases from the stagnant water that had mingled with the waste from the outhouses. For weeks, even after the ground had dried up, the air smelled like rotten eggs.

I remember Father putting his arm around Mother as they looked over the destruction, saying, "We are all safe, and that's all that matters. We can rebuild."

Soon after the hurricane, Father purchased the citrus orchard in north Ruby. Many of the trees had been uprooted and the orange crop destroyed, so the owner wanted to sell out. It's funny the way things turn out. Father was able to purchase the land because of a hurricane and now he had lost his citrus crop because of a freeze. Despite his wisdom, status, and promises, Father could not control the impact of nature on our lives, any more than he could control Mother's abrasive, yet accurate observations.

Chapter 6

We had just finished dinner when we heard a knock on the front door. "I'll get it!" Marta scrambled out of her chair and ran through the living room. "It's mariachis!" she announced after she had opened the door, her eyes flashing excitement. I saw my mother look at Father in surprise. I realized with some embarrassment that she thought that he had commissioned the serenade for her, though how she could have thought such a thing considering the way she had been treating him was beyond me. We abandoned our seats in the dining room and followed Marta outside.

"Está la señorita Isabel Caballero?"

I stepped forward and nodded shyly, accepting a long-stemmed red rose from the lead singer of the group. Standing behind him were men dressed in traditional charro outfits, black *pantalones* and matching short jackets trimmed with silver *conchas*, flowing scarlet bowties, and enormous felt sombreros embroidered with gold threads. The five men stood ready with their guitars, violins, and trumpet.

"From Señor Marcos Benavides," the lead singer said as he bowed.

Marta, Ellie, and Lupita all giggled, their hands covering their mouths. I glowered at them and glanced at Terre, who was leaning against the porch post, her arms crossed, a smirk on her face. She didn't think much of Marcos or "shallow" romantic gestures, as she referred to courtship rituals.

I turned my attention back to the musicians when the melody of "Solamente Una Vez" by Mexican composer Agustín Lara, began. *Solamante una vez a mé en la vida, solamente una vez y nada más.* I felt the blood pulsing through my veins. This song from the early forties was my favorite Mexican ballad, something I had once mentioned to Marcos. It was also my father's favorite song and one he had commissioned to be played for my mother every year on her birthday, though he had not done so for her last birthday a few months before. I felt as if I had stolen something from her, so mixed with my gratitude for this open display of Marcos' unabashed love, I felt disconcerted and guilty.

By the time the musicians had finished, many of our neighbors had gathered in our front yard under the mulberry trees. To say that I was embarrassed is an understatement. I have never been fond of center stage, and to have my private love announced to the world, well, I was mortified.

Father thanked the musicians and gave the lead singer a tip, sending them on their way. As we walked back into the house, he said, "So, Isa, you have an admirer. Has someone stolen your heart from me?"

"No one could ever steal my heart from you, Papá." I linked my arm through his.

He gave me a sad smile. "My Isa has grown up. I suppose I should be expecting a call from your young man soon, eh?"

"I think so, Papá."

Father nodded and walked to the back of the house while Mother instructed my sisters to clear the table.

"Marcos Benavides has a bad reputation, and he drinks," said Mother, after Father had gone, her arms akimbo.

"How did you know about Marcos and me?" I glanced at her, then away, focusing on the china cabinet behind her. It was a habit of mine, not being able to look a person in the eye when I was being reprimanded.

"We live in a small town, Isa, and I have friends in Westwood. News travels fast in these small towns, especially that kind of news."

"Why haven't you said anything?"

"I didn't want you to do anything rash. I know what it's like to be young and in love, though you might find that hard to believe. Think carefully before you make a commitment to this boy. From what I know of him, he doesn't have much ambition."

"You don't know him, Mamá. He's smart, and he does have ambition."

Mother just stood there looking at me, her dark eyes expressing love and concern. Then she just turned around and walked into the kitchen.

I went to my bedroom and lay on my bed feeling exposed, as if I had just walked naked through our neighborhood. But, in my head, I could still hear the words to the love song. As I recalled them, I felt fortunate that I had fallen in love with a man who had as romantic and tender a heart as my father.

You belong to my heart, now and forever,
And our love had its start not long ago—
We were gathering stars while a million
guitars played our love song;
When I said, "I love you," every beat of my heart said it, too.
Twas a moment like this, do you remember?
And your eyes threw a kiss when they met mine;
Now we own all the stars and a million guitars are still playing;
Darling, you are the song and you'll always belong to my heart.
*****

A few days later, three men called on Father.

"Who was at the door, Isa?" My mother sipped from her cup of *cafe con leche* at the kitchen table, where she was sitting with Doña Cuca.

"Three men in business suits for Father," I answered nonchalantly even though my heart thumped so loudly I was sure everyone could hear.

She exchanged knowing glances with Doña Cuca, who was going through her evening ritual of pouring beer into a frosty glass retrieved from the refrigerator. She waited for the foam to subside then brought the glass to her wrinkled mouth. She sipped the amber liquid, a satisfied expression on her face. She once told me that she had a glass of beer every night for medicinal purposes. "It keeps my digestive system running smoothly," she had said matter-of-factly. "Just one, though. That's all you need to keep yourself in working order." I suppose that's why I like to drink a beer every now and then, especially when I feel a bit clogged up.

"I wonder what they want?" Lupita plunged the last of the dinner plates in the sudsy water in the sink.

"Oh, don't be such a *tonta*, Lupita," Ellie said as she dried one of the stoneware plates with a cotton cloth and placed it in the cupboard. "They're here for Isa."

Marta, who was writing out her ABCs on a tablet at the table, giggled.

I smiled sheepishly, but said nothing. Marcos had told me he was going to propose according to custom, and it looked as if today was the day for the formal *petición de la mano*. I was sure that he had commissioned these men to ask my father for my hand in marriage on his behalf. I was anxious because I had no idea what father would say to the men's entreaties for Marcos.

I grabbed a dish towel and, though my hands were shaking, began to help Ellie dry the dishes. I suppose by now you're wondering why my sisters and I spent so much time cleaning while our maid visited with Mother. The fact of the matter was that Father hired Doña Cuca to help my mother, not us, as Mother so dramatically demonstrated one day about a year before after coming upon Ellie during a mutiny.

Ellie, who has always been the most assertive of all of us, had thrown a dish towel on the floor in the middle of helping with the dishes, stomped her feet, crossed her arms and said that she was through washing dishes. "We have a maid. Why do we have to wash dishes all the time? Why do we have to cook, mop floors, dust and make our own beds? It's ridiculous. What are we paying Doña Cuca for?"

Unfortunately for Ellie, Mother had just returned from the market and was stepping onto the back porch when Ellie was in the middle of her tirade. I cringe thinking about what happened next. Mother opened the kitchen door, set the two grocery bags on the table, dashed across the kitchen floor and slapped Ellie resoundingly across the face.

"How dare you question the way I run my household?" Mother's face flushed red and her dark eyes narrowed to slits. "What are *we* paying Doña Cuca for? *We*? Since when, Eloise, did you pay for anything in this house? You are spoiled and headstrong, and I am ashamed of you."

Ellie sobbed into her hands, her head bowed down, so that all we could see was a dark mass of wavy hair.

Mother's eyes scanned the room, taking in the five of us girls. Raul as usual was out with his friends. Heaven forbid he would have domestic duties. I looked down, focusing my eyes on a scuff mark on the red-tinted concrete floor beneath my loafers.

"All of you listen to me," Mother said, her voice harsh. "I will not have you grow up to be snobbish, idle women who have nothing better to do than to look your noses down on other people. Yes, we have more money than some. Yes, we have a maid and a gardener and your father has many people who work for him. But that has nothing to do with you. You have no idea who you might marry, or if you will marry at all. What if you marry a man who can't afford a maid? It's not as if hundreds of rich, eligible Mexicanos are running around the Valley. Who's going to do the cleaning and cooking for you? I would not be doing my duty as a mother if I allowed you to be idle. No, I will not let that happen. Now get back to work, all of you. And, one more thing. If you do not like the way I run my household, you are welcome to leave it." With that, she turned on her heels and left the kitchen with a toss of her wavy red hair, leaving us to put away the groceries.

Since that dreadful day, Ellie never complained again, nor did the rest of us. As I watched Ellie now, rubbing the dinner plates, her eyes twinkling when she looked at me, I felt a deep affection for her. I also felt a little guilty. You see, that day she had merely stated what we all were feeling, but were too afraid to say out loud. Over the years, for various reasons, Ellie was the one to voice her concerns on our behalf, causing my mother to go into fits of unprecedented proportions. But my sister never lost her spunk, no matter how often Mother berated her. I have always considered Ellie to be the bravest of all my sisters.

"Do you know who the men are, Isa?" Ellie had finished drying the dishes and opened the kitchen door just a crack, enough to see into the living room.

I stood next to her and whispered, "The plump one sitting on the far right end of the sofa is Señor De Leon. He owns the biggest grocery store in the northern section of Westwood. Señor Hilario, the thin one at the other end of the sofa, is the proprietor of Paco's Restaurant." Both were dressed in dark suits and ties, their hair slicked back with pomade, smelling of cologne and money.

"And the other one?"

I frowned as I glanced at the third man, who was dressed in the khaki uniform of a boy scout leader. He was beefy, and his face turned red at the slightest provocation. "I've never seen him before."

"Was Marcos a boy scout?" Ellie asked.

"Maybe so." I grinned at the sudden revelation. I found it hard to imagine that Marcos had been a boy scout.

"Girls, get away from the door," Mother commanded.

We closed the door quietly and joined Mother, Doña Cuca, Marta and Lupita at the table. "It's all so romantic, isn't it?" Lupita sighed as she fiddled with her hair, which fell like a curtain over her shoulders to her waist as she removed the rubber band holding it back.

"Yes, at the beginning it's always romantic, eh *comadre*?" Doña Cuca grinned, the deep wrinkles on her dark cheeks disappearing momentarily.

"Yes, it is. But the romance doesn't last long," she said wistfully.

As my mother and Doña Cuca commiserated about the demise of romance after marriage, I realized that Marcos' family must be well-respected in Westwood because Marcos alone could never have convinced such prominent men to vouch for him. Marcos had dropped out of high school and was known to frequent bars across the border in Reynosa. In those days, however, a family's standing was important, and I suppose the men, being men, considered Marcos' indiscretions as minor when compared to his parents' stellar reputation. It goes to show that a man's reputation has more to do with who he is rather than what he does—while with women, it's just the opposite.

After what seemed an eternity, the three men left. Father called for me and I heard Mother's chair scratch across the floor as she rose and followed me to the living room. I sat on the couch and Mother plopped down next to me.

"You know why these men were here, *hija*?"

"Sí, Papá." I looked at my hands.

"Do you love this young man, Marcos Benavides?"

"Sí, Papá."

He nodded thoughtfully. "Do you want to marry him?"

"Sí, Papá."

"I don't know that he is good enough for you. He did not finish high school."

I waited in suspense for him to continue, not sure where this conversation was headed.

He sighed. "However, he has been in the military service and was honorably discharged. His former troopmaster, Señor Ybañez, says that

Marcos is an honorable young man. The señores say that he comes from a respectable, if somewhat poor, family, and that he is a hard worker." He paused. "A few months ago, I might have said no to this young man's proposal. However, considering our reduced circumstances, I would feel hypocritical to do so now." He stopped and looked out the front window.

I followed his gaze. The bougainvillea on the front trellis was blooming and the fushia flowers looked lovely against the white slatted boards.

He continued. "When the men come back next week for the answer, I will give my consent, if that is what you wish."

I smiled and nodded, feeling as if the whole world had been given to me as a gift.

"So that's it?" Mother sat up, putting her hands on her hips.

"What do you mean?"

"What about me? Don't I get a say?"

"There is nothing for you to say, Beatriz," he answered tiredly. "Has it been so long? Have you forgotten what it was like to be young and in love? Don't you remember what lovers will do to be together, despite everything and everyone?"

Father's remarks stunned Mother to silence. I knew the story of my parents' elopement, but it was not something openly discussed in our home. Father had been from a prominent Monterrey family and although they had lost their money and status after the Revolution, they felt that Father would be marrying beneath him if he married Mother, who had been a servant in his uncle's employ. He defied them and married her without his mother's blessing, something that I am sure bothered him immensely as he doted on his mother. His mother and sisters eventually came to terms with the marriage, but there were still lingering feelings of ill-will on both sides, particularly between Mother and my tías.

Mother pursed her lips. "No, I have not forgotten, Miguel," she finally said. "Very well. If Isa is determined to marry this young man, then nothing I say will matter. But mark my words." She looked at me. "You will have troubles, Isa. And, when you do, don't come crying to me." She rose, wiped her hands on her calico apron in a gesture that reminded me of Pontius Pilate, and stalked out of the room.

Father scowled as he watched her disappear into the kitchen, then smiled when he glanced at me. "You know she doesn't mean it, don't you, *hija*?"

"I know, Papá."

"*Bueno.* You can go now and tell your sisters. I can see Ellie and Marta peeking through the kitchen door. Try to keep the squealing to a minimum. I'd like to read the paper in peace."

I glanced at the door, which slammed shut. "Oh, Papá, I don't squeal anymore."

He just smiled.

*****

I met my future in-laws for the first time three days after the men returned and my father gave his consent to the proposal. Marcos and his parents made the traditional visit to meet my parents and me at our home. Marcos' father was a small, wiry man, light-complected with thin bluish veins prominent on his hands and arms. He had the kindest eyes I had ever seen. Light brown, they exuded gentleness and warmth. He walked with a stoop in his shoulders, a malady that afflicted many agricultural laborers. Señor Benavides had picked cotton and vegetables for years before being hired by the Westwood School District as a groundskeeper at the high school.

While Marcos' father was gentle and quiet, his mother was dramatic and talkative. As stout as her husband was thin, and much darker complexioned than Señor Benavides, she had decidedly Indian features—a prominent nose and a large face with a strong jaw line. I understood immediately the comment Marcos had made earlier in our acquaintance when he had said that his mother ruled the house.

"Señora Caballero," she said, "You have the most beautiful hair I have ever seen."

"*Gracias*, Señora Benavides." Mother beamed, smoothing her hair with her hand. "But, *por favor*, call me Beatriz, or *comadre*, whichever you prefer. After all, we will soon be relations."

My future mother-in-law couldn't have known this, but she had touched upon the one thing that would endear her forever to my mother. Of all her physical features, my mother was most proud of her hair, which was a burnished copper, and until the day she died at the age of eighty, she kept it dyed as close to its original color as possible.

Señora Benavides returned my mother's smile, patting her own bluish hair, which was pulled up in a hair net. "Before this happened, I had dark hair, but by the time I turned forty, it had turned white." She sighed. "My daughters wanted me to dye it back, but what for? I suppose if God wanted me to have dark hair He would have kept it dark. However, if my hair had been red like yours, I would have changed it back in an instant."

Mother gave her newfound friend her most appreciative smile. "It looks so becoming the way it is now. I think you're right. I don't see a need to change it."

After the women had exhausted the subject of their hair, my father spoke. "So, Marcos, what do you think about this Longoria business?" he said, referring to a segregation issue involving a Mexican-American

GI and a South Texas funeral home that had been in the newspapers for the previous two months. That issue, along with the disastrous freeze, had been a major topic of conversation in the Mexican-American community (and I'm sure the Anglo community as well) since the news broke.

"It made me mad as hell . . ." Marcos said vehemently, then stopped. "I'm sorry, sir . . ."

"That's all right. Go on," Father said, his mouth turned up in a slight smile.

Marcos leaned forward, his expression intense. "Private Longoria died defending this country, defending the same gringo bigots who then said, 'It's okay that you put your life on the line for me, but don't even think about being treated as an equal when you get back. You might be a decorated soldier but you're still a worthless Mexican who doesn't deserve to be treated with respect.'"

Father nodded, pleased with Marcos' passionate response. Father had always admired assertive men. "It amazes me the lengths that some gringos will go to try keep us Mexicanos under their thumb, even after death." Father shook his head.

"Those gringos in Three Rivers probably feel like *tontos* now," Señora Benavides said with a smirk. "The Mexicano they didn't want in their chapel is now buried with full military honors in Arlington National Cemetery, thanks to Senator Johnson."

"I don't usually trust politicians," Father noted, "however, if I were a citizen of this country, Senator Johnson would get my vote."

"Why, I would have thought that you were an American citizen, Don Miguel," Señora Benavides said. "You have lived here for a long time."

Father's face clouded over, though his voice held no rancor. "Yes, I have lived here a long time, but my heart belongs to México." He then looked at Señor Benavides. "Do you have any ties to México, *compadre*?"

"All my family is now in Texas. I immigrated when I was fourteen during the early part of the Revolution, and my brothers came after. I do feel an emotional tie to the old country, but the United States is my homeland now. However, I have many friends who feel as you do."

Señor Benavides had answered matter-of-factly, with no defensiveness. I was amazed at his depth of perception. He sensed immediately my father's discomfort about this subject. Marcos had told me that both of his parents were illiterate, that they could neither read nor write, but obviously illiteracy did not equate with stupidity because Señor Benavides was not a stupid man.

"Then you will understand when I say that to give up my Mexican citizenship would be like renouncing my own mother. I will never renounce my homeland." Father sat erect, his mouth set in a determined line.

"I would renounce México in a minute if he would let me," Mother said to Señora Benavides, pointing her thumb at Father. "All I remember of México is heartbreak and hard times. That horrible Revolution took my father and then the flu epidemic took my mother."

Father scowled at Mother. "Now is not the time to speak of such things." He turned to look at Señor Benavides. "I am afraid my wife speaks when she should be silent. It is a failing, I have noticed, of many of the weaker sex."

To my relief, Mother said nothing, though her face flushed a peculiar shade of red. Marcos' father exchanged a quick glance with his own wife. Soon the conversation turned to less volatile topics and while our parents conversed, Marcos and I glanced furtively at each other. At one point, Father startled us both by asking Marcos how he intended to support me.

Marcos answered, "I'm working for American Fruit Growers and am in line for a promotion. I promise you that Isabel will want for nothing."

Father nodded, seemingly pleased with the response. But I knew what he was really thinking. Despite the uncertainty of self-employment, Father believed that working for yourself was the only way to make a good living. I could tell he was a little disappointed in Marcos' seeming lack of desire in that direction. However, after the Benavides' had gone, Father said that he was impressed by Marcos' bearing and declared him to be a good sort of young man. His parents he declared to be *buena gente*. That was all I needed to hear. The wedding plans would proceed.

Chapter 7

Marta came down with the chicken pox two days before Mother, Father and I were to drive to Monterrey to purchase my wedding dress. Mother begged off going on the trip, saying she didn't want to leave my youngest sister. I was more relieved than annoyed, not about my sister's illness, but about my mother's legitimate excuse to avoid the trip. When we visited Monterrey, we always stayed with my grandmother and although she was gracious to my mother, Father's other relatives, particularly his sisters, treated her with barely concealed contempt. Oh, it was subtle, nothing you could really put your finger on, but it was apparent, even to me, that they considered Mother inferior. My aunts would be talking and then stop when Mother walked into the room. They would be polite to her, but I never once saw them sharing a joke with her. Even in their home when they should have been the hostesses, Mother would end up in the kitchen, serving them.

It didn't take me long after Mother bowed out to think to ask Carmen, Marcos' sister, to accompany Father and me to Monterrey. Marcos had introduced me to his sister, Carmen, who was my age, early in our courtship. One of the first things I had noticed about Carmen was her sense of style. In those days, women wore dresses in public, not like many of today's women who wear unflattering blue jeans and T-shirts everywhere they go.

Carmen worked as a sales clerk at Crystal's Apparel Shop in Westwood. She got a discount on everything she purchased there, so she always dressed in the latest fashions, dresses with belted waists and either pencil-slim or billowy skirts that were calf-length (a result of the lifting of wartime restrictions on fabric use). She also wore matching accessories—necklaces, earrings, purses, pumps, and gloves.

Carmen was delighted when I asked her to accompany me to Monterrey. She was able to get off work with just two days' notice. Lucky for me, she had vacation time coming and was able to take the whole week off. On a sunny morning in early March, with $150 in my purse which Marcos had given me to buy my gown, Father and I drove to Westwood to pick up my future sister-in-law for our four-hour journey south.

*****

In 1949, Monterrey was a city of more than 300,000 inhabitants, its grand plaza surrounded by Spanish colonial palaces and cathedrals and post-modern buildings, an odd juxtaposition of the past and the present.

The landmark that defined Monterrey was the saddlelike profile of *Cerro de la Silla*, Saddle Hill, which rose like a great monolith to the east of the city. Monterrey was virtually surrounded by the Sierra Madre Oriental, and as we approached from the north and I saw the peaks of the rugged mountains towering to the sky, I felt my pulse quicken. This would most likely be the last time I would come to my father's birthplace as a single woman.

Terre and I had visited Monterrey often as children, staying for extended summer vacations with my grandmother. Several of my father's many relatives dropped by daily, so our stays were always festive. On Sundays, we would drive out to the family *rancho* in Villa Santiago, which Tía Ana, my father's elder sister, had purchased. From there, we often visited *Cascada Cola de Caballo*, Horsetail Falls, where we picnicked by the eighty-two-foot high waterfall and rode donkeys to the summit, enjoying the lush greenery and the coolness of the fall's mist.

As Father drove into the city passing Plaza Purísima on the city's west side, Carmen and I both commented on the new basilica on the west end of the plaza which had been designed with a system of enormous parabolic arches that reached to the sky. "What an unusual looking church," Carmen said. "It looks out of place in this neighborhood, don't you think?" She glanced at the turn-of-the-century, neoclassical-style residences surrounding the plaza.

"Yes," I said. "I think they should have renovated the church instead of tearing it down, but everyone said it was too old and too small. My grandmother and grandfather were married in the old Purísima Church and I thought grandmother would be heartbroken when it was demolished, but surprisingly she wasn't. She likes the new church."

Father turned onto Calle Aldama, stopping in front of my grandmother's house, a quaint Spanish colonial with an arched entryway and tiled floors. My unmarried aunt, Tía Isabel (we were both named after my father's grandmother), met us at the door and couldn't have been more exuberant if she had been getting married herself. There's nothing like a wedding to get the juices flowing in a Mexican family, particularly among the womenfolk. Tía Isabel, who was in her early thirties, took care of Mamá Grande, cooking for her and seeing to her needs. Tía shuffled us into the *sala*. My grandmother, in a black, crepe de chine short-sleeved dress, was settled in her favorite chair, a red velvet upholstered arm chair with gilded gold armrests. The French Provincial chair had always reminded me of a throne.

"*Mi'jo!*" She rose, holding out her arms. "It's so good to see you."

Father strode over to his mother and enveloped her in a big bear hug. His bulk momentarily camouflaged her so that all I could see were her fleshy arms around his back and tufts of white hair over his shoulder.

She spied me and pulled away from Father. "Isa, you look radiant, just like a bride-to-be should." Mamá Grande hugged me, then sat down, wearied by the exertion. Grandmother was almost seventy and although blessed with good health, her children had always waited on her so that now the slightest activity tired her.

I introduced her to Carmen and could tell by the way Grandmother gave her a quick full length glance, then smiled, her brown eyes glinting, that she was impressed by my future sister-in-law's appearance and manners, which were, as usual, impeccable. You would never had guessed Carmen lived in a tiny wood-framed house with an outdoor toilet.

We chatted with my grandmother for a while, ate the mid-day meal, and rested for a few hours. At about five o'clock, Father drove Tía Isabel, Carmen and me downtown, and dropped us off at Plaza Zaragoza, the city's main plaza. We visited several shops that evening, but it wasn't until two days later that I found the wedding dress of my dreams, an ivory satin gown, at a boutique near the old district. After taking my measurements for some minor alterations, the seamstress assured me that the dress would be ready the next day. Three days later (we were on Mexican time), the alterations had been made and we were able to pick up the dress. At Tía Isabel's insistence, we went to a portrait studio so that I could have a picture taken in my gown. I will be forever grateful to Tía Isabel for insisting that we do this. That picture turned out to be the only professional photo I had of me in my wedding gown because Marcos and I were so broke by the time the wedding took place that we couldn't afford to pay for a professional photographer. The only reminders of our ceremony were fuzzy black and white photos taken by a few family friends.

When we returned to the house later that evening and I tried my gown on for Grandmother in her bedroom, she cried. She sat on her bed and pulled out a handkerchief from the drawer of her night stand.

"Don't you like the dress?" I gave a quick, worried glance at Carmen. I looked down at the soft satin skirt of the gown as it flared out five feet around me. The dress was gathered at the waist and the bodice fit off the shoulders, with a delicate net material covering my shoulders up to my neck. The back of the dress had over fifty satin covered buttons.

"No, it's not that, *hija*," she finally stammered. "The dress is beautiful and you look beautiful in it. I was just remembering when you were born. Has it really been so long?"

"I guess it has," I said, suddenly feeling sentimental.

"Oh, I'm just being an old fool." She wiped her eyes and looked at me again. "You will be a beautiful bride. Your *novio* is very lucky."

On the verge of tears, I gathered up the skirt of my gown and rushed over to my grandmother, kissing her soft, wrinkled cheek. "Thank you, Grandmother. But in truth, I am the lucky one. Marcos is wonderful."

"Of course he is, *hija*. Of course he is." She patted my hand and smiled.

*****

Later that night, several of my father's siblings came to visit. Father had ten brothers and four sisters, most of them married with several children of their own. When even a few of them visited Grandmother's house, which was not spacious, all the rooms overflowed with people.

"So, you're going to get married, eh, Isa?" Tío Jorge, whom everyone called güerito because of his light hair and fair complexion, leaned nonchalantly against the doorway in shirtsleeves, his muscular arms crossed. "Let me see. What advice can I give you?"

"What advice can you give her?" Tía Teresa's eyes widened and her mouth formed a circle. "*Válgame Dios!* You have no business giving marital advice to anyone. How many times have you been married? Three? Four?"

"Just three, and this time for good." He glanced adoringly at his latest wife, a buxom brunette, with whom he already had two children.

"Sí, Jorge has changed his ways." Tía Rita, who was ten years younger than my thirty-three-year-old uncle, smiled smugly.

"A leopard without spots is still a leopard." Teresa shrugged. "If anyone should be giving advice, it should be Dalia and Pepe. They've been married twenty years now, right?" She glanced at her older sister.

There were about twenty of us congregated around the oak table in the dining room, with Tía Dalia and Tío Pepe seated opposite me and Carmen, Grandmother and Father at either ends of the table. Several of my uncles had pulled up chairs near Father.

"Isa already has the excellent example of her own parents," Dalia said, her voice soft. "What could I add to that?" There was no hint of maliciousness in my aunt's response. Of all my father's siblings, she had always been the kindest to my mother. She had married a man who was half Indian, and I suppose, she too, had had a hard time because of it.

I glanced at Father, who was drinking beer and talking with his brother Alejandro. Apparently he had overheard Tía Dalia's remark because his expression turned sour. "My Isa needs no advice from anyone," he said gruffly. "She's good natured and forgiving, two attributes essential but lacking in many marriages. Besides that, her young man has common sense and is hard-working, two things that a few of you might take heed of."

There was a palpable silence, everyone looking furtively at Tío Felipe. Father had aided Tío on numerous occasions with monetary contributions

51

and recommendations for jobs, but Tío Felipe was a spendthrift and lazy to boot. In his mid-thirties, he, his wife, and three children lived in a small colonial house in Monterrey's oldest district. The neighborhood was distinguished, but the houses were old and falling apart. Father often said that Tío Felipe coasted along on his charm and that was about all that was keeping him afloat.

The evening wore on and my uncles became increasingly more raucous proportionate to their beer consumption. Father was noticeably surly.

"So, what do you think, Miguel? I was hoping that you could lend me a couple of thousand pesos to invest in the new company." Roberto, the youngest of my father's siblings, had pulled up a chair near my father. His expression was expectant. "I'll pay you back with interest, of course."

I knew that Father was still upset about having helped to pay for Roberto's medical schooling only to have his brother drop out and get married. "I'll think about it," Father said.

"What's there to think about? You always said that working for yourself was the best way to get ahead in this world. Well, now I want to do what you've done. I want to start my own business here in Monterrey. Maybe we can be partners."

"I said I'll think about it!" Father roared, pushing the chair out from under him. He elbowed his way out of the crowded dining room.

Roberto looked at me. "What's wrong with him?"

"I don't know, Tío," I lied.

"I'm tired," Grandmother said, motioning for Tía Isabel to help her up. "I'm going to bed."

That was Grandmother's cue that the party was over. Fifteen minutes later, everyone had gone.

"Carmen, I have to go to the bathroom. I'll be back in a few minutes."

"Sure," she said, her voice weary. She dragged across the courtyard, stopping to take her shoes off before continuing on to the guest bedroom.

I crossed the small courtyard, looking up at the velvety sky dotted with pulsating stars. I loved open air courtyards, especially my grandmother's, which was filled with pots overflowing with sweet-scented flowers and shrubs. I felt a sort of melancholy, the kind of feeling one gets before a significant life change. As I approached the bathroom, I overheard voices coming from my grandmother's bedroom. I lingered in the arcaded walkway, breathing in the sweet aroma of roses blooming in a ceramic pot on the patio.

"*Mi'jo*, what's the matter? You were very short with Roberto tonight. That's not like you."

Father didn't say anything for a few minutes, then finally, he spoke.

"Mamá, I've lost a lot of money on a business deal. The fact of the matter is, I'm broke."

I know it must have been very hard for Father to tell his mother that. Father had always given generous amounts of money to his mother and siblings, and when they visited, two and three at a time, he drove them to Edinburg and McAllen to buy new clothes. They would visit for several weeks, and though Mother complained that they were eating us out of house and home, Father would tell her not to worry about it, that there was plenty of money to go around.

"Don't worry about it, *hijo*," Grandmother said. "You've kept your promise to your father. You have been a good son and a good brother. Your brothers and sisters can take care of themselves. It's time to concentrate on your own family."

I ran to the bathroom and locked myself in when I heard a door slam, not wanting to be caught eavesdropping. I was glad that Father had spoken to grandmother about his problems. Maybe now, relieved of his responsibility to his siblings with the blessing of his mother, Father would be able to come to terms with what had happened and start over again.

'

Chapter 8

"**T**he truth is, I don't like working in the packing shed."

I could tell by the hesitant way he spoke that Marcos thought I might be upset by his declaration. His eyes had narrowed, two worry lines appeared between his eyebrows, and he kept running his hand through his hair. We were sitting on the porch swing in front of my house. Now that we were engaged, with the wedding only a few weeks away, he came almost every evening to visit me. "So, what are you trying to tell me?"

"I got a letter from my brother, Josiah. Inside was an acceptance letter from the post office. I've been offered a job."

"That's wonderful, Marcos." I was truly excited, though I'm sure he couldn't tell by my calm demeanor.

"Yeah, well, the thing is, the job is in Chicago. There's no openings here, so we'd have to move to Chicago."

I let his words sink in. It had never dawned on me that we would move from the Valley, especially to somewhere as far away as Chicago. But I remembered how exciting it had been to live in San Antonio when I went to college the year before, and how much fun it was to travel with Father and Mother to Mississippi when I was a little girl.

When I didn't say anything, he said, "What do you think about moving to Chicago?"

"When would we move?"

"Well, we'd have to go right after we got married. They won't hold the position indefinitely. We could make it part of our honeymoon, since you've never been there. It's a big city. There's lots to see."

I didn't have to think about it too long. "Sure, I'll go with you to Chicago," I said, contemplating my forthcoming resignation from my job at the water office with delight rather than regret.

"You mean it? You really mean it?" His face broke out in a smile.

"Yes, I mean it, Marcos. I love you. And, besides, I want you to be happy with your job." I touched his hand, which was on my knee. The truth of the matter was, like most engaged females, I was blindly in love and would have agreed with just about anything he said. I still cringe when I think about it.

"I'm the luckiest guy around." He pulled me close to him.

"Yes, you are, and don't you ever forget it." I poked him playfully in the ribs.

*****

We were married at Sacred Heart Catholic Church at ten o'clock on a

Sunday morning, a bright spring day at the end of April. Father, looking solemn and regal in a dark suit, gave me away, while Mother, wearing a pink organdy dress, cried into a daintily embroidered handkerchief. Marta was one of my flower girls and Terre was my maid of honor. Afterwards, we had a reception at my parents' house. By late afternoon, I had changed into my traveling clothes, a green suit with a matching pill box hat, pumps, and handbag. Carmen had given me a gray silk scarf, which I had draped around my neck and which cascaded down the front of my jacket.

After a tearful farewell with our families, Marcos and I piled into Bernardo's Chevrolet and, after a harrowing ride, we arrived at the Greyhound bus station. Despite my happiness that I was now Mrs. Marcos Benavides and the excitement I felt about moving to Chicago, I also felt wistful, and even a little afraid. I clung to Marcos' arm realizing as I gazed up at him that I really didn't know much about him. What did he like to eat for breakfast? Did he snore? Was he as particular about his clothes as my father was? What brand of hair pomade did he wear? It's funny now that I think about it, but our knowledge of each other was superficial. For his part, Marcos didn't know that he had married a strong-willed girl who was also spoiled. For my part, I didn't realize that I had married a man who, despite his cavalier attitude, was very traditional and very Mexican in his thinking. Our first year together would be volatile.

*****

We lived in Chicago for only four months and most of that time I was in the bathroom of our rented room throwing up. By June, I was pregnant and so sick to my stomach I had worn a path on the linoleum floor from my bed to the bathroom commode. I cried for my mother and father, complained about how awful I felt, and was otherwise a crybaby of the worst sort. Poor Marcos didn't know what to do with such a whiney woman. I blamed him for my miserable condition and we had terrible fights. He would tear out of our room vowing never to return.

We shared a third floor apartment with another couple who were also from the Valley and I was always embarrassed to see them after one of our rows. But, thankfully, they never said anything to us. Later, Marcos would come home ashamed, swearing that he would never desert me. Finally, one day he came home early from work and told me he had resigned his job at the post office. We were going to move back to the Valley so that I could be properly looked after. I felt so relieved and so loved when he took me in his arms and told me that all he cared about was my happiness and the health and well-being of our baby. If that meant moving back to the Valley and his returning to the packing sheds, then so be it. All I could think about was that I would soon be home with Mother, Father, my sisters, and brother. I was going home.

*****

We went home, but not to my parents' house. Marcos said that until he was able to provide properly for me, we would have to live with his parents, that anything else would be improper. I loved my in-laws and they were very good to me, but, well, they were my in-laws. How many young brides want to live with their in-laws? Still, I didn't say anything. At first.

My in-laws' house was on a street perpendicular to and about five-hundred feet north of the Missouri Pacific railroad tracks. The street was zoned for both residences and businesses. On the lots nearest the tracks were an ice plant and an oil depot. Behind them were cotton gins. All along the tracks, as in Ruby, were vegetable packing sheds.

We moved into the house with nine others, including Marcos' three young cousins whom his parents were raising. The tiny wood-framed house, which was painted pink, had four rooms, a twelve by twenty-foot living room/dining room (where we slept on a sofa sleeper), the same size kitchen, and two small bedrooms. Marcos' parents slept in one of the bedrooms and his two sisters in the other, along with Lorena, their one-year-old cousin. His two younger brothers and two male cousins were relegated to a little shack behind the house. Next to the shack was another small building where the toilet was located. I was relieved that at least it wasn't an outhouse.

The walls of the house were of quarter-inch plywood, so what was said in one room could be heard throughout the tiny house. Mamá Benavides spoke incessantly, giving orders to Monica, Marcos' youngest sister, to clean this or that, to take care of Bert, the youngest brother, who was a little slow. Monica was about sixteen at the time and her only escape from her mother's unrelenting orders was when she was at school. One thing I have to say about both my sisters-in-law, they had a sense of humor. They laughed a lot and took things in stride. I suppose there was nothing else to do but go crazy.

By the time we moved into my in-laws' house, I was already at the end of my first trimester of pregnancy, so I was no longer throwing up all over the place. Considering that the toilet was outside, it was a good thing. Marcos started back to work at the packing shed, which left me with Mamá Benavides all day. My mother-in-law liked to talk, and in me she had a captive audience. I remember one of our first conversations. I think it is indicative of the kind of people my in-laws were.

I was sitting at the tiny Formica table in the kitchen feeding mashed potatoes to Lorena, who was in her wooden high chair. Mamá Benavides was mashing garlic cloves and jalapeños in a molcajete to make salsa. "How is it that you and Papá Benavides are raising Lorena and her brothers?" I asked.

She glanced up from the chopping board and sighed. "My niece, Maria, God rest her soul, died when Lorena was just eight months old. Gerardo, their father, is a migrant worker and gone a lot so he couldn't take care of the children. Several of the children's aunts and uncles offered to take them in. But some wanted just Lorena, others wanted only the boys. I didn't think it was right to split them up, so Ignacio and I offered to take them all in. We have a small house and not much money, but there's plenty of love to go around. We have managed so far, and with God's help, things will work out." She smiled at Lorena, touching the child's cheek. The little girl, who was dark-complexioned with black curly hair, grinned, showing two tiny front teeth.

I have to say this, she treated those kids the same as her own, admonishing and smacking her nephews just like her own sons and beaming when Lorena started walking.

It was a good thing my mother had insisted that I learn how to cook and clean house because there was plenty of housework to do. As I grew to the size of a hippopotamus, I helped cook, wash dishes, wash clothes, hang clothes, sweep and mop the floor, dust the furniture (what little there was), and then started all over again the next day.

It wouldn't have been so bad except that there were no modern conveniences. For example, at my parents' house, we had indoor plumbing and a porcelain kitchen sink with a drain. At my in-laws', although my father-in-law had rigged up a faucet in the kitchen, there was no sink or drain. We washed dishes in a tub, then had to carry the tub outside to throw out the dirty water. At my parents' house, we had the latest gas burning range; my in-laws had a wood-burning, cast-iron range which had been built in 1915, according to the date etched on the top. It would get mighty hot in the kitchen when that range was blazing.

Probably the job I liked the least, but spent the most time doing was washing clothes. I remember how sore my arm would get from having to pull the clothes through the wringer after they were done. Then I'd have to hang them up on the makeshift clothesline that stretched across the back yard between two ebony trees. It seemed like there were always clothes to be washed and hung.

I'll never forget the day Father and Mother drove over in the pickup to visit me. It was a cold November day, a rare day in the Valley when the sun wasn't shining. I was wearing a large shift (nothing else would fit over my big belly) and was hanging a pair of trousers on the line. I know I must have been a sight because before Father embraced me, I could see the mortification in his eyes. I think that when he saw me, his princess, looking and working like a scullery maid, it was all he could do to keep from grabbing me and taking me home with him and Mother. He didn't say anything, but he didn't have to. In fact, it was a good five minutes before he could speak at all.

"*Mi'ja*, you shouldn't be doing that in your condition." He led me to a metal lawn chair and helped me sit down. I remembered the stories he used to tell me about his own mother's pregnancies, how his father pampered her and wouldn't let her get out of bed, much less do work. But, of course, she had an army of servants and nannies to take care of the house and the other children. I was not so fortunate.

"Papá, I'm all right. I'm just pregnant, not sick." I smiled up at him and smoothed my hair down the best I could. I had not been able to visit a hairdresser in months, so it was longer than usual and unruly.

"She's not doing anything that I didn't have to do when I was pregnant, Miguel," Mother said matter-of-factly. She looked down at me. "How is Marcos treating you?"

"He's wonderful. He works real hard and is very good to me."

"Humph." She crossed her arms, her eyes taking in the ramshackle buildings in the back yard.

"Here, *hija*, take this." Father put ten dollars in my hand.

"No, Papá, I can't. Marcos wouldn't like it." I handed the bills back.

"Keep it, *hija*, please." He grabbed my hand and placed the bills back in it. "Marcos doesn't have to know about it. Buy yourself something nice. A new dress maybe." He looked down at my faded shift.

I didn't have the heart to say no. I know it was killing my Father that he couldn't do more for us, that he couldn't offer Marcos a better job, that he couldn't provide us a place to live. Once, he would have been able to do all those things. "*Bueno*, Papá, I do need to buy a few personal things. I could also use a new maternity dress."

My mother-in-law joined us a few minutes later, carrying a tray with an assortment of *pan dulce*, a coffeepot and coffee cups, which she set on a metal table by the lawn chair. The conversation shifted accordingly. Thirty minutes later, my parents left. I watched them drive off, the rear wheels of the pickup spewing dust behind them. I sighed when I saw the dirt settle on the white undershirts on the line. I think if I hadn't been so much in love with Marcos, I would have run after them.

Their visit rekindled my desire to move, so for the next few weeks I pestered Marcos relentlessly. Paramount in my mind was the stricken look on Father's face when he saw me that day. I just couldn't bear to have him see me in such a state again, and besides, I was tired of washing clothes for eleven people!

Chapter 9

The three-room, clapboard house we moved into the first week of December was just a block from my in-laws. Marco's older brother, Josiah, had purchased the small home a few years before when he was engaged to a Westwood girl. The wedding never took place, and Josiah moved to Chicago, renting out the furnished house. When the tenants moved out, Josiah told us we could move in.

The day Marcos and I took possession of the house, I strolled through each of the rooms and made a mental note of what I would need to make the house truly our own. The antique pine dresser and poster bed in the little bedroom were in good condition, though the mattress had yellow stains on it. I thought my lilac coverlet would look pretty on it. In the living room was a small sofa and an upholstered armchair of blue chintz with some dark discolorations on the armrests. I knew that a few of Mother's doilies draped strategically over the arms would camouflage the stains nicely.

The kitchen contained a wooden table and four chairs, a small ice box, and a two-burner gas stove. In the corner of the room rested an old-fashioned porcelain bathtub, a makeshift shower curtain rigged up around it. I was puzzled as to how we were supposed to get water in the house until Marcos showed me the hose connected to a water spigot just outside the back door. Although I still had to haul water in and out to wash dishes, cook, and fill the tub up for baths, the fact that I would be hauling it back and forth into my own house made it seem less of a chore. While we were outside, I observed with dismay the outhouse snuggled in the back corner of the yard. "Oh, well," I said to Marcos, "it's better than not having a toilet at all."

Mother had given me an old Singer sewing machine in a cabinet, the kind that had a treadle, so I spent the first week making curtains for the windows, yellow and blue gingham for the living room and the kitchen, and lilac for the bedroom. When I wasn't using the sewing machine, I used it as a side table in the living room. I often set a crystal vase filled with fresh flowers on it. Marcos and I had received many fine wedding gifts which I had never been able to use, such as the crystal vase, so for the first time, I was able to use some of them.

Our routine was that after Marcos left for work, I cleaned up the breakfast dishes and made our bed. After that, I usually rested on the sofa in the living room near the front window, drank fruit juice or hot chocolate, and perused the newspaper or a magazine. I would gaze out the front window and daydream, one of my favorite pastimes. From the window I could see all the way to Texas Boulevard, the main street of the city. I could also see the enormous ebony tree that marked the corner of my in-laws' property. The tree's branches reached fifty feet toward the sky, its dark green canopy of leaves glistening in the sunlight. Papá Benavides had told me that when he helped clear the land when Westwood was first being developed, he had saved that tree, using it as a marker for the lot he would eventually buy.

Sometimes I saw my mother-in-law, her gray hair pulled up in a hair net, hauling a laundry basket around back. I would feel a little guilty. On those days, I just shifted my attention to my reading material. After all, I was in my last trimester of pregnancy and my feet and ankles were swollen most of the time. It was not as if I could run over and help her.

By early March, I was as big as a house and the baby's due date wasn't until the end of the month, so I went on long walks to try to hurry things along. One Sunday afternoon, Carmen, Monica and I were strolling down Texas Avenue when two young women approached us. One of them, a rather experienced looking woman wearing a tight dress and dark red lipstick, pointed a finger at Carmen, her face contorted in rage. "Stay away from him, *bruja*. He's mine!"

She had stopped us in front of Garza's Grocery Store, which was closed, but there were more than a few pedestrians strolling down the street. Carmen glanced furtively around. I knew she was concerned that the news of this confrontation would get back to her mother. "I don't know what you're talking about," she said, starting to walk away.

Monica and I followed.

"You know damn well what I'm talking about. You stay away from Frankie. He's my boyfriend. We've been together for a long time."

Carmen stopped and looked back at the girl, her expression saucy. "If Frankie is your boyfriend, then you tell him to stay away from me. I can't help who comes into the store any more than you can help how ugly you are."

My heart skipped a beat. I admired my sister-in-law's feistiness, but wondered if it was a good idea to taunt the distraught woman. The look on the woman's face was menacing, her eyes opened wide in disbelief. She lunged at my sister-in-law and just as she grabbed onto Carmen's hair, I felt a stabbing pain in my abdomen. Our screams mingled.

"Ay! Ouch! Ay!" I hunched over, both arms supporting my belly and could feel a warm moistness between my legs.

"What's wrong, Isa?" Monica grabbed my arm.

"The baby," I muttered.

Monica jumped between Carmen and the woman, almost getting hit in the process. "Carmen, the baby is coming," she yelled.

Carmen pushed the woman onto the sidewalk. "See what you've done?" she screamed. "My sister-in-law is going to have her baby, and it's not due for another two weeks. You'd better pray that there's nothing wrong with it, because if there is I'm coming after you."

The next thing I knew I was being driven to my house and helped out of the car by two men I didn't know. Carmen and Monica, on either side of me, took each of my arms, thanked the men, and helped me into the house. Carmen sent Monica to get word to Marcos and to Tía Ana, my father's sister, who was going to deliver the baby.

After helping me to my bed, Carmen sat on a chair and held my hand. "Do you need anything? Are you thirsty?"

"No, but I sure would like to know who that girl was," I said slyly.

Carmen gave me a wry grin. "Her name is Verónica Montez."

"And Frankie?"

This time, Carmen blushed. "His name is Frank Solano, and he's just a man who visits me at the store occasionally."

"Just a man?"

She rose from the chair and walked to the window, her arms crossed. "I can't help it. I think he's wonderful. He's older than me, twelve years older. He's a car salesman, and he makes me laugh." She sighed and turned around. "He has a reputation. That girl was more than just a girlfriend, if you know what I mean. He told me about her. But he loves me and wants to marry me. Mamá would never allow it. I hate to think what she's going to do to me when she finds out about what happened. And she will find out. I saw Señora Maldonado in the crowd, and she's one of my mother's closest friends. I'm sure she's already giving her an earful. Oh, Isa, I dread going home."

"Stay here as long as you want." I felt sorry for my sister-in-law. Mamá Benavides in a normal situation was a formidable presence. I could just imagine what she would be like all riled up over this. I was glad I wasn't going to be around to witness the scolding.

Tía Ana swooped into the house a few minutes later, taking control like a military commander, asking questions, issuing orders, and surveying her surroundings as she set her leather medical bag on the foot of the bed, removed her stethoscope and placed the earpieces in her ears and the bell shaped contact piece on my abdomen.

My aunt was in her mid-forties, a tall woman who wore tailored dresses and kept her still dark hair pulled up in a French twist. She was the epitome of professionalism and while some thought her cold, I knew that her prickly personality merely shielded a tender heart. Tía Ana was a registered nurse with a speciality in midwifery. She had immigrated to

Texas the year before, moving to Westwood, and already had a thriving practice in many of the Mexican communities of the Valley. She had never married and had told me on several occasions that she never would. She regarded the opposite sex with disdain and suspicion, much like my sister Terre did.

When Marcos arrived, he rushed to me, kissing my hands and cheeks and forehead. "I came as soon as I found out. Are you all right, honey?"

"Look at all the dirt you tracked in here, Marcos," Tía Ana admonished. "You've contaminated Isa with all manner of germs. If you care at all for the health of your child, leave at once."

Poor Marcos looked so distressed when he left the room that I felt like reprimanding my aunt for being so harsh. But I didn't, and when my labor pains began in earnest, I totally forgot about anyone's distress but my own.

After twelve hours of labor, Marcos Benavides, Junior was born. He was two weeks early, and I had Verónica Montez, Frankie Solano's jilted lover, to thank for that.

*****

Father and Mother were in Veracruz when Marquitos was born, and although I was disappointed that they weren't around, I was happy to hear they were traveling together. They both loved to travel, and when I was younger, they frequently vacationed in México. Terre told me their trip to Veracruz was more of a business trip, however, which frankly, made me even happier. It meant that Father had snapped out of his lethargy and that he and Mother had made-up.

When they returned to town a week later, they rushed over to see me. Father seemed preoccupied, but he beamed when he saw his first grandchild. I felt a deep satisfaction that I had been able to do something to make him so proud. He sat in a wooden chair near my bed and cradled little Marcos in his arms. "He's a fine boy, *hija*, and strong. Look at that grip." The baby had wrapped his tiny hand around Father's beefy finger.

I had always wondered if Father was disappointed that he had had only one son and so many daughters. As I watched him gaze lovingly at Marcos, marveling at his maleness, I thought maybe he had been, though he had never let on. He had showered all of his daughters with affection, though I couldn't help but notice that it was Raul he confided in, Raul he occasionally took with him on business trips, Raul for whom he had bought a pony, Raul he introduced to his associates in a different tone of voice, saying, "This is my son," like he was just a tad more special than his daughters. But maybe I'm making too much of it. Besides, everyone knows I was Father's favorite.

Mother hovered near Father and the baby, her eyebrows knit. "He looks just like José." She burst into tears.

Father and I exchanged commiserating glances. José was my mother's younger brother. When I was eight years old, he had gone to México to visit some friends and disappeared. Father had organized a search for him, even hired a private investigator, but my mother's nineteen-year-old brother was never found. The police suspected foul play, but with no body as evidence, there was nothing that could be done. Because there was no proof that he was dead, we couldn't have a funeral, and that was particularly hard on Mother and her sister, Candelaria. For months, Mother came home from outings saying that she thought she saw José at a church or a market or at a store. She often said that not knowing what happened to him was worse than knowing.

After my uncle disappeared, I cried when Father went on his business trips. I was afraid he would not return. It was many years before I could watch him leave without giving in to melancholy.

Mother pulled a handkerchief out of her purse and dabbed her eyes. "Beatriz," Father said gently. "With all due respect, your brother had red hair and freckles. Look at this baby. His hair is brown, his complexion clear. I think he looks like a Caballero. Look at those big, dark eyes."

"I suppose you're right," she said with a sigh.

"I think he looks like Marcos," I interjected, hoping to steer the conversation away from my unfortunate uncle.

"He does have Marcos' dimples," Mother said, her equilibrium reestablished.

The conversation continued until Marcos came home from work, tired and dirty, bearing two bags full of freshly harvested beets and carrots.

*****

I sometimes wonder what would have happened to us if there had not been another disastrous freeze. There is a saying, "No bad comes that does not have good in it." My grandmother Alicia told me this years ago and now I understand what it means. But then I thought the freeze of 1951 was the worst possible thing that could have ever happened. In retrospect, I now realize that for Marcos and me, it was the best.

It was so cold that January that when I washed the baby's diapers and hung them up on the line, they would be frozen stiff thirty minutes later. By February, it was clear that there would be no spring harvest in the Valley so Marcos was laid off work. With so many agricultural employees out of work, the few menial jobs that were available to Mexicanos were filled, and Marcos could not find another job. Then Marquitos got sick. He had been plagued with ear infections almost since the day he was born, and now at eleven months, I noticed the familiar tugging and pulling on his left ear again.

"We have to take him to the doctor, Marcos." I rocked my howling baby in my arms. "He needs antibiotics."

"I know," he said, his forehead creased in concern. "But let me take him. There's no need for you go out in the cold. We can't afford for you to get sick again."

I didn't respond. I had just gotten over a bout of the flu, and it had been awful. "All right. But make sure he's bundled up properly. Keep his face covered." I handed our squalling baby to my husband.

A few minutes later, I watched from the window as Marcos, wearing a straw cowboy hat to protect his head and dressed in an Army jacket over blue jeans, sauntered down Emerald Boulevard toward Texas Avenue in his worn brown cowboy boots carrying our son in his arms. When he hadn't returned two hours later, I started to get perturbed. I knew by the ache in my breasts that it was time for the baby's feeding, so I stood by the window getting angrier by the minute at Marcos' thoughtlessness. As the minutes stretched to another hour, I began to dredge up the grievances I had against my husband. A couple can't be married for a year and not have grievances against each other, as anyone knows who has been married for any length of time. I recalled with disdain the times Marcos had stayed out all night with his friends. The last time he had done it, a few months before, I told him that if he ever did it again I would leave him. We had gotten into a terrible fight.

"You listen to me, Marcos Benavides. You are a married man now," I had said when he stumbled in at six o'clock in the morning. "Don't you have any respect for me?"

"Aw, honey." He stepped toward me, his eyes bloodshot. "I respect you very much. But a man needs to get some steam off. It has nothing to do with you. We weren't doing nothing wrong."

"Anything wrong," I hissed, correcting his English. Marcos and I spoke both English and Spanish to each other, and I had found that his grammar skills in both languages left a lot to be desired.

He frowned, stopping in front of me. He hated when I corrected him. "I'm a man and I will do as I please," he exhorted, standing a little taller, thrusting out his chest.

"Then you will be a man without a wife. I promise you that if you come home again like you did this morning, I will take Marcos and leave you." I stood before him, my hands clenched.

"Don't threaten me, Isabel. I will never let you take my son away from me."

"Don't threaten me, Marcos." I suddenly felt scared about the direction our conversation had taken. "I love you with all my heart. But I will not be made a fool of. Don't think I'm stupid. I know that you and your friends go to Reynosa and dance and who knows what else with those women over there. Elvira told me that Arnoldo Ramirez gave his wife gonorrhea. Do you want to do that to me?"

Marcos' eyes opened wide, a surprised expression on his face. "I have never been with another woman since we've been together. I would never do that to you," he said vehemently.

"You'd better not, Marcos, because I will put up with a lot, but I will never put up with a philandering husband." Even as I said it, I felt hypocritical though I didn't know why.

Marcos didn't respond. He just looked at me, an odd expression on his face, as if he didn't know whether to be angry at my insinuation or proud that I had stood up to him. "I'm tired," he had finally said, dragging off to our bedroom.

He hadn't come home late since then, but it had only been a few months, so I wasn't discounting the possibility of it happening again.

I finally caught a glimpse of my husband and child at the far end of the street. Marcos stopped every few minutes to show off the baby to whoever happened to be walking by. As he neared our house, I saw his dimples flash as he allowed Señora Zamora who lived two houses down to peek into the bundle of blankets at our son. I shook my head. How could I be angry at such a man?

When he finally got home, I scolded him for being gone so long, but not too harshly. Marquitos had fallen asleep, but awoke when I thrust my breast into his little mouth. As he sucked, the rock hardness of my breast gave way along with my anger.

"I took so long because people along the way to and from the clinic admired Marquitos, and they had to touch him to ward off the evil eye."

"Do you really believe in the evil eye?" I asked, my mouth turned down.

He furrowed his eyebrows. "Not really, but why take a chance with Marquitos?"

It was hard to argue, especially since our baby was involved. Better to err on the side of superstition than risk our baby's health.

*****

A few weeks later, Marcos surprised me when I was visiting my parents' house. It wasn't a pleasant surprise. I was sitting on the swing on the front porch watching my sisters play with Marquitos when Marcos drove into our driveway in a little Ford coupe. He jumped out of the car and rushed over to us, grinning from ear to ear.

"Who's car is that?" I said.

"It's ours, honey."

"Ours? You don't even have a job. How are we going to pay for it?"

His words tumbled out in a torrent. "Manuel Garcia works at the Ford dealership in Westwood. You remember Manny. Anyway, he gave it to me on credit, said I could start making payments next month."

Ellie, Lupita, and Marta rushed over to admire the car, leaving me alone with Marcos and the baby on the porch.

I sat there wondering what kind of a *tonto* would sell a car to an unemployed man. Then I wondered what kind of a *tonto* would go out and buy a car when he had no way of paying for it. "Are you crazy?" I jumped out of the swing. "We can't even afford to buy food or pay your brother rent and you went out and bought a car? I don't know who's crazier, you or Manuel."

"Ah, honey." He picked the baby up, for protection, I remember thinking. "Let's not fight. Come and look at it. I'll take you and Marquitos for a ride."

"Now, you listen to me, Marcos Benavides, you had no business going out and buying a car without consulting me first. We're married and all major decisions should be made by both of us. And how you could have even considered buying a car when we can barely afford to eat is beyond me. Now, take it back."

"I won't take it back," he said defiantly. "I'll find a job. You'll see."

A few days later, after running out of gas about a block from our house and pushing the car home, Marcos (who didn't have money to buy gas) called Manuel and asked him to come get the car. Unfortunately, his friend told him it would be a week or so before he could retrieve it. I say unfortunately because a few days later, in a moment of desperation, Marcos removed all four tires from the car and sold them so that he could buy food for us. When Manuel finally showed up with a tow truck, he was momentarily speechless when he saw the car propped up on cinder blocks. "What happened to the tires?" he finally asked.

I know I should have kept quiet but I just couldn't. Before Marcos could reply, I said, "What happened to the tires is what happens when you sell a car to an unemployed person. We ate them." Then, I turned on my heels and stalked into the house.

Two weeks later, Marcos joined the Air Force. I now realize that it really was the best thing that he could have done, but at the time, I was devastated. This was worse than being in agriculture, I remember thinking. He would be sent to another country, and I would never see him. It was too horrible to contemplate.

In August of 1951, he was deployed to North Africa for an eighteen-month tour of duty, and I found myself once again back in Ruby living with my parents, this time the mother of an eighteen-month-old baby, not exactly what I had envisioned when I got married.

Chapter 10

After Marcos left, I spent my days alternating between being angry at him and missing him, but when his first paycheck arrived, I began to just miss him. I realized after I received the paycheck that I was entrusted with our family's livelihood. It was a sobering thought. I had never been one to save. When I worked those few months for the water company, I had spent every cent I made on dresses, shoes, lingerie, cosmetics, perfumes, magazines, and books. After Marcos and I got married, we used what little money we had on necessities—food and medical expenses. Now I had a monthly check of more than two-hundred dollars, and I realized that I needed to save as much of it as possible. And so I did. I opened a bank account at the Ruby Bank and Trust and deposited one-hundred dollars a month in a savings account.

I knew better than to offer money to Father for the baby's and my room and board, but I secretly gave twenty-five dollars a month to Mother, who was only too happy to accept the money. Their trip to Veracruz the year before had not resulted in new business for Father. I remember he had once said, "To make money you must spend money." Unfortunately, he had only a small amount of cash to invest. Mother had told me that his contacts in México were not willing to finance any business ventures without collateral, and the only collateral they had at that time was the house in Ruby, the orchard, and several residential lots Father wanted to keep. Mother had adamantly refused to allow Father to put up the house for his business scheme (not that he would have even considered it), and Father refused to use the orchard as collateral, so they had come home, according to Terre, in a stony silence.

But the biggest blow of all came when Father lost every last one of his orange trees in the 1951 freeze. Mother, of course, could not resist reminding him about her advice to sell the orchard to Señor Greene two years before. Terre said that after that fight, Father was surlier than ever, then sunk into a deep depression. He would get up in the morning, eat breakfast and lock himself in his office and read. He would accept no visitors. One afternoon after I moved back in, Father and Mother had such a row concerning what she called his laziness that when Father later left the house, I was sure he was never coming back.

"We need money, Miguel. We have our children to feed, taxes to pay. Dora told me that Pancho could get us all work on his picking crew," I heard her say to Father as I rocked Marcos to sleep on an oak rocking chair that Mother had put in my old bedroom.

"No!" I heard the thud of what was probably his book as he threw it against the wall. "I forbid you to take my children to pick cotton. We have money. I told you I will provide for this family. Why do you keep pestering me, *mujer*?"

"Why do you sit here all day long and do nothing? Working in the fields is honorable work. When you first came here from México, you worked in the fields. Ah, but I know. You are too proud. You have always been too proud. The great Don Miguel Caballero working in the fields. You can't stand it, can you? You would have to work beside the very men who once worked for you. Your pride put us in this position, and your pride is keeping us here."

I could just picture my mother's twisted lips and raging eyes, and my Father's wide-eyed incredulity at her audacity. No one spoke to Father like that, ever. I felt my pulse quicken. My head began to ache as I waited for Father's response.

I heard Father's chair skid against the floor. "If I had pride I would have left you long ago," he thundered. "What kind of a man am I to stay married to a woman who continually harangues me and questions my every move? My mother never spoke to my father with such disrespect."

"Don't bring your parents up. You forget I know what happened between them," she said. "But I think with you Caballero men it doesn't matter what kind of wives you have; they are never enough for you."

I cringed, and then, as if on cue, Marcos began to wail. I wasn't able to hear Father's response, but I think that the baby's crying startled my parents into realizing that they had an audience. A few minutes later, I heard the screen door slam and Father storm down the driveway. Mother came into my bedroom, her face flushed, her eyes dark and glinty, the way she always looked after a fight with Father.

"Well, there he goes to the cantina again. He should just move over there," she said with a smirk as she moved the curtain in front of the bedroom window to peer out.

"He just might after what you just said to him," I mumbled.

"What did you say?" She narrowed her eyes.

"I just said I have a headache."

"Ay, my head is killing me, too." She rubbed her temples. "I'm going to lie down for a while. Try to keep Marquitos quiet."

I nodded and looked down at my son. He grinned at me showing his tiny front teeth. I glanced at the photograph of my husband on the dresser. Marcos had worn his military uniform for the sitting. He was smiling, his crooked teeth and dimples prominent. Tears began to fall down my cheeks, and in a few minutes I was sobbing.

*****

Father returned later that night, but he and Mother stayed clear of each other for a while. Then, a few days later, Mother prepared his favorite meal for supper: carne guisada with rice and beans, fresh corn on the cob, and for dessert, flan. Father nodded at Mother when he had finished and that was that. Equilibrium was established once again, at least for a while. I never heard them apologize for the horrible things they said to each other. Mother had said Father was proud, well, Mother had her share of that sin, too.

Now that I was married, I tried to analyze my parents' relationship in light of my own and that of my in-laws'. Marcos and I had had our share of arguments, but they mostly involved the struggle for power. Luckily for me, his mother pretty much ruled the roost when he was growing up, so when I made demands or gave an opinion, he would listen thoughtfully. On the other hand, I remember once when I had contradicted him in front of another couple, he had been very angry. He told me that I had embarrassed him in front of his friends and that it was my duty as a wife to always go along with whatever he said. Well, you can imagine my response. "I don't know where you get your information about wives, Marcos," I had said. "What you just described is a parrot. If you want someone who will go along with everything you say, get a parrot." Needless to say, he wasn't very pleased by that remark. He slept on the couch that night.

His parents' relationship was an enigma to me. Papá Benavides was a gentle soul who, after he retired, went to the six o'clock Mass every morning until he died. He loved to work in the garden and, as a result, their little pink house was surrounded by lush, flowering gardens and the scent of gardenias. He barely spoke a word, and when he did speak, he did so quietly and deliberately. That's not to say he was weak. Marcos told me that when he was a boy, he had been whipped plenty of times by his father, and there was nothing weak about the way he wielded a belt. But he also said that Papá Benavides preferred less physical ways to get his point across. Once, when Marcos, Josiah, and two of their friends had played hooky from school (they were in junior high at the time), a neighbor told his father that he had just seen the boys skinny dipping in the canal a few miles from the school. Papá Benavides strolled over to the canal and grabbed up all their clothes, every stitch. As he was leaving, he called out, "You all think you're so smart that you don't have to go to school? Well, then, figure out how you're going to get home with no clothes." Then he left. Marcos said they stayed in the canal until night fall and then ran home in the cover of darkness. "When we got home Mamá was waiting with a long, thin branch in her hand, and she whipped our naked butts as we ran through the house." He laughed, then added wryly, "We never played hooky again."

Mamá Benavides was a chatterbox as I mentioned. She complained, worried, and yelled. I often heard her scold Papá Benavides when he came home a little late from work. "Ay, you know how I worry when you come home late, *viejo*," she'd say, hugging him to her ample bosom, as if she hadn't seen him in a year. "I have visions of *la migra* taking you back to México." He would assure her that everything was fine. He always carried his green card with him, didn't he? But she would go on for the rest of the evening, lamenting about the sad treatment of *los mexicanos*.

My mother did her share of haranguing, but in our house, Father was the boss, no question, at least when he was home. I think that one of the problems between my parents was the fact that Mother had become so Americanized over the years, while Father had remained staunchly Mexican. He hated that she was so independent, not realizing that it was because of his continued absenses that she was compelled to become independent. She did everything when Father was away, including paying the bills, running the house, and dealing with the servants, repairmen, and storekeepers. I remember once she organized an English class for the women in the neighborhood. Every Saturday afternoon for an hour, several of our neighbors would settle themselves on our front porch and Mother, who could barely speak English herself, would bring out our Spanish-English dictionary, then write English words on a chalkboard telling the women to repeat after her as she pointed at the word, "Cat, dog, run, ball." She would always finish the lesson by reciting a sentence that Terre or I had helped her with the night before, a phrase that would be useful, such as, "How much does it cost?" or "How much to bail him out of jail?" I think if Mother had been interested in politics, she would have been a great grass roots organizer.

But Father didn't encourage Mother's leadership abilities. When he returned from his migrant trips, Mother had to disband the English classes because Father didn't like the "cackling" of so many women on his front porch. I suppose I don't blame him; the volume did get pretty loud with ten women reciting disjointed English and numerous children screeching and laughing as we ran around the yard.

In the end, I realized that I couldn't analyze my parents' marriage any more than I could analyze my own. So many things are left unsaid, so many things happen behind closed doors, and so many things are just nobody else's business.

*****

Almost every day, I walked to the post office to mail letters to Marcos and pick up my family's mail. Going to the post office became the day's highlight. During the week, I would go alone or take Marquitos along, but on Saturdays, one or more of my sisters would accompany me.

On a Saturday in the fall of 1951, Ellie and I were crossing the tracks toward the post office when she suddenly stopped. "Isa, look. Isn't that Mr. Walton's daughter-in-law going into that abandoned packing shed?"

I looked at the boarded-up building Ellie had pointed at and saw Janice Walton open a side door and go in. I knew it was Janice because she had been featured on the society page of the Ruby newspaper when she became engaged to marry the postmaster's son, Jason, two years before. She was no beauty, certainly not like Jason's sister, Noelle, who had been chosen Citrus Queen at the 1947 Valley Citrus Festival, but she had long curly brown hair and an hour-glass figure.

"I wonder what she's doing in there," Ellie said. "Let's go see."

"No!" I attempted to grab her arm, but she was already hurrying down the tracks.

"It's none of our business," I whispered loudly as I ran after my sister, my shoes making a crunching sound on the gravel around the railroad track. "Come back."

She ran from window to window of the old canning shed looking for one that was not boarded up.

"Ellie, get away from there." I must admit I was as curious as she was to see what Janice was doing in that shed, but as her elder sister and a mother, I realized that I had to set an example. However, by the time I got to her, it was too late. She had found a window that was only partially boarded up, and as she peered into the building, I saw her mouth drop and her eyes bulge. I edged up next to her and looked in. Janice Walton and a man I didn't recognize because his back was to us were going at it on a wooden table in the middle of the shed. The man's pants were down around his ankles and the cheeks of his buttocks were glowing white in the dusky room. I was horrified and intrigued. Ellie, probably for the first and only time in her life, was speechless.

I finally gathered my wits and pulled her away from the window. "Let's get out of here," I whispered. We stumbled away from the building back onto Main Street.

"Who was she with?" Ellie asked, her face flushed. "Was that her husband?"

I shook my head. Mr. Walton's son was short and stocky like him. The man Janice had been with was tall and slender. "Don't you dare mention this to anyone, Eloise Caballero."

"Oh, Isa, can't I tell Lupita? She won't say anything."

"Fine, but don't tell Marta. She couldn't keep a secret if her life depended on it."

When we entered the small building that housed the post office, Mr. Walton greeted us cheerily like he always did. I felt so bad for him, and even a little guilty. But it wasn't my fault, I reminded myself self-righteously. I hadn't been the one anxious to spy on Janice. I scowled at Ellie, who returned my gaze with a puzzled expression.

"Ah, there you are! There are two letters for you from your husband, Miss Isabel, and one for your sister, Teresa, from that nun friend of hers in San Antonio," the postmaster said gallantly, whisking the letters out of a drawer beneath his counter.

"Thank you, Mr. Walton." I retrieved the fat envelopes from him.

Mrs. Walton emerged from the back room, her crinoline undergarments swishing under her dress. The postmaster's wife was plump like her husband, and she wore her short, dark hair in waves around her face. She aways wore a lot of make-up, and today she looked like a Cupie Doll, with cherry red lips and bright pink cheeks. "Oh, hello, Isabel. I have some pictures to show you of Noelle's baby." I had gone to high school with Noelle, and though we hadn't been close friends, she being Anglo and all, her mother always kept me informed of her activities. She had married Samuel Alberts, a handsome former football player who had graduated from Mercedes High School and who now worked as an insurance salesman.

As I oohed and ahhed over photos of Mrs. Walton's granddaughter, I heard the door open and Ellie gasp. I turned around and saw Janice stroll in with Noelle's husband.

"Guess who I saw as I was driving down the street after one of my calls?" Samuel said much too exuberantly as he took off his fedora.

"Yes, and wasn't it nice of him to offer me a ride ?" Janice said all smiles.

"Well, how nice," Mrs. Walton commented. "Did you have lunch with Jason, Janice?"

"Oh no, I ate a sandwich at the soda fountain. Jason had too much work at the bank, so I was just going back to the house when Samuel drove by. He offered to take me home, but he had a letter to mail."

He handed the letter to his father-in-law.

"I was just showing off your new daughter to Mrs. Benavides here," Mrs. Walton said, eyeing her son-in-law.

Samuel nodded at me and glanced over my shoulder. "She's a beauty, all right," he said smugly.

"Yes, she is," I mumbled.

"Well, we'll be off." He put his fedora back on his head.

The room was still as we watched the couple get into Samuel's car and drive off. I looked at Mrs. Walton and saw her and Mr. Walton exchange quick glances.

"We have to go now, Mrs. Walton. Your granddaughter is lovely. You should be very proud." I retrieved my letters from the counter and walked to the door with Ellie.

"Oh, yes, thank you, Isabel. See you Monday," she said somewhat absentmindedly.

Ellie and I didn't say anything for at least five minutes as we walked down Main Street. Then she said, "Did you notice that his pants were unzipped?"

I nodded.

*****

I remember those last few months in Ruby with fondness, laughing with my sisters and gossiping with my friends. On weekends, we often visited the Río Bravo rancho that Father had leased in México so that he could grow cotton and watermelon for market. It was a lovely rancho with horses that we could ride.

But I missed my husband and was overjoyed when he returned in March of 1953. He had orders for his first stateside tour of duty in Wichita, Kansas. This time, Marquitos and I would go with him, and I was ready. In the eighteen months I had stayed with my parents as a single mother, I had grown up considerably. We used the one-thousand dollars I had saved as a down payment on a three-thousand dollar, green 1951 Fleetline Chevrolet. This time there would be money to make car payments.

Father threw us a going away party, and all of Marcos' family attended, including Carmen and her husband, Frankie, and their one-year-old daughter, Ninfa. Carmen and Frankie had eloped in 1951 and moved to Corpus to escape the wrath of Mamá Benavides. Monica told me that when her mother found out about her eldest daughter's elopement, she had raged for days. Unfortunately, Monica was the one who suffered. All excursions came to a screeching halt, and Monica became like a prisoner in her own home.

However, after Ninfa was born, Mamá Benavides' heart softened. When Carmen and Frankie finally came home to Westwood a year later, baby in tow, my mother-in-law accepted them into her home with a few choice words of chastisement and many words of praise for the beautiful, bouncing baby girl, her first granddaughter.

The day Marcos and I left Ruby is a poignant memory etched in my mind. It was April, when cotton is planted, and acres of carrots, onions, tomatoes, and peppers are ready for harvest. It was a sunny morning, a slight breeze ruffling the branches of the enormous ash trees on the side of my parents' house. My sisters and brother gathered with my parents to say goodbye to us. They passed three-year-old Marquitos one to the other, kissing and hugging him as if they would never see him again. Only Father, Marcos, and Raul were not crying. Father shook Marcos' hand and exhorted him to be good to me, then he embraced me. "Take care of yourself, *hija*," he said. "If you need anything, you call me, *bueno*?"

Tears streaming down my face, I nodded. I looked at him and my heart constricted when I saw that his eyes were moist. Mother came between us and hugged me, uttering a blessing. "*Que Dios te bendiga, hija*," she said, holding me tight. She then looked at Marcos and told him something that would become her mantra to all her sons-in-law over the years, "*Portate bien, hijo, que nada te cuesta.* Behave yourself, son, it doesn't cost anything."

As we drove down the dusty street, I turned around to take a last look at my family and the house. Terre was leaning against the porch post, her arms crossed. She had just been hired as a teacher at the Latin American elementary school by our house, and I am happy to say that I was instrumental in helping her land the job. I hoped that she would be happy for a change now that she would be doing something she had always wanted to do. I also hoped that she would find a nice man to marry, though I knew that was a tall order, given her perfectionistic tendencies.

Raul, whose nineteenth birthday we had just celebrated, had enlisted in the Air Force and would soon be leaving the flock. I smiled, remembering what he had said after taking Marquitos for a ride in Father's pickup. "I'm not ever taking Marquitos with me again, Isa. He called me Daddy in front of Connie Esparza," he had said with exasperation. "He's going to ruin my reputation." But the next day, Marquitos was in his usual spot next to Raul when he took off on an errand.

The jasmine was in bloom, as were the bougainvillea and rose bushes. The Queen Palm tree that Father had planted for me when I was a little girl was now over twenty feet tall. I recalled the day I had seen the unusual looking palm tree when we were driving through one of the Valley towns, and I had remarked to Father that I thought it was beautiful. A few days later, he brought home a Queen Palm sapling that was about five feet high and planted it in the front yard in direct view of the porch swing, because that was where I liked to lounge.

Mother and Father stood under the palm, its delicate, feathery leaves fluttering over them. I saw my sister, Marta, who had been standing next to Ellie and Lupita, walk between Mother and Father. Mother draped her left arm over Marta's shoulder and with the other hand, waved at us. Father waved, then dropped his hand to his side. I waved back and entreated Marquitos to do the same.

That was one of the last times I saw my parents together.

Part II

Terre
The Second Daughter

1942-1955

Chapter 11

Isa always had a blind spot when it came to Father, and now, these many years later, I think I understand why. I remember the time Mother mailed a photograph of Isa and me in a letter to Father when he was on one of his contracting trips. Isa must have been about six in the photo. I was five. In his reply, he wrote, "Isabel smiles; her eyes twinkle. Terre frowns, very serious. My Isa looks at the world through rose-colored glasses, but Teresita sees the world, warts and all. Put on Isa's glasses, *mi'ja*, you will have a much happier life."

But I never did. I couldn't. Isa and I have always been different. She could put her head in the sand, ignore the discord, make excuses. I could not. I will say this, though. Sometimes I wish I could be more like my sister. To be able to forgive easily, to dispense with grudges, to live a life unfettered by bitterness. I have struggled all my life to do what Isa does without effort. I prayed the Lord would change my stony heart. But, after all these years, when I think of my childhood, all the rage and bitterness resurfaces, and I am aware that I have not forgiven or forgotten. Maybe Isabel is right. Maybe writing about it will help to finally free me.

Isa believes Father's bankruptcy was the beginning of the end of our parents' marriage. Actually, their marriage began disintegrating long before Father lost his fortune. I can trace their decline as far back as 1942, the year that Marta was born, the year that Father took that woman with him to Mississippi.

*****

Ellie's and Lupita's birthdays are only a few days apart in November, and that year we were going to celebrate them together. Ellie was going to be five and Lupita three. I remember how carefully Mother measured out the cup of sugar into the cake batter. The war was raging in Europe, and sugar was one of the first food products to be rationed, so she wanted to make sure she didn't waste any.

We were gathered in the kitchen—Ellie and Lupita anxiously waiting to lick the spoon and bowl, Isa holding baby Marta, and me reading the cake recipe to Mother. Señora Cavacho was visiting that day, sitting across from Mother at the kitchen table as Mother stirred the white cake mixture.

"We stayed at a very nice motel in east Texas, *comadre*, one that had a restaurant. Ay, the food was delicious. I had a thick, grilled hamburger. Jerónimo had fried chicken smothered in gravy, Don Miguel had liver and onions, and Lucia had a hamburger, like me."

Mother lifted her eyebrow and stopped stirring. "Lucia? Lucia Guerra went with you to Mississippi?"

"*Ay, Dios,*" said Mother's friend, her face turning red. "*Pues, sí.* She wanted to come. She needed the money," she added, a note of defensiveness in her voice.

"Where did she stay?" Mother let go of the spoon and it sank half-way into the cake mixture. She put her hands on her hips.

"*Pues,* I don't know, *comadre.*"

"You do know, Concha, and you will tell me right now if you know what's good for you."

Señora Cavacho frowned. "Ay, *comadre,* it was nothing, nothing. Just a little fling. It gets lonely for a man away from home."

Mother's dark eyes smoldered. "You set the whole thing up, didn't you?" she said as she walked slowly around the table like a cat stalking its prey.

I was only thirteen at the time, but I knew something bad had happened between Father and Lucia and that something bad was about to happen to Señora Cavacho. I gathered up my sisters, and we fled to the living room. By then Ellie and Lupita were crying and two-month-old Marta was wailing. But above the din, I heard Señora Cavacho scream, the crash of dishes, and the thud of chairs falling to the floor. Soon, several of our neighbors were at our front door inquiring about the ruckus, the absolute last thing we needed.

"Everything's fine," I yelled through the screen door, making up my mind to stop the fight. I ran to the kitchen and grabbed Mother from behind. I was already a head taller than she was, so I restrained her without too much effort. "Mamá, stop it. She's not worth it," I said.

Señora Cavacho, her nose bleeding, scrambled up from the floor. "You'll pay for this, Beatriz. I'll have the law on you." She stumbled out of the kitchen through the back door.

I let go of Mother after Señora Cavacho had gone and she just stood there, all the fight knocked out of her. "Ay, my head is killing me." She grabbed her head in both hands. "I'm going to lie down."

After she staggered out of the kitchen, I looked around. The kitchen was in a shambles, chair legs turned upward, white cake mix dripping from the stuccoed walls and pine cabinets onto the red concrete floor. My sisters crept into the kitchen and Ellie and Lupita began to wail all over again when they saw what was left of the cake batter.

"*Cállense,*" I commanded. "Everything will be fine. Isa and I will clean up, and I'll make another batter. Don't worry. You'll have your birthday cake." Despite what happened, I wasn't going to let that big mouth Concha Cavacho ruin my sisters' birthday.

*****

Lucia Guerra was one of Señora Cavacho's boarders. She had moved to Ruby from México in early spring, 1942. She was the talk of the neighborhood because she was a young, voluptuous woman who always dressed provocatively. The first time I saw her she was sauntering down the street, her mules flip-flopping on the concrete sidewalk, in bright green, skin-tight pedal pushers and a sleeveless white blouse that was tied in a knot at her waist. Her long, wavy hair was auburn, like Mother's, but unlike Mother's, her hair color was not natural. I could tell by her black roots.

When she went for her daily walk at precisely seven in the evening, many of the men on the block suddenly appeared on their front lawns, ostensibly to wash their cars, water the grass, or to drink a beer on their front porches. It was really rather amusing watching them gawk at her as she sashayed by. At least I thought so until the day she stopped on the sidewalk in front of our house and beckoned for Father.

I was in the living room looking out the window, so I didn't hear their conversation. But, from Father's demeanor, I could tell he was flattered by her attentions. He thrust his chest out and nodded thoughtfully as she spoke. Father was about thirty-seven at the time and still fairly trim. He was meticulous about his appearance, always insisted that his shirts be starched and his trousers ironed with a crease down each pant leg. That day, his shirt sleeves were rolled up to just below his elbows, and he had been sitting on the porch swing drinking a beer when Lucia walked by.

Father had always been gallant around women, but what I witnessed between him and Lucia that day wasn't mere gallantry. It was the mating dance, a ritual I have observed frequently in my life and something I became very much aware of in connection with my father.

Father was an imposing man. He was not traditionally handsome, but he had an aura of authority that made men respect him and women desire him. That he had money also proved to be a powerful aphrodisiac. Of course, I didn't know all these things at the tender age of thirteen. All I knew then was that a Jezebel had set her cap on Father, and I hoped he would put her in her place. Father had often spoken with conviction about honor and integrity, and it didn't occur to me that he could actually be a willing accomplice in an adulterous deception. So, after I found out about his trip, I felt as if he had not only deceived Mother, but that he had lied to me, and the immense respect I had for him began to ebb away, slowly, but surely.

*****

"I'm sorry to disturb you, Miss Caballero, but I need to speak to

78

your father. Is he home?" Police Chief Whetstone stood at the front door in his khaki-colored uniform, clutching his Stetson hat in his enormous hand.

"He's not home, sir," I said through the screen door, hating Señora Cavacho more every second that the law man stood there.

"Do you expect him home soon?"

"Yes, sir. He took my brother with him on some business calls. But he should be back any minute."

"Is your mother home?"

"Yes."

"Could I speak to her?"

"Well, she's in bed with one of her migraines."

"I see." The police chief looked around the front yard, his eyes resting on my sisters' wicker doll carriages on the front porch. Police Chief Whetstone and my father were friends. In fact, he and his family lived on the México side of town, one of the few Anglo families that did. Father had bailed many a field worker from the Ruby jail over the years and, in that capacity, had befriended the Anglo law man. The police chief was a tall man with long, gangly arms that hung down almost to his knees, and he spoke perfect Spanish. "I'll come back. . ." He stopped when my father's pickup rolled into the driveway. "Well, speak of the devil." He smiled at me, then turned and strolled to the pickup.

I saw Father speak to Raul, who then loped to the house. "What's going on?" my brother asked as the screen door slammed shut and my sisters rushed to the living room from various parts of the house.

"Mamá got in a fight with Señora Cavacho," I said.

Raul arched his eyebrow. "What does that have to do with the police?"

"She broke her nose," chirped Ellie.

"Who broke whose nose?" Raul asked.

"There was blood everywhere," Lupita said in her three-year-old voice.

"Mamá broke Señora Cavacho's nose," said Ellie.

"We don't know that for a fact," Isabel interjected.

"What are you all talking about?" Raul said, his eyes round.

Mother walked in just then, her face haggard, her eyes red.

Raul turned to her. "Mamá, what's going on here? The police chief is outside."

"Is your father here?"

"Sí, he's talking to Señor Whetstone."

"Isa, Terre, take your sisters and brother with you to your room. Stay there until I call you."

"But, Mamá, . . ." Raul stammered.

"Just go."

We reluctantly made our way to my bedroom.

*****

I heard the police car drive away a few minutes later and then the front screen door slam as Father entered the house. In the end, it didn't matter that we were in the bedroom, the confrontation between my parents was so loud, we could have been in the next county and still heard them.

"How could you? Have you no shame?" Mother screamed.

"Me? I'm not the one acting like a fishwife. Where's your decency, your respect for yourself?" Father volleyed. "It's going to cost me a lot of money to patch things up. You broke Concha's nose. Did you know that?"

"I would have broken her neck if I'd had the chance," retorted Mother. "But this isn't about what I did to that poor excuse of a friend. This is about you and that little *puta*, Lucia Guerra." She paused for a moment. "Ah, now you understand."

My father said calmly, if somewhat loud, "I've told you before, I am a man with a man's needs. What am I supposed to do? Wait for months at a time until I can be with you again, and then wait to see if you are agreeable? No, it is intolerable. I give you everything you need. I support you and the children as a good husband and father. But I will not give you my manhood."

"I don't want your manhood. But I don't deserve to be humiliated. I could understand your other one night stands. But this, this is more than a wife should have to bear." Mother's voice sounded tinny, tremulous. I knew she would be in bed for days with one of her migraines.

"And this is more than a husband should have to bear. Coming home to meet the city police chief in my driveway because my wife has gotten into a catfight with another woman. In México, no one makes a fuss about such things. Men are expected to be men and women behave like women. You have become contaminated by this culture."

"This is not México," screamed Mother. "And I thank God for that."

There was another bout of silence, then Father barked, "Enough! I'm hungry. Get me something to eat."

"Get it yourself," she retorted.

I heard Mother's footsteps in the next room. She opened my bedroom door. "Terre, go fix your father something to eat. Isa take care of the children. I'm going to my bedroom. Don't disturb me. My head is aching."

*****

Father sat at the kitchen table reading the newspaper as I prepared the evening meal. I could not believe how calm he was after what had just transpired. It was as if nothing had happened. He sat there, unruffled, like a king ready to be served. I could feel the blood rushing through my body as I turned on the burner to reheat beans and rice. I recalled my parents' conversation. Obviously Father had been unfaithful to Mother before Lucia Guerra, and it made me furious to think about it. I turned from the stove, putting my hands on my hips. "How could you do that to Mother?" I said. "You always talk about honor and integrity yet you do such a dishonorable thing. How could you?"

Father looked up from the paper, his expression incredulous, then menacing. He slapped the paper down. "You dare to talk to me in that tone of voice and about something that is none of your business?"

"But it is my business. You're my father. What you do reflects on this family," I said in a more subdued voice.

"That's right, I am your father and as the head of this house, I forbid you from ever discussing this with me again." He stood up. "You've spoiled my appetite. It's a sad day when a man is treated so shabbily in his own home. I will eat elsewhere." He stalked out of the kitchen.

I learned that day that avoidance is a powerful weapon in domestic warfare.

Chapter 12

Mother and Father maintained a stony silence for several weeks after the Lucia Guerra revelation and Mother took out her frustrations and anxieties on us. She flew into rages at the slightest provocation. When Ellie accidentally spilled a glass of milk, Mother slapped her hand and made her cry. As my little sister wailed, Mother went into a screaming tirade accusing the rest of us of plotting to cause her to have a nervous breakdown. When I yelled at her to stop, she slapped me.

I clutched my stinging cheek, tears streaming down my face. "Why are you doing this? Why are you screaming at us when it's Father you're mad at?"

She raised her hand to strike me again, but stopped herself. "Go to your room this instant and don't ever question me or what I do again."

I gladly took refuge in my room. Although Mother didn't appreciate my interference, I think what I said made her realize how badly she had been treating us because her verbal assaults against us ceased.

*****

That Christmas, Mamá Grande, my father's mother, came to Ruby with three of her daughters, Ana, Isabel, and Teresa, and her youngest son, Roberto, my father's nineteen-year-old brother. Although my sister, Isa, and I shared the same names as my aunts, the four of us were actually named for my grandmother's mother, Isabel, and my grandfather's mother, Teresa. Our brother, Raul, was named in honor of my father's father. At that time, it was a custom for children to be named after a grandparent or great-grandparent and so it was not unusual for several generations to have the same name. Since my aunts went by their given names and Isa and I by nicknames, we rarely encountered confusion.

On Christmas Eve, we feasted on tamales and salsa, empanadas filled with picadillo, buñuelos, cinnamon-flavored cookies, hot chocolate, and an aromatic punch made with piloncillo, cinnamon, and tecojote fruit. We went to midnight Mass, and when we returned home, we exchanged presents. Father had money then so the gifts were lavish, particularly his gift to Mother. I remember the surprised look on her face when she opened the large box, pushed aside the white tissue paper, and gazed at the mahogany-colored mink coat. A peace offering, I thought. Did he really think he could make amends by buying her a mink? Mother smiled tremulously as she pulled the fur out of the box.

"Try it on, *mi amor*," Father said expansively.

My aunts oohed and aahed over the coat as he helped Mother put it on. Mother liked expensive things. Who doesn't? But I could tell by the furrow between her eyes and the tightness of her lips that she was having a difficult time refraining from saying something nasty to Father as she would have if her in-laws had not been there. Come to think of it, I have no doubt now that Father asked his family to visit that Christmas for the very reason that he knew Mother would hold her tongue in front of them.

"It looks lovely on you, Beatriz." Grandmother beamed from Father's upholstered armchair, her white hair glistening in the lamplight, as she bit into her favorite treat, a *marranito*, a ginger cookie shaped like a pig.

"Gracias, Mamá." Mother slipped the fur off her shoulders, returning it to the box. "It is a beautiful coat, though I won't be able to wear it often around here."

"You like it?" Father looked expectantly at her.

"What's not to like?" She walked toward the kitchen, avoiding his gaze. "Does anyone want something more to eat or drink?"

Father knit his eyebrows together and pursed his lips, not pleased with her response. What did he expect? Did he want Mother to throw herself on him, kiss him wildly, and thank him profusely after what he had done? Did he really think a mink coat would make up for the humiliation Mother suffered because of him? I was proud of Mother. I know she loved that coat, but she would not be bought off.

*****

Grandmother Alicia was an avid Chinese Checkers player. She was so good at the game she often said if she had one peso for every game she had ever won she'd be a millionaire. Late on Christmas morning, Mother, who enjoyed games of chance, challenged Grandmother to a game betting a dollar that she could beat her. Grandmother's face lit up as she accepted the challenge. The atmosphere in our living room became charged with excitement. We, that is, my aunts and uncle and siblings, gathered around and watched as Mother and Mamá Grande set up the Chinese Checkers board on the little round table between them, Grandmother choosing red marbles and Mother choosing yellow. We knew better than to take sides. That would have been undiplomatic. We cheered them both on as they progressed through the game. Grandmother leaned forward on her chair, a pensive expression on her face, never taking her eyes off the marbles, and Mother, trying to appear nonchalant, sat back and smiled, making comments to us kids, acting generally distracted. When Mother won the game by one jump, Grandmother didn't say anything at first, but I could tell by the sour expression on her face that she was not pleased. "You made an illegal move earlier in the game, Beatriz." She shrugged. "*Pues, ni modo.*"

"That's not true, Mamá Alicia. I won fair and square."

83

"Well, if that is what you call winning fair and square, then fine."
She turned to Tía Isabel. *"Mi'ja*, get a peso out of my purse for Beatriz."

"No, wait," Mother said. "I don't want your money if there is any doubt that I am not the clear winner. Why don't we play again?"

Grandmother calmly reset the game board. "I think that's best."

Mother lost the second game. I always wondered if she lost it on purpose, and now looking back, I think she did. Mother was much smarter than Father gave her credit for.

Later that day, Tía Dolores and her daughters, Ramona and Raquel, joined us for Christmas dinner. Tía Dolores was my grandmother's sister. She was two years older than my grandmother and, according to my mother, had been a great beauty in her youth. Now in her early sixties, vestiges of her beauty were still apparent. Her eyes, though slightly hooded with sagging lids, were yellow-green and penetrating. Her once blond hair, now steely gray, crowned a face that was far more wrinkled than my grandmother's, but nonetheless striking. Her high cheekbones, thin nose, and piercing eyes gave her a haughty appearance, though she was quite the opposite. She was also slender, unlike my grandmother Alicia. When Isa and I visited her at her rancho outside of Mercedes, she was always doing one of four things: working in her vegetable plot, tending her flower gardens, milking the cows in the barn, or riding her horse on her property. Like my grandmother, she had grown up as the pampered daughter in an aristocratic Mexican family that lost its fortune during the Revolution, but unlike Grandmother, she had gotten over it.

I don't mean to denigrate my grandmother. She was a kind and loving woman. But it bothered me the way everyone treated her. She never lifted a finger to do anything. Her daughters waited on her hand and foot, and so did my mother. She could barely walk. I think her legs were atrophied from disuse. She did like to sing, though, and I still remember her singing lullabies to us when we were children.

Anyway, that Christmas our house was bursting with people in an atmosphere of contrived conviviality. There was noticeable strain not only between my parents, who barely spoke a word to each other, but also between my great-aunt Dolores and her niece Ana. The tension between the two women was an ongoing thing, though Tía Ana seemed to be more affected by my great-aunt's presence than the other way around. All I knew was that their rift was about something that had happened in México many years before, an incident that no one would discuss.

About five in the afternoon, we finished our Christmas meal, a thirty-pound turkey packed with a sausage stuffing, mashed potatoes, corn, green beans, sweet potato pie, and biscuits, a traditional American Christmas dinner. Isa and I helped clear the table, and after we finished, we strolled to the front porch, where we heard a rather heated exchange between Tía Dolores' daughters, Ramona and Raquel, who were seated on the porch swing.

"I don't like the way Ana treats Mamá, or us, for that matter," Raquel was saying. "She has always treated her with scorn. She looks down on us, and I don't like it one bit. One of these days I'm going to tell her off."

"Ana didn't say anything to Mamá."

"She didn't have to. Didn't you see the way she rolled her eyes when Mamá was talking about how difficult it has been to milk Sofie? Why she actually looked disgusted, as if she couldn't believe that Mamá would degrade herself doing farmwork. Heaven forbid her mother would foul herself in such a way."

"You're being mean."

"You know what your problem is, Ramona? You can't forget that she is your half-sister, even though she wouldn't acknowledge such a thing if she had a gun to her head."

I glanced at Isa, whose eyes looked as if they were going to pop out of their sockets. I cleared my throat.

Raquel turned around, her face red. "Oh, hi, Terre, Isa. Come and sit with us."

We moved the Adirondack chairs that were positioned in front of the swing so that we could face my father's cousins. At twenty-four, Raquel was the younger of the sisters, petite, with long, straight black hair and small, dark blue eyes, almost Asian in appearance. The two years older Ramona was tall and robust, with dark brown hair and large, amber-colored eyes. She looked remarkably like my father's youngest sister, Teresa, who was about the same age. Once when I had mentioned their similarities to my aunts, the room had gone absolutely still and then Tía Ana had mumbled, "I don't think they look anything alike."

"I couldn't help overhearing what you said, Raquel," I commented.

She exchanged glances with Ramona.

"Oh, don't mind Raquel. She's just spouting nonsense," Ramona said.

No one said anything for a while. I glanced at the basket of red poinsettias that adorned the corner of the porch and wrapped my sweater tighter around me. It was cooler outside than I had anticipated.

"I think we should tell them," Raquel finally said. "They're old enough. I was thirteen when Mamá told us."

Ramona scowled. "But why? As far as I'm concerned, Antonio Rommel Ramos, may he rest in peace, was my papá. No one could have had a better father. That's all anyone needs to know." Tears began to flow down Ramona's cheeks and she wiped them away quickly. "Ay, forgive me. I just miss Papá so."

Isa leaned forward and touched my cousin's hand. "We all miss him, Ramona."

I shifted on my chair and glanced away. I have never been one to wear my heart on my sleeve, so emotional displays have always been uncomfortable for me. While my sister and cousin commiserated, I thought about my great-uncle's untimely death and my great-aunt's odd behavior afterward. Tío Antonio had fallen off his horse and broken his neck three years before. At the funeral, Tía Dolores had carried herself with dignity, but when she returned to the rancho where everyone gathered afterward, she began to rage. We all heard her cursing someone named Francisco, saying that it was because of him that Antonio had died. "If you hadn't broken his leg all those years ago, he would never have fallen off that horse. I hope you are rotting in hell you son-of-a-bitch!"

Mother later told us that Francisco was Dolores' first husband who had died in 1910. I was ten and Isa eleven at the time we learned this. We had both been dumbfounded by the revelation because it meant that my great-aunt had been married three times. Though each husband had died leaving her perfectly free to remarry, it still seemed scandalous. "Who was he?" I had finally managed to ask.

"A rich hacendado from Chihuahua. He was twenty-five years older than she was. The story is that he saw her at her quinceañera dance and fell madly in love with her, and her papá agreed to the marriage. *Pobrecita*, she married him when she was only fifteen and they were married for fifteen years. He took the best years of her life."

"Fifteen years? But if he died in 1910 that means that he, and not Tío Antonio, was Tío Gabriel's father," I said, remembering that Gabriel had told me that he was born in 1903, two years before Father.

Mother had given me one of her looks, the one that meant the subject was closed. "Antonio was Gabriel's father. That is all you need to know. Whatever you do, don't ever talk about it to your aunt. She doesn't like talking about that time or about Don Francisco. I don't think he was a very good man."

Isa and I had both nodded, acknowledging Mother's warning. However, for the next few days, we talked to each other at length trying to decipher our great-aunt's checkered past, to no avail. What we were to find out from Raquel that Christmas day three years later made Mother's revelation seem trivial.

"I thought your father was a Frenchman from Monterrey," I said to Raquel after Isa had consoled Ramona. "Mother said that he died when you and Ramona were toddlers."

"Let's go for a walk," Raquel said, rising from the swing.

We all rose, stepped off the porch onto the lawn, and then strolled onto the sidewalk. The temperature was in the low sixties, average for winter, though a wind from the north made it feel cooler. The late afternoon sunlight peeked through the clouds, however, giving the impression that it was warmer than it really was. Several children were playing with new toy cars, bicycles, and doll carriages in their front yards. As we sauntered by them, Raquel spoke. "Luis LeClerc, my mother's second husband, was my father. But your grandfather, Don Raul, was Ramona's father."

I glanced at Isa, who looked absolutely dumbfounded. I could tell she was dubious about what Raquel had admitted. She hated to think ill of people, especially those who were related to her.

"Are you certain about this?" she asked.

"Why would I lie about a thing like that?" Raquel stopped walking and put her hands on her hips.

"I didn't say you were lying. It's just so hard to believe. I mean, I've heard so many wonderful things about Grandfather, how devoted he was to Grandmother. They had fifteen children, didn't they? Doesn't that mean anything?"

Raquel smirked. "It means that he was a randy old goat."

Isa's lips tightened. "That's not very nice."

"Oh, Isa, she's right. And it explains a lot of things, doesn't it? Why the tías treat them so badly," I said.

"But it's not their fault. Why blame Raquel and Ramona? They have no control over what happened."

"No, I suppose not. But feelings can't be controlled," I said.

Raquel looked at me. "You'd better keep this to yourself."

"What do you think I am, nuts?" I said, then added, "What I don't understand is how my grandmother and your mother can be so close after such, such . . ."

"Betrayal?" Ramona gazed at me, her blue eyes searching.

I nodded.

"Yes, it's crazy, isn't it? Mamá says that your grandmother forgave her many years ago. She said that both of them had many things to forgive. I don't understand myself. If my sister slept with my husband, much less had a child with him, I'd kill her." She shot a menacing glance at Ramona.

Ramona looked mortified. "Oh, Raquel, I'd never do anything like that to you. You know that."

"But Tía Ana didn't forgive your mother," I reflected.

"No, Ana is a hard woman. That's why she never married, I think. She doesn't trust men."

Later that night, I lay on the living room sofa trying to get to sleep but my mind kept wandering to what I had learned that day. I also remembered a sermon I had heard at Mass one recent Sunday. The priest had talked about the sins of the father being visited upon his children for several generations. Was it the third or fourth generation? Would this curse of infidelity end with me, or would one more generation of Caballeros have to suffer through it?

Chapter 13

As far as I know, Father never again lived with another woman like he did that spring and summer of 1942, but he was involved with other women continuously, if sporadically, in the ensuing years. Isa won't like my mentioning the following story, but I'm going to anyway because it shows a pecularity in my father's choice of women, evidence of a guilty conscience, if not a warped mind.

After Isa married Marcos, he continued to play around. I don't mean like Father, running around with other women, but he was known to frequent bars in Reynosa. He liked to dance, and I have to say, my brother-in-law was, and still is, a great dancer. More than once, I have seen groups of people encircled around Marcos on a dance floor, clapping and yelling while he rumbaed, mamboed, or jitterbugged with Isa. Even Isa, who is a pretty fair dancer herself, would admit that the adulation is more for Marcos' fancy footwork than for hers. He is that good. Anyway, Marcos often went to Reynosa with his buddies to dance and drink, and according to him, nothing else. Well, if Isa believes him, who am I to say differently?

After one of his excursions to Reynosa, Marcos told Isa and me that he had seen Father. I was visiting them one Sunday afternoon at their house in Westwood when he shared this information. Isa and I were sitting together on the sofa, and Marcos sat across from us on an armchair. He had averted his eyes when he mentioned seeing Father, making me realize that there was more to the story.

"Who was he with?"

Isa looked at me and frowned. "Why do you think he was with anyone?"

"Come on, Isa, we're talking about Papá here." I looked at Marcos, who glanced at Isa, a worried expression on his face. "Well? Who was he with?"

"Nobody," he said.

He refused to talk about it with Isa around, so I waited until one of her frequent visits to the outhouse. She was in her eighth month of pregnancy, and the pressure of the baby's weight on her bladder was severe.

"Who was he with?"

"Listen, Terre, I'll tell you, but don't tell Isa. She's real protective of your father." He crossed the room to sit on the sofa next to me. "He was with a woman who looked so much like your mother I nearly went up to them to say hi. Pretty stupid, huh? As if your parents would be happy to see their son-in-law in a club in Reynosa without his wife. The woman had red hair and was small like your mother. Boy, all I could think about was getting the hell outta there without being seen. I hid behind a post until he went to the men's room, and then I hightailed it out."

I was mildly amused at the thought of my swaggering brother-in-law slinking behind a post but was too disturbed by his report about Father to poke fun at him.

"She had red hair?"

"Yes," he said.

Lucia Guerra had had red hair, too; however, she didn't resemble my mother, to the best of my recollection. Who was this new redheaded woman? Later, when reports came back to me about Father and other women, invariably the women had red hair. What are the chances of that happening accidentally? I think that Father might have been rationalizing his infidelities by being with women who resembled Mother. Maybe it lessened his guilt. Maybe he actually thought he was with Mother. Either way, I felt no sympathy for him. I was, in fact, appalled.

*****

After Isa and Marquitos left for Kansas, and then Raul left to go to basic training, our house felt unbalanced. I didn't know much Catholic theology then, but now thinking back, I can see that the effect their absence had on our family was a clear example of the biblical image of the Christian community as the body of Christ. As all Christians together form the body of Christ, we are all dependent on each other. If one part of the body ails, say, the head aches, the functioning of the entire body is affected. In our case, Isa had always been the heart of our family and Raul the brain. Without our heart and brain, we felt a void, a void that had to be filled. Lupita, with her compassionate nature, eventually became our heart, though in reality, no one could really take Isa's place. I stepped in as the brain, not too difficult a move for me. After all, I've always thought I was smarter than Raul, and had I been a boy, I'm sure Father would have thought so, too.

I missed Isa, Marquitos, and my brother, but I know that Father felt his favorites' absence even more keenly than I did. He was surly, and the drought that had been plaguing the Valley for five years, threatening to dry up our only source of water, didn't help his attitude. The Río Grande—that ancient river that runs along the Texas border from El Paso to Brownsville—was a major source of irrigation and drinking water for the Valley, but it was running dry. At the end of June, 1953, the river actually did run dry from Laredo to the Gulf of México for the first time in history.

The Caballeros of Ruby, Texas

*****

We stood on the sandy riverbank, Phoebe and I, gazing at the parched, craggy bed of the Río Grande about a hundred feet downstream from the nearly completed international bridge in what would eventually become the town of Progreso. It was odd to see this great expanse of steel yawning over a dry basin, but I knew that the rains were long overdue, and soon enough, water would again flow down the twisting bends of the river.

"They're looking at us," Phoebe whispered, putting her hand to her mouth.

"Who?" Behind me was nothing but a thicket of underbrush, sage bushes and mesquite trees. On the opposite bank, the scenery was much the same except that there were several Mexican citizens lolling on the riverbank.

"Those two immigration agents by the bridge."

I glanced upstream and saw two young men, one dark-headed, the other blond. Both wore sky blue shirts with epaulets and navy pants.

"The one on the right is cute," Phoebe said. "I've always liked *güeritos*."

"Oh, Phoebe, you're as bad as Isa ever was."

She ran her hand through her dark curly hair. "I'm not getting any younger. Mamá says that I'm way past my prime. She says that a girl is most beautiful when she is sixteen. After that, it's all downhill."

"That's crazy."

She laughed. "Well, maybe so. But you know my mother and her worries about my marital status. When I turned twenty-three, she lamented for weeks that I would become an old maid, like her sister, Teodora."

"What's wrong with that? Not everyone is cut out for marriage, you know. Should women be insulted and treated like second class citizens simply because they choose to remain single?"

"Why are you getting mad at me? If you don't want to get married that's fine with me. But I do."

"I never said I didn't want to get married. I just don't think I'll ever meet a man I can trust."

Phoebe gave me a wry look, her hazel eyes narrowed. "What does trust have to do with it?" She glanced back at the agents. "Oh, look."

I followed her gaze. The two men were talking to one of the workers who was pointing at something under the bridge. Other workers were clustered in groups at various points on the bridge peering beneath it.

"Let's go see what's up," Phoebe said, already making her way along the riverbank past mesquite and huisache trees whose canopies stretched over us.

I followed, a knot stuck in my throat. "Phoebe, I don't think . . ." I was interrupted by a man's voice calling out, *"Es un esqueleto!"* I felt shivers run down my spine even though I had known it would be something gruesome like that. It was not unusual to read in the newspaper about a body found in the river. Mostly these "floaters" were accidental drowning deaths. But sometimes the bodies showed signs of trauma: gunshot and knife wounds or a broken skull. Many Mexicans met untimely deaths perpetrated by the very people who they hired to help smuggle them across the river. There were also drug running-related deaths, not so many then as there are now, however.

When we arrived at the bridge, the blond agent—the "cute" one—was herding everyone away from the area underneath the bridge. The other agent ran into the trailer, which housed the temporary immigration office. Before long, we heard a siren announcing the arrival of several patrol units of the Hidalgo County Sheriff's Department.

"We'd better go." I grabbed Phoebe's arm.

"Don't you want to see what happened?"

"We can read about it in the paper tomorrow."

"Just a minute." She picked her way over sage brush and rocks to the worker who had spoken to the immigration agent. I waited under the shade of a spindly mesquite tree. A few minutes later she came back. "He said a skull and bones are partially buried in the riverbed under the bridge. It looks like they've been there a long time."

We were silent as we drove up Highway 88 in Phoebe's red Chevrolet convertible a few minutes later. On either side of us, sugar cane and cotton fields blanketed the countryside. An occasional farmhouse dotted the horizon. Soon we saw the towering palm trees on either side of Westwood's main street. Highway 88 turned into Texas Avenue in Westwood and then back to Highway 88 on the town's northern outskirts. We drove up Texas under the swaying palms.

"I wonder who that poor person was?" I finally muttered when we reached the outskirts of Westwood and continued on Highway 88 to Ruby.

"Probably some poor Mexican."

"Probably."

The next day, a newspaper article in the Westwood Gazette reported that Justice of the Peace Hernán González had pronounced the individual whose skeleton was found, officially dead. The remains were sent to the Westwood Mortuary. According to the article, no wallet or even bits of clothing were found on the skeleton, so chances of identification were slim. When Father mentioned the story to Mother, she became agitated saying that the skeleton could be that of her brother José, who had disappeared in 1936. She insisted that Father make inquiries. Grumbling that it couldn't possibly be his brother-in-law, but not wanting to upset

Mother further, Father left for the mortuary immediately. When he returned a few hours later, he said that several other people had also been there making inquiries about the skeleton and that the pathologist had given them sketchy information. "He said that the skeleton belonged to a man between the ages of twenty and thirty and that he had been dead for several years. He also said that he could not pinpoint the exact year of death, but that he could very well have been in the water for over ten years. He said that the man was probably murdered. The skull was fractured. There were also remnants of a rope wrapped around a cinder block near the skeleton."

Mother grimaced, tears in her eyes. "Could it be José?" she said softly.

"*Pues*, it's possible, but unlikely," Father said. "Remember, Beatriz, José was last seen in Monterrey, more than a hundred miles from the river. I don't think it's him."

Poor Mamá. It would have been a blessing had she known for sure if the skeleton belonged to her brother. The pathologist told Father that if he had José's dental records, he might be able to do a comparison with the skeleton's teeth. Unfortunately, my uncle had never been to a dentist, so there weren't any dental records to match. In those days, we didn't have anything like DNA analysis, like we do now, so there was really nothing more we could do.

No one ever claimed the victim's remains, and eventually he was buried in a pauper's grave in the county cemetery, the Mexican section, of course. Who else would have met such a sad end in the Río Grande but a hapless Mexican?

*****

The town of Río Bravo, México, is ten miles southeast of Reynosa. Like the Río Grande delta on the American side, the land in and around Río Bravo from Reynosa to Matamoros contains rich alluvial soil and was, and still is, an important farming area in México. Father had leased twenty hectares in Río Bravo from a Monterrey businessman that included agricultural fields, a farmhouse, and several outbuildings. There was also a barn that stabled four horses. Father paid the businessman a percentage of the profits from the sale of cotton and watermelons grown on the land in exchange for its use. The money Father earned from these crops had at one time simply supplemented his other income, but was now one of his main sources of revenue.

In August, we drove to the Méxican rancho for a week-long visit so that Father could supervise the cotton harvest. Unlike other crops, cotton doesn't need a lot of water, except early on after planting, so Father was not worried that the drought had affected production. However, this year the watermelon yield would be minimal, because even with the underground irrigation system on the property, the drought had affected that crop adversely.

He and Mother took the pickup, and I drove Ellie, Lupita, and Marta in our seven-year-old Buick. It was a humid day. Rivulets of perspiration formed on my face when I lifted my suitcase into the trunk of the car. Once on the road, the hot air felt gritty as it blew through the open car window onto my face.

After crossing the Hidalgo International Bridge into México, we drove on packed earth roads—narrow, bumpy, and jarring—quite different from the asphalt roads in Texas. As we neared the farmhouse, I saw several fields of fluffy, white cotton ready for harvest. During our trip to the rancho two months before, thousands of white flowers had covered the plants. My father had once told me that pollination occurred when the flowers bloomed, and that after the flowers withered a boll formed. It took about two months for the boll to mature, and then the cotton would be ripe for the picking. Judging from what I saw as we drove by the fields, we would have a bountiful harvest.

When we reached the farmhouse, a white wooden structure with a red clay tile roof and covered verandah, Guadalupe and Severino emerged with their three-year-old son, Manuelito. They were the caretakers of the property, and Severino also oversaw the crop planting and picking. We piled out of the vehicles, and Father immediately took Severino aside and disappeared out in the fields, while the rest of us took up residence in the big house.

Guadalupe, a Tamualipan Indian woman who cooked and cleaned for us when we visited the rancho, transferred her belongings to the smaller house next to the barn when we moved in. After I deposited my suitcase in the bedroom I would share with my sisters, I strolled outside. A large ebony tree grew in front of the big house, while yellow esperanza and fuschia bougainvillea bloomed in beds in front of the verandah. Large tins in which grew aloe vera, purple verbena, and pink and yellow moss rose lined the porch. I thought the tin cans bearing such brand names as *Café Colombia* and *Jalapeños Juárez* looked tacky, but Guadalupe didn't believe in wasting anything or buying anything unnecessarily, and I had to admire her thrift.

I scanned the corral and saw the pinto horse that Marquitos had ridden the summer before and felt suddenly melancholy. I had not realized until then how much I missed my little nephew. He had brought a lot of joy to our home, as small children are apt to do; it seemed that when he left, he took the joy with him. I walked toward the corral and the horse cantered over to me. There was no grass for him and the two other horses to munch on; the ground was parched, sort of the way I was feeling. As I stroked his muzzle, I felt a plop on my head. When I looked up to see what had hit me, another drop of water plopped in my right eye. I ran to the house yelling, "It's starting to rain!"

Within a few minutes, the sky opened up. Father and Severino ran across the cotton field to the front porch where we had all gathered. Father was the picture of despair as the rainfall continued unabated through the night. He stood by the screen door, his thick eyebrows knit together, his lips turned downward. Even Mother knew better than to say anything to him. By the next morning, the heavy rain had dislodged much of the cotton. White lumps dotted the field. The rain continued for several days, and by the time it stopped, the entire cotton crop had been washed away.

Our trip back to the Valley was somber, and I was grateful that I wasn't in the truck with Mother and Father. When we arrived at the international bridge that ran between Reynosa on the Mexican side and McAllen on the American side, we had to turn back. The Río Grande was not only flowing again, water was lapping over its banks and across the bridge. Although I was grateful for the sight of water in the river, I wondered why it couldn't have rained a week or so later so that we could have harvested the cotton crop. Who knows why things happen the way they do? It did seem to me, however, that God was making Father pay for his transgressions in the only way that might get his attention—financially.

People can do many things when they are faced with a crisis or tragedy. They can rail against God, they can become despondent and refuse to accept any new challenges, or they can accept it as God's will and go on. Father did all three. In the weeks to come, he muttered and stomped around the house. He fought with Mother more than usual. He stayed away from home, spending much of his time drinking in the neighborhood cantina. Finally, at the end of September, he resumed his business activities. I saw men coming and going from his office at the back of the house throughout the day, and often he would take the pickup and drive to Edinburg to carry on some business transaction at the city offices. He didn't mention the rancho, and we never visited there again.

Chapter 14

During the fall of 1952, the third-grade teacher Miss Sorenson, who taught at the Mexican school next door to our house, was killed when her car collided with a cow on Farm Road 491. I was shaken by her death, because she was not much older than I was. I asked Mother why God had allowed Miss Sorenson to die so young, and she commented with her usual fatalism, "Her time was up and it is useless to question God."

The news of the teacher's untimely death traveled like lightning through our small community and so did the news that school administrators were having a difficult time finding a teacher to replace her. Not many certified teachers were anxious to work at Mexican schools where the pay was substantially less than at the Anglo schools. Isa was the one who convinced me to apply for the teaching position.

"You ought to apply, Terre," she said one afternoon when we were playing with Marquitos on the front porch. "You always wanted to be a teacher."

"But I don't have a degree."

"So what? You have one year of college, and Miss Peabody always said you were smart as a whip. Besides, they're desperate." She grinned at me, her smile impish.

Miss Peabody, the principal of the Mexican school, had been my fourth grade teacher at the Anglo school and had been one of my most encouraging teachers. I remember how disappointed she had been when she saw me working at the soda fountain.

I had always wanted to be a teacher and had attended college with that intention, but when Father went bankrupt and I wasn't able to complete my education, I had put my dream aside. I took the job at the soda fountain as a way to forget my ambition, as a penance for having wished for something too grand. After all, weren't Mexicanas only good for service and domestic jobs? Isn't that what had been hammered into my head since elementary school, where teachers pushed home economics—sewing, cooking, cleaning—as the preferred course of study for Mexican girls? Had it not been for Father's insistence that we be taught an academic course of study, I might not have had such high ambitions. I might not have been so let down when my college career ended almost before it began.

What did I have to lose? I was tired working at the soda fountain, and if Miss Peabody said no to my application, I would be no worse off.

But if she said yes, well . . . I dressed carefully the next morning, putting on my gray tailored suit, nylons and pumps, then walked passed Señora Sanchez's house and across the street to the school. I entered the small building that served as the principal's office. A middle-aged woman with curly blond hair, who looked like an older and chubbier version of Shirley Temple, looked up at me from her wooden desk. "Can I help you?"

"I'm Teresa Caballero, and I've come to apply for the teaching position."

"Oh, just a minute," she said, suddenly excited. "Let me see." She rummaged through her desk. "I know I saw an application in here a minute ago. Oh, here it is." She held it out to me and stood up. "Just sit right here and fill it out." She gestured to an empty chair by a smaller desk. "When you're finished, just tell me and I'll give it to Miss Peabody. In the meantime, I'll tell her you're here. What was your name again?"

"Teresa Caballero."

She knocked on the principal's door and rushed in, closing the door behind her. A few minutes later, Miss Peabody came out and greeted me. My former teacher was in her late sixties. She had a receding hairline and white wispy hair cut close to her scalp. She wore circular wire-rim glasses and a dark tailored dress that was snug across her ample hips.

"Teresa, I'm so glad you came to apply for the position." She glanced at my partially completed application. "Finish up and come in when you're done."

"Thank you, Miss Peabody."

A few minutes later, I sat across from my former teacher, a wooden desk separating us.

"My, my, what a fine young woman you've turned into."

"Thank you, Miss Peabody."

She perused my application. "I was sorry to hear about your father's setback, particularly when I learned that it would prevent you from continuing your education. If anyone deserved to go to college it was you."

I looked away, glancing at the framed degrees on the wall behind her. "I appreciate your sentiments, Miss Peabody."

"How is Isabel?" she asked abruptly, noticing my discomfiture.

"She's fine. She got married and has a little boy."

The principal smiled. "Yes, I sometimes see her in the front yard with him. What a beautiful child. That's how I always pictured Isabel, as a housewife and mother. Isabel wasn't academically inclined as I recall, though she did like storytime."

I felt insulted for my sister though I didn't know why, because Miss Peabody was right. Isa was more suited to domestic life than the business or academic world. Even she would have agreed.

"But you, you were always at the top of the class. Smart as a whip. Probably one of the sharpest Spanish girls I ever had. Perhaps someday you'll be able to finish college." She looked at me, her brown eyes kind. Though I know she meant well, I felt piqued that she had felt the need to classify me as Spanish, particularly since I had consistently made better grades than all the other students in my class, male or female, Anglo or not.

"I know you don't have a teaching certificate, but I believe you would be a good teacher. I would like to hire you to take Miss Sorenson's place for the remainder of this semester and possibly until the end of the school year. I'm having a hard time filling the position, and I believe the superintendant will allow me to hire you under a hardship clause. Now, you understand that your salary will be less than what the other teachers are getting since you have no degree?"

"Yes, ma'am."

"Could you start on Monday?"

"You mean, I'm hired?" I stammered, wondering how I would be able to prepare for the class in one week.

"Why, yes. If you still want the position."

"Oh, yes."

"I want you to meet with Miss Friedrick, our fourth grade teacher, after school tomorrow. She'll be able to help you with the curriculum." She rose and walked around the desk. "And don't worry about a thing; you'll do just fine."

I stood up and we shook hands. She walked me to the door and as she opened it for me, she said, "Oh, Teresa?"

"Yes, ma'am."

"Some of the children are still struggling with English, but I don't want you to feel sorry for them and speak in Spanish. They must learn English and become good Americans, like you and your brother and sisters have. Do you understand?"

"Yes, ma'am, I understand."

*****

The next day after school let out, I walked over and found Miss Friedrick in her classroom. A middle-aged teacher, she had shoulder-length black hair and wore cherry red lipstick on rather thin lips. She was standing at the front of the room gazing out the screened window nearest the chalkboard. Twenty-five wooden desks were crammed so closely together in the small room, I had to sidle up one of the narrow rows to get to her.

The teacher turned her head and gave me a practiced smile when I reached her. "Oh, hello, you must be Miss Caballero. My, isn't it a hot day?" She lifted her hair off her neck and turned back to look out the window.

I followed her gaze, my eyes resting on a rusty swing set in the center of a field of overgrown weeds.

"It's difficult getting the children to concentrate on their schoolwork when it's so hot. Oh, but that's not the worst of it, I assure you. Half the textbooks we use have pages missing. Today, we were reading *The Adventures of Huckleberry Finn* from the English textbook, and all the books had several pages missing. How they expect us to teach these children to read and write competently is beyond me." She suddenly stopped talking and looked at me, a surprised expression on her face as if she didn't remember I was there. "Oh, but I'm rambling."

She gestured at a chair next to her desk. "Please have a seat. Miss Sorenson was working on the multiplication tables with the children and also cursive writing." She handed me a book. "That's the third grade curriculum book and Miss Sorenson's grade book. You'll get the hang of it. Just read through the teacher's guide and you'll be fine. I've found that most of the children are a bit slow, but I suppose that's to be expected, given their background."

"What do you mean?" I felt the hair stand up on my neck.

"Well, you know," she said uneasily. "Most of the children are lower class Mexicans, not Spanish like your family."

"Oh, I see," I mumbled.

"Anyway," she continued, back on track. "They are well-behaved and are mostly quite motivated. Of course most of them will drop out after the fifth grade, so it really seems a waste of time." She looked out the window again, her expression wistful.

"Thank you for your time, Miss Friedrick." I rose from the chair.

"Oh, call me Winifred. We're colleagues now." She gave me a pathetic smile and held out her hand.

I didn't want to shake her hand, but I did. As I walked home, I felt soiled, as if I had just been let in on a dirty secret to which I shouldn't have been privy.

*****

When Isa and I attended the Mexican school in north Ruby in the 1930s, it was comprised of one square, clapboard building used for all six grades. Weather-worn with a mottled gray shingled roof, it was quite different from the brick elementary Anglo school in south Ruby. My father transferred Isa and me to the Anglo school when we were in the third grade. The school was sparkling clean, with rooms for every grade level, and was equipped with modern conveniences, such as indoor plumbing. When I began teaching at the Mexican school in October of 1952, the disparity between the schools hit me full force. I wondered how I could have been so blind to the inequity before.

By the early 1950s, several wood buildings had been added to the Mexican school so that when I began teaching, the school was comprised of seven clapboard buildings surrounding an unkempt field. The buildings that comprised the Mexican school were of wood, unpainted and poorly constructed, some of them frame buildings with no interior finish, unlike the pristine brick Anglo school. Bathroom facilities consisted of two outhouses and a cement water trough and fountain outside the main building, unlike the Anglo school that had indoor plumbing and modern toilet facilities. Each classroom had six small windows, three on each side of the room and only one light bulb that hung in the middle of the room from a low ceiling. It would get quite hot on warm days and quite difficult to see on cloudy days. Our textbooks were discarded, out-of-date volumes, many with no covers and missing pages, passed to us from the Anglo schools. The supplies—chalk, pencils, crayons, paper—were always in short supply, so we had to ration and re-use what we could.

Although we had to teach in less than ideal surroundings, the children didn't seem the least concerned about it. After all, they had not known anything but deprivation for most of their young lives, many of them being children of migrants and service workers who barely earned enough money to put food on the table. Most of them lived on the outskirts of town in two-room shacks with no indoor plumbing. Even those who lived in town had outhouses behind their box-like homes, rather than indoor toilets.

On my first day of class, Miss Peabody introduced me to the students, mostly dark-skinned, dark-haired Mexican children, many of them older than eight, the usual age of a third grader. I was startled when they bellowed in a loud chorus, "Good morning, Miss Caballero."

I smiled. "Good morning, children."

The principal admonished the children to be on their best behavior, and with a nod in my direction, she left the room. After she left, I remember feeling suddenly adrift, like a disabled boat in the middle of the ocean. I finally stammered, "I am very sorry about what happened to Miss Sorenson, and I know you are, too. I will try to do my best to make the transition smooth."

Blank stares.

"First, I would like to go down each row and have each of you tell me your name. We'll start here." I pointed to the row on my right, where in the first seat, a girl with two braids looked up at me, her brown eyes alert and intelligent. "What is your name, young lady?"

"Sonia Hernández," she answered softly.

I nodded, then glanced at the boy behind her. I went down each row thus so, hearing such surnames as González, Abrego, Cuellar, Martínez, López, and Treviño. In the last row sat a boy with dark green eyes, emerald in color, that flashed impishly when it was his turn to introduce himself. "Pedrito Infante, no relation to the singer," he said matter-of-factly, then grinned.

I laughed. He had a disarming smile, all innocence and dimples.

"Mees," he continued in a serious tone.

"Yes, Pedrito."

"Isn't Caballero a Mexican name?"

"Yes."

"Are you Mexican?"

"I'm Mexican-American."

"Then how did you get to be a teacher?"

His question stopped me cold. I fidgeted, stood straighter, smoothed my dress, pursed my lips. Finally, I answered, "Do you think it's odd that I'm a teacher?"

"*Pues, sí.* I mean, yes," he stammered, looking around at the other students. "I thought only gringos could be teachers."

"Well, you are wrong, Pedrito," I said firmly.

"Miss?"

"Yes, Sonia?" I glanced at the little girl in the first row.

"Pedrito spoke in Spanish. Will he have to stay in for recess? Miss Sorenson marked down every time we spoke Spanish, and we had to write the correct sentence in English fifty times during recess."

"If that is what Miss Sorenson did, then that is what I will do. Pedrito, stay inside during recess and write, 'Well, yes,' fifty times."

"Yes, ma'am." He looked down at his desk.

"Now, let's see how well you all can read. Get out your reading books."

The children obediantly pulled their worn English texts from inside their wooden desks.

Later, during recess, I overheard two of my students talking underneath one of the windows of my classroom. I didn't mean to eavesdrop, but their voices were loud.

"It's hard to believe Miss Caballero is a Mexicana," said a female voice.

"Papá calls Mexicanas like her *agringada*," said her friend.

"What's *agringada*?"

"Mexicanos who act like gringos."

Pedrito, who was at his desk writing his sentences, glanced up at me. He had heard, too. I smiled at him and then looked out the window

101

at the cloudless, blue sky, trying to appear unaffected by what I had heard, though inside my stomach was churning. *Agringada.* I realized that these children had been taught to believe that Mexicanos and professional attainment were not synonymous, that only gringos could be professionals. They had been taught this not just by their Anglo teachers, but by their parents as well.

How was I to combat such ignorance?

Chapter 15

I finished out the school year and was rehired again for the next academic year amidst a spatter of controversy. On the one hand, most of the parents liked the idea of having a Mexican-American teacher as a role model for their children. On the other hand, a few parents, under the tutelage of Señor Zuniga, the landlord of a few rental properties in north Ruby and one of our town's prominent citizens, complained that my employment as a teacher was yet an another example of the inequality of Mexican schools. "The principal of the Anglo school would never hire an uncertified teacher, much less a Mexicana," he griped.

Señor Zuniga's complaints fell mostly on deaf ears. He couldn't rally enough people in our community to his side because the majority chose to remain loyal to my father, which translated into loyalty to me. Instead, several citizens visited the principal and lauded her for hiring me. To justify their approbation, I was determined to be the best teacher possible, and so spent much of my spare time studying books on elementary education teaching practices. The ensuing two years were the most challenging and exhilarating of my life.

Then I met Diego Gómez.

My sisters and I had gone to the 1954 Cinco de Mayo celebration on the grounds of the new Sacred Heart Catholic Church. Built on land Father donated, the new church, which had been completed the year before, had a seating capacity of five-hundred, was made of brick, and had a hefty mortgage. Father Carmody, aware that Cinco de Mayo was one of our town's most important holidays (since so many Méxican nationals and Méxican-born immigrants lived in our community), welcomed the celebration as a perfect opportunity to earn money to help pay for the new church building. Proceeds from raffle ticket sales and profits from the food and game booths went straight into the church coffer.

A southeasterly wind from the Gulf of México blew that night, as it did most of the time, and I could smell the salty sea breeze. The conjunto band, situated on a platform in the center of the parking lot, had already begun playing when we strolled onto the church property. Several couples were dancing to the lively beat of ranchera music.

"Oh, there's Maria," said Ellie, touching her hair. She had sprayed half a bottle of hairspray on her hairdo, a teased flip with bangs, and it looked like a stiff helmet on her head. She smoothed her hands on the billowy skirt of her aqua dress and rushed off to her friend in a flurry of petticoats.

Soon Lupita, her waist-length hair caught back in a pony tail, and twelve-year-old Marta, her auburn locks curling all over her head, ran off with their friends, leaving me to search for Phoebe. On the telephone, she had told me that she was bringing someone for me to meet, and I begged her not to. I hated blind dates, and she knew it. I hoped against hope that she would not do this to me again. The last blind date she had set me up with had been with a cousin of hers, a widower with two children. His eyes were droopy and his lips turned downward in a "woe is me" sort of look. Phoebe and I met him and a friend for dinner and a movie in Edinburg. During the meal he reminisced about his wife and talked about how much his children needed a mother. If that wasn't bad enough, he stank of cheap cologne and spent much of the time picking wax out of his ear. At the movies, "The Beast from 20,000 Fathoms," I spent much of the time swiping his hand off my leg. As the night wore on, I began to find the beast in the movie more appealing than the man I was with. It was all I could do not to run out of the theatre screaming.

I shook my head thinking about that night. I lingered at the edge of the parking lot by a food booth where tamales were being sold. Several of my students sauntered by, greeting me with embarrassed smiles and furtive hand waves. Finally, I saw Phoebe and her *novio*. Leopoldo was from a wealthy ranching family in Edinburg, and the couple had gotten engaged just a few months before, much to Phoebe's satisfaction and her mother's delirious relief. As they approached me, I saw that Phoebe had indeed brought someone along. The man was wearing pressed trousers and a white short-sleeved shirt that was open at the collar in a V, a small clump of dark chest hair exposed. He was exceptionally hairy with dark hair on his arms as well. There was something very primitive and masculine about him that mesmerized me.

"I'm sorry we're late," Phoebe said, her hazel eyes twinkling, "but Papá wanted to talk to Leo about the wedding."

"That's all right." I felt awkward under the intense scrutiny of the stranger's gaze.

"Terre, this is Leo's cousin, Diego Gómez."

I looked into his dark eyes and, in that moment, I felt everything around me slow down—the music, the breeze, the dancers—everything seemed to move in slow motion, and Diego stood out in sharp relief—his primitive maleness, his quiet demeanor, his sensuous smile, his intelligent eyes. He put out his hand.

"I'm glad to finally meet you. I've heard a lot about you."

When our hands touched, I felt a jolt of electricity shoot through me, and I yanked my hand away. "I'm sorry," I stammered looking at my feet. I looked back at him. "That is, I'm glad to meet you, too."

"Let's go dance, Leo." Phoebe gave me a wry smile and led her *novio* away.

"Would you like to dance?" Diego held his hand out again.

"No! I mean, not now, thank you." What was wrong with me? What was it about this man that got me so riled up?

"I see a vacant bench over there." He pointed to the front of the church. "Let's go sit down."

He put his hand on my elbow and led me to the wooden bench under the canopy of an ash tree. He pulled a cigarette from his shirt pocket as we sat down. "Do you mind if I smoke?"

"Yes."

He looked at me in surprise.

I frowned. "I just don't like cigarette smoke. I think I might be allergic to it or something." My father occasionally smoked cigarettes, and I hated the acrid smell that sometimes lingered on his clothing.

He put the cigarette back in his pocket and sat back, both arms resting on the top rim of the bench. "Most girls would have said they didn't mind."

"I'm not most girls."

"I can see that." He gazed at me, his expression curious.

It was getting dark and the lamp posts on either side of the church entrance flicked on. In addition to the lamps, strands of red, green, and white light bulbs that encircled the tops of the food and game booths and bandstand illuminated the area.

"Phoebe tells me you're a school teacher."

"Yes."

"Do you like teaching?"

"Yes, I do."

He nodded, then started to glance around.

I realized that if I wanted to encourage his attentions, and I really did, much to my surprise, I would have to carry on a conversation, something I was not used to doing with a man, particularly one in whom I was interested. "What do you do?"

"I work at Magness Produce Company in Westwood. I'm an assistant accounts manager. I work by commission, which is fine with me since I can sell anything."

"I believe you can," I said, instantly embarrassed. I could hardly believe my flattering tone.

He grinned, then rose and held out his hand. "Come on. If you won't let me smoke, you've got to dance with me."

I put my hand into his, and he led me to the parking lot turned dance floor and took me in his arms. It was a slow number, and we danced with a six-inch space between us as was proper. Throughout the night and until the end of the fiesta, Diego lingered by my side and we danced several times. He even danced a polka with Marta. He was an adequate dancer, certainly not the caliber of my brother-in-law, Marcos, who was an expert in technique and style and who exuded joy when he danced. However, Diego had other attributes that I admired. He had ambition, and more important, during the time we were at the celebration he never looked at another woman. When he asked if he could call me, I said yes.

*****

I never knew waiting for a phone call could be so torturous. Every time the phone rang, I felt my temperature go up, and I began to sweat profusely. At least that's what happened the first few days after I met Diego. I couldn't believe how giddy I felt and was thoroughly disgusted with myself. It wasn't as if Diego was the only man who had ever shown interest in me. When I was in high school, Arturo Ramírez, who was a senior, sent me fifteen red roses for my fifteenth birthday. I remember how flattered I had been. But even though he was quite handsome, I felt no emotional connection to him other than friendship. There were others, boys who drove by the house in their jalopies, whistling, honking and waving when Isa and I lounged on the front porch. There were boys at school dances and community fiestas. But no one had ever touched my heart.

Isa once said that I was too serious and demanding, that I would never find a man to live up to my standards. Well, at least I had standards! Isa could find merit in a one-legged toad in a leap frog contest! Okay, maybe I'm not being fair to my sister. But I digress.

When Diego hadn't called by the following weekend, I had regained my equilibrium. "Well," I thought, "he's just like the rest, unreliable and untrustworthy. It's a good thing I found this out now instead of later."

Then on Sunday night, he called. "I'm sorry it's taken me so long to call you," he said over the phone. "I went out of town on a business trip and just returned yesterday."

"Oh, that's all right. I've been so busy grading papers and preparing for school that I've hardly had time to think about anything else." What a liar I was!

"Well, then," he said in a subdued voice. "Ah, I was wondering if you'd be able to go out with me on Friday night. To the movies or something."

"I'll have to ask my parents."

"Sure, of course. What if I call you back tomorrow evening?"

"That would be fine."

"Well, talk to you then," he said.

"Okay."

After I put the phone back on the receiver, I sat down at the kitchen table and tried to gather my wits. During our conversation I had done my best to sound normal, even disinterested. Inside, I was a raging bundle of nerves. I had no idea how Mother or Father would react to my request. Frankly, I felt foolish to be having to ask for their permission to go out on a date. After all, I was twenty-four years old and employed in a prestigious profession. But that didn't matter. I was an unmarried Mexicana and under the authority of my parents.

That night during dinner, Father was in a rare good mood. He teased Marta and complimented Mother, telling her that she looked exceptionally pretty in the new dress she was wearing, a polka dot dress with a full skirt. This was the time to plunge in. "Papá, I met a young man at the Cinco de Mayo celebration last week. He's Leopoldo Gómez' cousin. His name is Diego Gómez, and he works for Magness Produce Company in Westwood. He wants to take me to the movies on Friday night. Would that be all right?"

"Diego Gómez?" Father gave me a searching look. "The name is familiar. Is he kin to Pedro Gómez of Mercedes?"

"Don Pedro is his father."

"Don Pedro owns a dry goods store in Mercedes," he affirmed, nodding.

"His mother, then, is Yolanda Vera, from the Veras who own the meat market in Mercedes," interjected Mother, a pleased expression on her face.

Father nodded. "If Diego has half the business sense that his father has, he will do well in life." He paused. "So, this gentleman wants to court you?"

"Papá, I don't think it's called courting anymore."

"Whatever it's called, it means the same thing," he said gruffly. "*Bueno*, you may accompany him to the movies with one of your sisters. I'd like to meet him when he comes to pick you up."

"Of course, Papá."

He smiled. "Teresita, this is good news. I was beginning to wonder if you were going to end up like your tía."

Father hadn't called me Teresita in years, and although I wanted to savor the moment, I couldn't resist replying, "Tía Ana doesn't have such a bad life. She makes a good living and doesn't have to answer to anybody."

Father's eyes narrowed. "You'd better learn to keep such opinions to yourself, now that you've finally got someone on the hook. Otherwise, you'll end up like your tía."

This time I resisted the urge to reply. I looked down at my plate, pursing my lips together. Why did Father have to make everything a contest of wills?

On Friday, Diego spent half an hour talking with my father about the produce business. By the time he, Lupita, and I left the house, I knew that he had won Father over. However, instead of feeling relieved, I felt uneasy. I had been Father's adversary for so long that his approbation seemed suspect. I glanced at Diego as we drove down our dusty street in his sleek, red Chevrolet with sweeping tail fins. He was clean shaven, smelled of soap, and was dressed in dark slacks, jacket, and a tie. I was powerfully attracted to him in a way that scared me. Even so, all I could think of was the proverb my mother used when she wanted to make a point that someone's exterior appearance did not always tell the whole story—*Aunque me visto de lana, no soy borrego.*

Although I may be dressed in wool, I am not a lamb.

Chapter 16

More than half my students didn't finish the school year. In April, they said their farewells and departed with their families on their annual migrant trip up north. Many wouldn't return until October. I was distressed when the children left, especially my students who were bright and thirsty for knowledge. I mentioned this to Miss Friedrick one day after school toward the end of the 1954 school year, though for the life of me, I'm still not sure why considering what I had learned about her over the course of my teaching tenure.

"You musn't get so emotionally involved with these kids," she said. "They're different from you and me. They're little better than work animals when you really think about it. They like working in the fields or they wouldn't do it year after year. Let's face it. Agricultural work is what these Mexican kids were made for."

My mouth fell open. I must have looked as mortified as I felt, because Miss Friedrick asked me what was wrong—I could never get used to calling her Winifred, which to me denoted a closeness I never felt with her.

"Nothing," I stammered. "That is, do you really believe that?"

"Don't you?"

Had I become so *agringada* that this *gringa éstupida* did not realize she was talking to a Mexicana? I rose from the chair in which I had been sitting and spouted off in rapid Spanish, "You are the most ignorant, stupid woman I have ever met in my life, and I am ashamed that you are my colleague. It is no wonder that these children never get out of the fields with people like you as their teachers. And, furthermore, I am ashamed of myself for being a part of this conspiracy to keep my people down. Yes, my people!" I slapped my hand against my chest.

I was shouting by the end of my tirade, and Miss Friedrick looked absolutely terrified. Her thin lips were plastered against her teeth and her blue eyes were opened wide in fright. The door to the classroom flew open and Miss Peabody lumbered in.

"What on earth is going on in here?"

Miss Friedrick jumped out of her chair, edged around me and ran to the principal, knocking a few desks along the way. "We were just talking, and she began screaming at me in Spanish." She crouched behind the principal and pointed at me.

I glared at the teacher, my arms crossed.

"Teresa," Miss Peabody said sharply, "we have rules about not speaking Spanish here, and they go for the teachers as well as the students."

"I realize that and I apologize, Miss Peabody."

She gave me a quizzical look. "Please come to my office."

"Of course." I followed the principal down one of the aisles to the back of the room. Miss Friedrick spoke after Miss Peabody disappeared through the doorway. "What did you say to me?"

I glanced back. "Believe me, you don't want to know." I turned on my heels, leaving her gaping at me.

*****

"Teresa, I heard some of what you said to Miss Friedrick."

I blushed. I had forgotten that the principal was proficient in Spanish. She gave me a sad smile. "She really is a rather ignorant woman, isn't she? But she is in a minority. The others don't feel as she does. Even so, the children are lucky to have her."

"I don't think so."

The principal gazed at me. "Teresa, I have been very happy with your work here. The children love you and so do their parents."

I felt my cheeks get hot.

"But I can't have you insulting a teacher and defying the rules of this school district."

I sat up straight. "So, you're not going to renew my contract."

"I didn't say that."

"What are you saying?"

"If you ever again insult Miss Friedrick or any of the other teachers, for that matter, and if you speak Spanish again on these school grounds, I will fire you. Understood?"

The unfairness of the reprimand stung. If anybody should be apologizing it should be Miss Friedrick, I thought. She was the one who insulted me. "Understood." I said, rising.

"Good. Now I want you to go and apologize to Miss Friedrick for speaking in Spanish. But for heaven's sake, don't tell her what you said."

I would have rather run in front of a moving train than apologize to that mealy-mouthed *sonsa*, but I trudged over to her classroom and mumbled an apology. She simply nodded, keeping her distance. I gathered my purse, school books and supplies from my own classroom and marched home.

*****

I banged into the house a few minutes later, slamming my books on the dining room table on my way to the kitchen. Father was perusing the newspaper, drinking a cup of *cafe con leche*, and snacking on a pink frosted *mollete*, a sweet bread confection that he loved. He looked up from the paper. *"Que pasó, mi'ja?"*

"Where's Mamá?" I avoided his question.

"She's visiting one of her friends," he said as I pulled out a pitcher of lemonade from the refrigerator. I poured myself a glass and sat down across the table from him. He continued to look at me. "Did something happen with Diego?"

"No, Papá, everything's fine with Diego."

"That's good. I've been hearing a lot of good things about him." He folded the paper and set it next to his coffee cup, giving me his full attention. "I understand that he has brought in more customers for the produce company than any of the other salesmen. I think in a few years he will be able to strike out on his own."

"What about his loyalty to the company?"

"Loyalty is important if you are being treated fairly, but Diego is a Mexicano working for a gringo. How fairly do you think he's being treated?" He gave me a wry look.

"Actually, Papá, something happened at school today between me and a gringo teacher that has a lot to do with that very subject." I related the incident, feeling somewhat disconcerted as I spoke. Father and I never had heart-to-heart discussions, mostly because I avoided him as much as possible. But since Diego had come into my life, I had noticed that Father seemed more benevolent toward me. Come to think of it, there was something about Father that day that made me feel a little tender toward him, a unique experience to be sure.

Father was forty-nine years old and looked every bit his age, if not older. He had grown corpulent over the years. He weighed more than two-hundred-fifty pounds. He had a double chin and thick jowls, and an enormous paunch, but he was as meticulously groomed as ever, his gray-streaked hair combed back, every hair in place, his pressed white shirt tucked neatly into his gray trousers. That day, despite his well-groomed appearance, he looked vulnerable and endearing. Looks can be so deceiving.

When I had finished my recitation, Father crossed his arms and leaned back on the spindly legs of the metal chair. "Terre, although I understand your concern for these children, it is a mistake to identify too closely with them. You are not like them. You are from a long line of aristocratic Spaniards. My father's parents came to México directly from Spain in the late 1800s and my mother's family was one of the founding families of Monterrey, pure Spanish, educated, as white as the definition requires."

"And Mamá?" I couldn't resist asking.

"Though your mother was an orphan and knows little about her heritage it is obvious that she has Spanish blood. Her red hair and white skin attest to that."

"And that's all that matters?" I asked with barely concealed contempt.

"In this gringo society, the only thing more important than having white skin is having money," he said derisively. "My advice to you is to not get too involved in the problems of these migrant children. If there is one thing I have learned in life it is this—no good deed goes unpunished." His voice was bitter. "I saw it during the Revolution. My parents treated our servants, most of them mestizos and indios, like members of our family. They fed and clothed them, gave them shelter and good salaries. And how did they repay my parents? When the first revolutionary troops came through the city, almost every one of them fled our home to join the Revolution, calling my parents aristocratic swine. After everything my parents had done for them and their families, that was their thanks."

"But this is different. This is the United States of America. We are supposed to have a classless society."

"If you believe that about this country, then you have learned nothing. Nothing," he roared.

"What's going on in here?" Marta trudged into the kitchen behind Ellie and Lupita and set her satchel on the table.

"Nothing." I scrambled out of the chair and ran to my bedroom. I closed the door behind me, blinking away my tears.

*****

I managed to make it to the end of the school year without getting into any more trouble. Although on the surface I was minding my p's and q's, inside I was in turmoil. I had always known that my father was class conscious, but never had he articulated his feelings on the subject so forcefully. Nevertheless, I felt he was wrong. If Mexicanos such as ourselves, who were more readily accepted, or should I say tolerated, by Anglos, did not do something to help these children, then who would?

Despite Father's advice, I was determined to help in some way. My first plan of action was to visit the homes of my students to stress the importance of an education. I remembered the times Mrs. White, the school nurse, visited our home when Isa and I were in grammar school. In her starched navy dress with white collar and cuffs, white hosiery and shoes, and a pristine white nurse's cap, she looked so formidable and efficient that I nearly swooned in awe. In those days, the school nurse made visits to our homes to teach hygiene, and to admonish us to watch for signs of polio, which was the most feared disease at the time. Because Mother could not speak English and Mrs. White could not speak Spanish, I had to translate their conversation, which turned out to be tricky.

"Mrs. Caballero, it is very important that you instruct the children to wash their hands thoroughly with soap after they use the toilet. Polio is caused by a virus that is passed by germs from dirty hands."

Mother crossed her arms. "Does she think we're pigs around here? That we don't know about washing up? I may not have gone past primary school, but I do know about such things as cleanliness."

Mortified, I looked at Mrs. White's expectant face. "My mother says thank-you very much for your advice. She will do as you say."

The nurse beamed, and Isa gave me a sideways glance.

I recalled the nurse's visits as Lupita and I trudged to Colonia Caballero one Saturday afternoon in June, vowing to do my best not to offend anyone during my calls. Of course, I had to take one of my sisters along and Lupita was the obvious choice. One, because she had a soft heart for anyone in need, and two, because Ellie and Marta had more important things to do, like setting their hair in curlers.

"Can you believe that Father once owned all this land?" Lupita waved her hand gesturing at the housing project, which encompassed about twenty acres of land subdivided into almost two-hundred residential lots.

"Easy come, easy go," I said flippantly as we strolled up the first dusty street of the colonia.

"Terre, don't be like that," scolded Lupita. "Papá worked hard to purchase this property, and you remember how awful he felt when he had to sell it to Señor Greene."

"He didn't sell all of the land, if you recall, he kept several lots."

"Twenty lots out of two-hundred is not much. But at least the colonia still bears his name. Papá will be remembered for years to come because of that."

I rolled my eyes, but said nothing. "Let's see." I pulled out my list of addresses from my pocketbook, then glanced back up at the row of box-like clapboard houses situated on narrow lots on either side of the street. Ebony and thorny mesquite trees adorned the front yards of most of the tiny houses, which were painted an array of bright colors—pinks, blues, yellows, and greens—most trimmed in white with dark shingled roofs. Only a few of my students lived in this colonia. Most of them lived on the outskirts of town on rural property, but since the colonia was walking distance from my house, I wanted to visit them first.

As my sister and I strolled up the street, I noticed that several of the houses were boarded up, the homes of migrant owners who spent summers up north picking vegetables and/or cotton.

"There's two-five-five," I said. "That's where Pedrito Infante's grandmother lives."

"Why do you want to see her?"

"It's not her I want to see. One of my students told me that Pedrito didn't go with his parents up north this year because he wasn't feeling well. He's staying with his grandmother. I want to see how he's doing," I said as we walked to the front door of the yellow house. Through the screen door, I saw an elderly woman sitting on a chair. I knocked on the frame of the door.

The old woman, wearing a floral housecoat, her short hair a mixture of white and gray, shuffled to the door.

"*Como está, Señora.* I'm Señorita Caballero and this is my sister, Lupita. I came to visit Pedrito. I was his third grade teacher at the Latin American school."

"*Pásale, pásale*, Pedrito is in the back room. He's been very sick. Ay, I don't know what to do anymore." She wrung her hands as she escorted us to the back room of the small house.

The house was comprised of three rooms, a living area, kitchen, and bedroom, all simply furnished. Pedrito was in the tiny bedroom lying on a full-size bed. Only his face could be seen above the chenille bedspread. I was alarmed by his wasted appearance and labored breathing. I approached him and he opened his eyes. Once a vibrant jewel-like green, his eyes now looked like murky pools.

"How long has he been like this?" I glanced at his grandmother.

"When his parents left last month, he had a fever and sore throat, and said he felt weak. Then he began complaining about a stiffness in his neck and back, and said his throat still hurt. Now he can't move his legs. I took him to a curandero and he has been treated for *mal ojo* and *susto*, but nothing has worked. I think he was not a very good curandero." The grandmother shrugged.

"Have you consulted a doctor?"

She shook her head.

"Why not?" I demanded.

"Gringo doctors don't understand us. They call us stupid and then charge us too much money."

"Señora, Pedrito is very sick," I whispered, pulling her toward me so that Pedrito couldn't hear. "He must be seen by a doctor."

"Ay, señorita, I have no money for a gringo doctor."

"I'll take care of it," I said, sending Lupita off to fetch Doctor Taylor, Ruby's resident physician.

Less than an hour later, Doctor Taylor arrived. When he emerged from Pedrito's room after a few minutes, his expression was grim. "How long has he been unable to eat?"

I translated for the señora. "Two days. She had been giving him broth because his throat hurt, but two days ago he couldn't even drink that."

"Wasn't he inoculated in March with the rest of the school children?"

"I'm not sure, doctor. Pedrito was not in my class this year." I paused. "You mean, he has polio?"

"A severe case of it, I'm afraid. Were you and your sister inoculated?"

I glanced at Lupita, whose eyes were opened wide in fear. "Why, yes."

"Good." He strode into the living room. "Tell his grandmother that I will try my best to save him, but even if I can manage that, he will be paralyzed for the rest of his life."

✦✦✦✦✦

Pedrito died two days later of respiratory failure brought on by bulbar poliomyelitis. His funeral was one of the saddest I had ever been to, even considering the funeral of the Alleluia's eighteen-year-old son who had died in Sicily during the war. Raul had played taps on his trumpet at Manolo's funeral, and it was wretchingly sad. Even so, I didn't cry at Manolo's funeral, not like I did at Pedrito's. I cried as much for the senseless loss of a beautiful ten-year-old boy, as I did for the ignorance that contributed to his death. Because by then I knew that his own family had prevented him from attending class the day of the inoculation. His grandmother because of her primitive folk beliefs had convinced his parents that Pedrito did not need to have a "gringo" shot. And the Anglo school administration did not do their part in following up with the children from the Mexican school who had missed the polio vaccine. Ignorance and prejudice, I have found, are two evils hardest to combat in this world.

Father forbade me from visiting the rest of the colonia residents after what happened with Pedrito. In truth, I was so overcome with grief and overwhelmed by the seemingly indomitable task before me, I was grateful for his intervention.

115

Chapter 17

Diego took my sisters and me to Delta Lake the Sunday after Pedrito died. I didn't much feel like going but he insisted that I needed to get out and have some fun. Delta Lake, an off-channel of the Río Grande, was just a few miles north of Ruby. The area in and around the lake encompassed about two-thousand acres, and it was a popular recreation area for Valley families. Father and Mother often took us to Delta Lake when we were kids to fish and swim, so the place held happy memories for me.

I spread out a quilt on the loamy ground near the murky lake, and Diego and I sat down. Several young men standing on the bank under the droopy branches of a cypress tree ogled Ellie, Lupita, and Marta as they strolled to the water. Lupita, always the modest one, wore a one-piece black swimsuit, while Ellie and Marta pranced around in two-piece swimsuits. Ellie's was red with white polka dots, and Marta's was green with white hibiscus flowers.

"You want to get in?" Diego glanced at me.

"Not yet." I smiled, trying to avoid looking at his almost naked body. It wasn't that I didn't like what I saw; it was that I liked it too much. He was wearing navy swim trunks, and his muscular and very hairy legs were stretched out and crossed at his ankles. He had a thatch of thick hair on his chest that crept down in a V underneath the band of his trunks. Just looking at him made me want to swoon.

For his part, Diego seemed at ease, nonchalant even, and for some reason, his indifference made me a little angry. Didn't he find me attractive? I looked at the white terry cloth cover-up I was wearing over my aqua one-piece swimsuit. The belt of the cover-up was pulled tightly around my waist and just the bottom portion of my legs from my knees down were showing. I smiled to myself. I wasn't exactly projecting a sexy siren image, was I? Truth be told, I was probably more modest than Lupita was.

"Ellie sure is feisty." He interrupted my thoughts.

"Yes, and if she doesn't watch it, she's going to find herself in serious trouble. She's boy crazy just like Isa was."

"Did Isa get in trouble?"

"Well, no," I admitted.

"Then what makes you think Ellie will?"

"She's more daring than Isa was, more willing to flaunt herself. Just look at her." My sister smiled coquettishly at one of the boys who had whistled at her. She splashed water in his direction.

"If you ask me, Ellie is all talk and no action. I wouldn't worry about her."

I frowned, wondering how he would know such a thing about my sister. "What makes you think that?"

For the first time that afternoon, he seemed ill at ease, or maybe it was just my imagination. He sat up from his lounging position. "Men know about such things, that's all. I've been around, Terre. I'm not a boy scout."

"I know, Diego," I said softly, suddenly realizing that I knew very little about Diego's past. We had been dating for only a few weeks and we saw each other only on weekends, though occasionally he drove by during the week in his sleek Chevrolet to say hello. There had been two weekends in six that we had not seen each other because he had been in San Antonio on business. I remember how odd I thought it was for him to have to stay over an entire weekend when everything was closed on Sunday, but I didn't say anything. He had called me on those Sundays telling me how much he missed me and so had allayed my suspicions. Yes, I admit I was suspicious of him. Given the fact of my father's less than honorable behavior with other women, who could blame me?

"Come here." He lifted his hand to my cheek and attempted to pull me toward him.

"No, not here. Not in front of everybody." I pulled away.

"No one's looking, *hermosa*." He tried to kiss me again.

"Let's go swimming." I jumped up.

"Fine." His voice was edgy. He stood up and strode to the lake and did a shallow dive into the water, not even waiting for me.

I wanted to kick myself. Why did I act that way when I wanted him so badly? Why did I push him away when what I really longed for was to feel the caress of his arms around me and his lips on mine? Why did I act contrary to what I felt?

He came up from the water and shook his head, water splashing all over Lupita, who was nearest him. She squealed, and he laughed, a carefree chortle, then he looked at me. I had taken off my cover-up and was standing on the shoreline of the lake.

"Come on in, Terre. The water feels great." He gave me a disarming smile.

I jumped in the water, determined to make it up to him, determined to loosen up, as Ellie said I needed to do. When I was within three feet of him, he lunged at me and dunked me in the water. When I came up he was no more than a foot away from me. We stood in the lake looking at each other, water dripping from our hair. I was just about to reach out

117

and touch his shoulder when I saw his eyes dart around me and then heard a syrupy voice.

"Hi, Diego!"

I turned around and saw a young, somewhat plump girl in a flesh-colored, two-piece swim suit. She had long, dark wavy hair and large breasts. She was with a friend, an equally sleazy looking girl, and they were both wearing dark sunglasses.

He simply smiled and gave a little wave and the girls strolled away.

"Who was that?"

"Actually, I don't remember her name," he said. "She's a friend of one of my sisters."

"Oh," was all I could say. I didn't believe him. If there was one thing I could see a mile away, thanks to Father, it was a woman on the prowl. And that girl not only was on the prowl, she wanted to sink her claws into Diego. What perplexed me was Diego's behavior. He certainly didn't act guilty. After the girl sauntered away, he began to splash water at my sisters as if she had never walked by. After a few minutes, I joined in, to his surprise and mine. Later, when we were back on the quilt resting after our water war, I leaned over and kissed Diego full on the lips, brazen as the bright June day.

"What's come over you?" he murmured when we had finished.

"I'm you're girl, right?"

"My favorite one," he said, "especially now."

As we kissed again in view of God and creation, I considered what he had said. I didn't like the implication of his words, but soon I could no longer think about anything but the sensations his wet kisses stirred in me.

*****

At the end of June, Isa and Marcos and four-year-old Marquitos came down from Kansas for a visit. They had only been in Ruby a few days when a ferocious storm blew in. But not even Hurricane Alice could dampen Father's spirits now that Isa and Marquitos were home. As the storm raged around us, Father sat in his armchair in our living room, cuddling my whimpering nephew in his arms.

"There's no need to be afraid, *mi hito*," he crooned. "Abuelo's here." He kissed Marquitos' forehead and smoothed his whispy hair.

As I watched Father soothe Marquitos, memories of another hurricane came to mind. I had also been four when a storm barrelled into the Valley and I have a vivid memory of Father and several of our neighbors holding onto the rafters of the little house we used to live in so that the vibrating roof wouldn't fly off. Mostly I remember that after the storm subsided, Father had gone over to Mother, Isa and me and held his arms out, not for me, but for Isa. It was Isa Father comforted, Isa who cuddled on his lap, Isa he crooned to. I had clung to Mother, but it was Father I had wanted, I am ashamed to admit. Even then I knew that Father preferred Isa to me. I don't begrudge my sister that. But I do hold it against my father. Parents shouldn't favor one child over another. They should treat their children with equal love and affection. But I sound bitter, don't I? I don't mean to. Mother held me close, crooned in my ear and rocked me back and forth. So why does the memory of that night hurt me so?

*****

A few days after the storm, Diego braved the still muddy roads to meet Isa and Marcos. I had been on pins and needles the whole day hoping that the meeting would go well and that Isa would like Diego. Now, looking back, I realize that my concern was ridiculous. Unlike me, Isa is predisposed to like everyone. She always has been.

We sat on the front porch, Isa and Marcos on the swing, Diego and I on the Adirondack chairs. The air smelled of mildew and mire due to the heavy rain of the previous days.

"How do you like living in Kansas?" Although Diego had looked at Marcos when he asked the question, it was Isa who answered.

"Oh, I like it. Marcos and I have met such nice people, haven't we, honey?" She turned to Marcos whose right arm was draped possessively around her shoulder. Before he could respond, Isa continued. "You know, gringos in the military are not prejudiced like the ones down here."

Diego nodded. "I've heard that before. When I travel for my job I find that the only gringos who give me trouble are the low-class ones, the white trash hillbillies. Unfortunately, there are a lot of them."

"Isn't that the truth," Marcos said with a smirk.

I mostly listened as my sister and Marcos conversed with Diego. But rather than being concerned if Isa approved of Diego or not, I found myself fascinated by a subtle change in Isa's relationship with Marcos. When they had first married they had immediately become entrenched in a power struggle, with Marcos insisting that as a man he could do as he pleased and Isa confronting his macho stance with various methods of resistance—stony silence, arguments, and stormy departures from their house to ours.

It seemed that Marcos had finally come to terms with the fact that he was a married man and was quite content in the role. Isa seemed more worldly, more sure of herself, and she certainly seemed to have Marcos under control. By then they had been married five years and, I must say, they were a glowing recommendation for marriage, something that I hoped wouldn't be lost on Diego.

119

Mother emerged from the house a few minutes after we had settled outside, and Marcos and Diego immediately jumped out of their seats. "Mamá, sit here," Marcos said gallantly gesturing to the swing. He turned to Diego after Mother sat down. "How about a smoke?"

Diego's face lit up. "Sure."

"Isa, we're going to walk down to Garcia's store. Do you want anything?"

"Bring me a chocolate bar," she smiled impishly, her plump cheeks dimpling. Isa had gained a good twenty pounds since her marriage, as had Marcos, another sign of domestic bliss, I suppose, but one which I did not approve of.

"Do you want anything, Señora Caballero? Terre?" Diego asked.

"Nothing for me," I said firmly, giving Isa a sidelong glance.

"Go by Tencha's Cantina and see if you can pry my husband out of there," Mother said with a laugh though her eyes were not smiling.

"Mamá!" I looked at her aghast.

"Bring me an orange cola, *por favor*," she said, ignoring my cry of protest.

As the men sauntered across the lawn, Isa called out, "Don't be long, honey."

Marcos turned and waved, his expression pleasant, but he didn't answer.

"So, what do you think of Diego, Isa? He's a good catch for our Terre, eh?"

"He's very nice, Mamá, and very handsome." She grinned and winked at me.

"More important, he comes from a good family and has a good job."

"You both talk as if he's already asked me to marry him."

Mother and Isa gave each other knowing glances. "Terre," Mother said, "are you the only one who can't see that Diego is in love with you? A marriage proposal will come soon enough. Mark my words."

Although Diego was an ardent lover—he called me daily, brought me gifts, serenaded me—I must admit I still felt as if he were a stranger. I have never been able to understand men. Perhaps it's because my first reaction has always been to distrust them. "Mamá, how did you know that Papá was the one for you?"

Mother seemed as startled by my question as I was that I had even asked it. She didn't say anything for a while, then she spoke, her voice wistful. "It was a bright, sunny day, I remember. Candelaria and I were playing in the courtyard of the Hacienda Santa Elena, your great-grandfather's hacienda where my grandmother was a cook. The Villistas had already been through and had left the hacienda in a shambles. They had torn down the church and taken most of the livestock, including Don Félix' racing horses. It was 1916, six years into the Revolution. A motor car came through the hacienda gates and in it were two men and two boys. They got out of the car, one of those old Ford Model T's, and Don Daniel greeted us. I had a vague recollection of him. He was Don Félix' son, the one who had lived at the hacienda before the worst of the fighting began. He introduced my sister and me to Don Raul and the boys. Your father was about ten years old, but already he had the bearing of an aristocrat; he stood tall and proud. He was wearing a dark suit and bowler hat, and when he took my hand, he smiled at me. He had the kindest eyes I had ever seen. I fell in love with him then and there."

"But if Father was ten, you must have been only five!" I sputtered.

"That's right." Mother smiled. Her features softened as she remembered. "After Don Daniel brought us to Monterrey to work for him, I saw Miguel occasionally when he and his parents visited his uncle. He was so handsome. He actually made my heart flutter when I saw him, but I dared not hope that he felt the same about me. We were of different social classes, and in México, well, that meant we might as well be living in different countries. In fact, when I was fourteen, he made that quite clear when he asked me to be his mistress."

"Papá asked you to be his mistress?" Isa stammered.

"What did you say?" I asked, fascinated.

"What do you think I said?" she retorted. "I was a good Catholic girl. I slapped him and told him to go to hell."

"Mamá!" Isa and I both cried out in unison.

Mother grinned at our response, then continued. "After my grandmother died, I came to Texas where Candelaria and her husband had moved with my little brother, José, God rest his soul wherever he is." She made the sign of the cross over her chest. "I saw your father again in a field between Ruby and Westwood. Imagine how astonished I was when I saw him picking cotton. The son of Don Raul Caballero, prominent Monterrey businessman, and grandson of Don Félix Guzmán Hernández, a hacendado, picking cotton. It was a sight to be sure." She laughed. "But surprisingly, he was not embarrassed. Even dressed in dirty clothes, sweat running down his face, your father had a dignity that no one could match. He walked through the rows of cotton when he saw me and said, 'Señorita Beatriz, you are a vision of loveliness and a welcome sight. Permit me to call on you tonight.'

"Mind you, I was dressed in nothing more than rags and was wearing a tattered wide-brimmed straw hat. It had been almost a year since the last time I had seen him, the time when I slapped him. I told him he could call on me if his intentions were proper and he assured me that they were. That night I found out that his father had died and had left his family in the poorhouse. Within a few months, he asked me to marry him."

"I never knew that."

"There are a lot of things about your father and me that you don't know, *hija*," Mother said matter-of-factly, glancing at me.

Isa and I were still exclaiming over my mother's revelation when Father drove up in his pickup. He eased out of the vehicle slowly. I could tell he was drunk by the deliberate way he put one foot in front of the other as he wobbled toward us. He stumbled on the first step of the porch. "How are my girls?" he said expansively, steadying himself on the railing.

He lurched to the swing and put his arms around mother, nuzzling his face against her neck, something he only did in public when he was drunk.

"Get your hands off me." She leapt off the swing. "You're drunk."

Father's eyes narrowed. "Not as drunk as I'm going to be."

She stalked into the house, Father stomping behind her.

A few minutes later, Marcos and Diego returned from the store reeking of cigarette smoke. Isa didn't seem to mind, but I hated the odor and moved my chair away from Diego's. I thought about the story Mother had told us, thinking about her relationship with Father now. Was that what became of marriage? The blush of love, the longing—did they always deteriorate into fighting and disdain? I found myself observing Diego, watching his every gesture and expression, looking for some indication that he could become like Father. But I saw only what I wanted to see (I realize that now), a clean-shaven, handsome face, a quiet demeanor, a man whom I longed to be near in the most intimate sense.

Later, when we kissed before he left, my apprehensions ebbed away like the dimming dusk.

Chapter 18

That summer flew by and I began my third year of teaching in the fall of 1954. Diego continued to travel a lot, going to San Antonio several weekends a month, and I became accustomed to his absences. Looking back, I wonder how I could have been so naïve. It's funny now that I think about it. Because of Father I had initially been distrustful of Diego, but also because of Father I overcame my suspicions, much to my detriment.

My relationship with Father was complex. On the one hand, I despised his macho posturing, his Mexicanness, if you will. On the other hand, I craved his approval. When Diego came into my life, I felt Father's approval as I never had before, and pathetic as it sounds, I basked in his warm smiles and tender affirmations.

Though it may seem that Father was progressive—he did, after all, send Isa and me to college—I think his reasons for sending us had more to do with the fact that he could do it, financially, I mean. In those days, few Mexicanos went to college. In fact, only two other Mexicanos from my hometown continued on to college, children of well-to-do businessmen. It was a matter of pride, I think, for Father to send his two eldest children to college. It just so happened that we were daughters. I don't think he really believed in his heart that women truly benefitted from college since, in the end, marriage was the ultimate goal. Also, though he seemed proud when I began teaching at the Mexican school, I think to him it was just a productive way for me to spend my time until the real reason for my existence presented itself—marriage.

Though I seem to be putting all the blame on Father, in truth, Mother was no better. She was beside herself that I had "caught" someone like Diego. After he asked me to marry him in November of that year, she seemed to walk taller and took great pleasure in announcing to all her friends that I was engaged to be married, finally! I had never seen her so happy.

I cringe just thinking about it. How could I have allowed myself to be swept up like some weak-kneed school girl in this illusion of romance and parental approval? I, who was above such nonsense, was swept along like a cork in a mounting tidal wave, and soon enough would find myself battered against a ragged, rocky shoreline.

*****

In early spring of 1955, Father made an announcement that would ultimately be the beginning of the end of our family.

"I'm going to California next week." Father wiped his mouth with his white linen napkin and set it on the side of his plate of carne guisada. He gazed at us defiantly, or so I thought. The six of us were eating dinner in the dining room.

"Why are you going to California, Papá?" Marta set her glass of milk on the table and looked at Father inquisitively. My youngest sister was twelve, a bit naïve, and like Isa, oblivious to Father's faults.

"I've been told of a foreman's position at a packing shed near Soledad in the Salinas Valley. A Texas company owns the shed, and I know the owner of the company. I'm going to go over to make arrangements for us to move there."

"What?" Ellie stammered, spitting bits of food out of her mouth.

I looked at Mother who was sitting opposite Father, closest to me. Her lips were set in a thin line and she didn't look at all pleased.

"What is the matter with you, Eloise?" Father demanded. "Where are your manners?"

"I'm sorry, Papá." She wiped up the mess. "But I'm just surprised, that's all." She glanced at Lupita, Marta and me, trying to gather some support, I think. But we were all too shell-shocked to utter a word.

Father glanced out the dining room window, his thick eyebrows knit together. "I think it's time to make a fresh start." He looked back at us. "I'm done here in Ruby. I've been trying for five years to re-coup my losses, and I keep coming up against brick walls. "It's time for a change. Of course, this won't affect you, Terre. By the time the arrangements are in place, you will be married to Diego and, of course, your place is with him."

"But Papá, next year is my senior year," Ellie blurted out. "I don't want to spend my last year in a strange high school where I don't know anybody!" She looked at Mother, her expression pleading. "Mamá, do you want to leave Ruby and all your friends? What about Doña Cuca? What will she do? She's been with us for years, and I know that Señor Domingo will not let her leave Ruby."

"*Pues*, I don't want to leave Ruby, either." Mother averted her eyes as she played with her spoon. "But your father thinks it's necessary, and he is the head of this house."

I felt my pulse quicken. I hated when Mother acquiesced to Father, especially when she was against what he was proposing. "But if nobody else wants to go," I couldn't resist saying, "why does Father's wish have to prevail? Shouldn't a family be run like a democracy?"

Father scowled at me and then smashed his fist against the table sending silverware and glasses flying in every direction. "There will be no more discussion on the subject." He rose heavily from the table. "We're moving to California and that's the end of it." He stalked out of the room.

Mother, my sisters and I sat at the table looking at each other, stunned into silence. Finally, Lupita spoke, her voice soft. "I've heard that California is beautiful. Maybe Father is right. Maybe we do need a new start."

Ellie shot out of her chair. "Oh, shut up!" she said before storming to her bedroom.

*****

Father left for California at the beginning of April. He was gone for over a month. When he returned, he was in an unpredictably benevolent mood. "I think it would be best for Ellie to finish out her senior year here in Ruby," he said magnanimously the morning after his return.

"You mean it, Papá? Ellie looked up from her dusting chore, the china cabinet in the dining room. Marta had just been teasing her, calling her Aunt Jemima, because of the red cotton scarf that was wrapped around the enormous curlers on her head.

"Yes. In fact, I think it's probably best if all of you stayed until Ellie graduates." He glanced at Mother, who had been helping Doña Cuca thaw out the refrigerator. "There's no need to disrupt their education, don't you think, Beatriz?"

"But that's a full year away!" Mother said.

"Just nine months, actually." Father poured himself a cup of coffee. "I need to tie up loose ends here during the summer and then there's Terre's wedding in August. I'll leave after that. Of course, I plan to come to Ruby frequently during the next year, and you will come up to Soledad for short stays. Don't you think it's a better idea for Ellie to finish high school here?"

Mother's eyes glinted with suspicion. "If you say so," she finally answered, glancing at Doña Cuca, who was busily scraping ice chunks from the freezer, acting as though she hadn't heard a word.

"Then it's settled," he said, pleased. "I'll be in my office." He sipped his coffee as he headed to the back of the house.

My sisters squealed after he left, jumping up and down in the kitchen until Mother admonished them to get back to work. I went back to dusting the stretch of bookcases in the living room, wiping the leather spines of the books in fast, angry strokes. There could only be one reason for Father's change of heart concerning Mother's and my sisters' move— another woman. He must have found himself a paramour in California and didn't want them in the way. Perhaps it was wrong of me to think that Father had ulterior motives for leaving Mother and my sisters behind for a year, but it just made sense given his less than honorable past.

Mother stalked into the living room. "Marta, there are streaks here." She pointed at the glass pane of the dining room window that overlooked the gravel driveway and a great ash tree. "Clean it again."

I could tell by the sour tone of her voice that she was thinking the same thing about Father that I was. Poor Mother. What did she do to deserve such a husband?

*****

As Father prepared for his imminent departure, I faced the end of my teaching career. In those days, married women were not encouraged to work and as I was about to become a missus, I was on the way out. On the last day of school, my colleagues and students gave me a going away party in my classroom. Miss Peabody's secretary brought in a vanilla-frosted cake with the words, "We'll Miss You, Miss Caballero!" scrawled in curlicue letters across it. I was on the verge of tears and seeing the cake didn't help. Still, I kept my tears in check.

"The children have something for you, Miss Caballero." Miss Peabody glanced at Reynaldo González, one of my students, a thin boy with dimples and a dark stock of hair. He stepped forward and handed me a stack of papers.

"We've been working on these all month, Miss Caballero. Some of us wrote poems, others drew pictures, and some wrote letters to you."

"Thank you," I mumbled, a knot in my throat as I took the papers from his hands.

"I would like to recite my poem if you don't mind, Miss Caballero," he said boldly.

I nodded, giving him a wistful smile.

He walked to the front of the room and the principal and I and the other teachers moved to the sides of the classroom so that we wouldn't block the other students' view. I smiled as Reynaldo geared himself up for the recitation. He had always been one of my more vocal students and had a theatrical flare.

"My Teacher," he began with a wave of his hands. "She is tall. She is nice. She is always fair. She makes me do my classwork, even when I don't care. She taught me how to read and write, better than I could. She taught me that I could do anything that I set my mind to do. She made me laugh when I felt sad and smiled her pretty smile. My teacher is the best in the world. I'll miss you, Miss Caballero." He finished with a flourish, bowing.

The tears that I had been desperately trying to keep in finally broke loose and I could feel them streaming down my face as I walked over to my student and gave him a hug. "That was beautiful, Reynaldo," I stammered.

126

He nodded and grinned, though I could tell he was a little embarrassed. He went back to his desk and a few of his classmates slapped his back in affirmation as he sat down.

I wiped the wetness from my face. "I would like to thank all of you for the work you did on these cards and poems and drawings." I looked down at the stack of papers in my hand. "I will treasure them always. It has been a great privilege for me to be your teacher and I will always look upon this time of my life with fondness. Now, why don't we cut the cake!"

The children jumped out of their chairs and rushed to my desk. I spent several minutes calming them down, and then I cut and placed pieces of the cake on small plates for them. Within minutes they had devoured the cake, and after a plethora of handshakes and hugs, the children and teachers began to leave.

Miss Peabody lingered behind. "Teresa, I just want to say it's been wonderful seeing you grow as a teacher," she said after everyone had gone. "It seems as though just when a good teacher is trained, she leaves us. Usually, it's marriage that takes her away."

"It doesn't seem fair, does it, Miss Peabody?"

"No, it doesn't."

"I don't understand why a woman can't work after she gets married if she wants to, especially if she has no children."

"Most men don't like their wives working outside the home. I once had a chance to get married, but I knew I'd have to give up teaching." She sighed. "I guess I just loved teaching more than Jim."

"Have you ever regretted your choice?"

"I'll be honest with you. Sometimes I have. I think I would have been a good mother." Her eyes misted.

"I think so, too, Miss Peabody."

"No use crying over spilt milk," she said, her no-nonsense tone back. "I suppose I'm as happy as anybody has the right to be." She touched my arm and smiled. "If my opinion means anything, I think you're making the right choice." She made her way between the desks to the door and then turned back to look at me. "Come back and visit when you can."

After Miss Peabody left, I lingered in the classroom wondering if, indeed, I had made the right choice.

Chapter 19

Diego stopped his car in front of a small house in south Westwood. Pink bricks ran waist-level across the front wall of the house. In front of the single story house stood a row of boxwood shrubs, neatly trimmed. "What do you think?" he asked.

"It's nice. Who lives here?"

"We do. That is, we will after we get married next month."

"It's ours?"

"I put a down payment on it yesterday."

I frowned, perturbed that he hadn't asked my opinion on the house before he decided to purchase it.

"Let's go inside," he said, oblivious to my displeasure.

"You have the key?"

He dangled a silver key in front of me and grabbed my hand, pulling me out of his Chevrolet. As we strolled up the concrete walkway to the front porch, he pointed out features of the house much as a real estate agent would. "As you can see, it's got brick in the front and it's been freshly painted. There's no trees in the front yard, but in the back there are several ash and chinaberry trees. It doesn't look big, but it's got more room than you may think."

We reached the front door, which was painted white and had three rectangular windows at the top positioned vertically in a stair step configuration. Diego jiggled the key in the lock.

"Are there many Mexicanos in the neighborhood?" I asked as the door opened.

"There are several families," he said. "I talked with the next door neighbor yesterday. Her name is Señora Balderas. She said that every time a Mexicano family moves in, more Anglo families move out."

"Their loss is our gain," I said. Since the war, more Mexicanos, particularly veterans taking advantage of their VA benefits, had begun moving into the nicer southside neighborhoods in all the Valley towns. Many of the Anglo homeowners showed their displeasure by moving further south. Heaven forbid that they would have a Mexicano for a neighbor.

As Diego showed me around, my displeasure that he had selected the house without me gave way to a reluctant feeling of gratitude when I realized how fortunate we were to be able to afford such a home. We walked hand in hand on the wood-plank floor of the small living room, the only distinguishing feature a fairly large picture window on which hung heavy gold-colored drapes in desperate need of cleaning. We moved onto the grayish linoleum floor in the kitchen. I could tell the porcelain sink had once been white, but now it was stained yellow. Likewise, the once white stove had a layer of urine-colored grease on its hood and the burner areas. "Anglos are always calling Mexicanos dirty," I sneered. "But just look at this kitchen. Mother would have a fit if she saw how dirty it is."

Diego frowned. "But it's fixable, right?"

"Of course it is." I squeezed his hand.

Anxious, I suppose, to get me out of the offensive kitchen, he guided me into a hallway that led to two small bedrooms on either side of a bathroom, then through each room. The bathroom, like the kitchen, needed a once over. This time, I kept my opinion to myself. We went into the hallway and back to the living room.

Diego stopped and looked at me expectantly. "It's a good starter home, don't you think? I know it's small, but one day, I'll buy you something grand, a huge house out in the country."

"Small? Why it's twice as large as what Isa and Marcos had when they got married, not to mention it's got an indoor toilet. I don't need anything bigger than this, Diego. It's a wonderful house."

He grinned and then pulled me toward him. His arms felt good around me and I leaned against him. When I looked up at him, he gave me a soft kiss on my lips and before I knew it, we were kissing passionately, our tongues intertwined. He pulled at the zipper of my dress. At the same time, he began to push me to the floor.

"No, Diego, no," I protested between kisses. It's funny all the thoughts that went through my mind as he caressed my body. I've always been a cerebral person, thinking, thinking, thinking, not feeling enough as Ellie would say. True to form, I was sprawled on the cold wood floor, my rational mind fighting against my bodily sensations. I thought about the postmaster's daughter-in-law who had run off with her brother-in-law a year before and the havoc their infidelity had caused. I remembered Ellie telling me that she and Isa had seen them together in an abandoned packing shed. I had been scandalized and intrigued. What was it about sexual attraction that caused men and women to throw caution to the wind? I had never understood the power of sex until I met Diego. I was ready to give myself totally to him when it came to me that no matter how much I wanted to, if I gave in to these sensual feelings, I would be no better than Janice Walton and Samuel Alberts, no better than my father, no better than all those people who allow themselves to be led by their physical responses and emotions, rather than by their heads. I had seen the results of such unions and I wanted no part of it.

"No," I said forcefully as I pushed Diego off me. I scrambled to my feet pulling my zipper back up.

"What's the matter with you?" Diego spat. He got up slowly and rearranged his trousers.

"We only have one more month until we are married. I want our wedding night to be special. I want us to do things right."

"I wish you had told me that before you let me get this far, Terre." He ran his hand through his hair in a gesture of exasperation.

We stood there looking at each other for a few minutes, Diego's heavy breathing mingling with the cicadas buzzing outside on the hot July afternoon.

"Come on, let's pick up your sisters," he finally said as he threw open the front door.

We picked up Ellie and Lupita from the five and dime in downtown Westwood where we had dropped them off before going to the house. My sisters immediately began to chatter, not noticing the chill in the air between Diego and me.

"Terre, you have specks of dust all over the back of your hair," Lupita said from the back seat. She began to swat at my hair with her hand. "What have you been doing?"

I was more than a little embarrassed by the question and as I formulated my response, Diego said, "She rubbed up against one of the curtains in the house. It was full of dust."

"What house?" Lupita asked.

"The house your sister and I are going to live in when we are married."

"Oh, show it to us!" Ellie said.

"Not today, girls. I need to get you home because I need to pack for my trip."

"You're leaving today?" I said. "But it's Saturday."

"Yes, well, I have some unfinished business in San Antonio. I'll be back by tomorrow night."

I didn't respond. Considering what had just transpired between us, I thought it best not to say anything.

*****

A few days later, Phoebe drove me to Edinburg so I could buy gifts for the wedding party. We were strolling down the perfume aisle of J.C. Penney's Department Store sampling myriad scents when we ran into Daisy Zambrano, a girl we had gone to high school with. Heavy-set with thick eyebrows and bushy hair, Daisy, whose dainty name did not match her formidable physique, gushed when she saw us.

"*Dios mío!* It's been so long since we've seen each other," she exclaimed. "Three years at least."

"Didn't you move to San Antonio?" Phoebe asked.

"Yes, I got married to Joe Estrada, and when he joined the Air Force, we got stationed there."

"Do you like it?"

"Yes, it's beautiful there. On Sundays, we almost always go to Brackenridge Park. It's got a river flowing through it and huge trees. Oh, by the way, I saw Diego Gómez a few weeks back. Aren't you and he engaged, Terre?"

"Yes," I said, a lump in my throat.

"In fact, Joe and I have seen him several times. Once I thought he was with you. The girl he was with looked a lot like you, but when I got closer, I realized it wasn't you at all. Plus, she was out to here." She encircled her arms in an arc over her stomach.

Phoebe gave me a piercing look then turned back to Daisy. "Are you sure it was Diego?"

"Joe went to high school with him and he introduced us. Actually," she said, her tone confidential, "Diego did seem a little ill-at-ease when Joe and I approached him. He was by himself that time sitting on a bench, but he kept looking around as if he was expecting someone. Oh dear, look at the time." She glanced at her watch. "I'd better go. I wish you the best, Terre. I'm sure Diego will be able to explain what's going on. The girl is probably his cousin or something," she added slyly.

It's hard to describe what I was feeling as Daisy related her story. I realized that she must have really hated me to tell me what she had. She actually looked triumphant as she lumbered off, all two-hundred pounds of her.

"Are you all right, Terre?" Phoebe gazed at me, her hazel eyes sympathetic. She put her hand on my shoulder.

"I don't really know. But suddenly, everything makes sense. About Diego, I mean."

"You don't believe that *bruja*, do you? She's always been jealous of you. Don't you remember in high school when you were voted most beautiful Mexican girl and she ran around telling everyone that it was only because of your father that you won? As if she would have been selected, the ugly cow."

"This isn't about Daisy, Phoebe. It's about Diego and what I have been suspecting all along. She just confirmed it." I stomped out of the store without making any purchases.

Phoebe followed me. "What are you going to do?"

"I'm going to Westwood."

"Why?"

"I need to talk to Diego," I answered as I walked onto the sidewalk.

"Terre, don't do anything rash. Give him a chance to explain things." She grabbed my arm. "Even if he has done something that you might not consider honorable, well, remember, he's still a good catch and you may never find anyone like him again."

"A man who has gotten a girl pregnant while he is engaged to another girl is a 'good catch' ?"

"You don't know that for sure, Terre. Don't jump to conclusions."

I looked at my best friend. "Do you know more than you're telling me? Your husband is Diego's cousin and he probably knows something. If he knows something, so do you."

"Do you honestly think I would betray you like that? If I knew that Diego was two-timing you, I would have told you. Surely you know that?"

"I don't know anything anymore," I said. "But I'm going to find out."

*****

The produce company where Diego worked in Westwood was situated along Highway 83 parallel with the Missouri Pacific railway line. When Phoebe and I drove into the parking lot of the company, I saw Diego standing on the loading dock of the company warehouse conversing with some other workers. His white shirt sleeves were rolled up above his muscular biceps. As always, the sight of him tugged at my heart. I knew that if what Daisy said was true this would be the last time I would ever see Diego. I would never again be able to feel his arms around me, his wet kisses against my lips. I would never again be struck by the sheer manliness of him. As I sat there watching him, he spied Phoebe's car. He grinned as he sauntered across the dock, bounding down the concrete steps.

"Hey beautiful," he said, leaning into the open car window, giving me a peck on the cheek. "What a nice surprise."

"I need to talk to you," I said tersely.

"I'm kinda busy now."

"It's important."

"Give me a minute," he said, his expression worried. He went inside the building and returned a few minutes later.

I got out of the car. "Phoebe will wait here. Let's go over there." I pointed to a grassy area near the building were several picnic tables were scattered about.

"All right." He put his arm around my shoulder and it felt as heavy and awkward as a two-by-four.

I sat at the first table we came to and plunged in before I could lose my nerve. "I saw Daisy Estrada today."

"Who?"

"She's married to Joe Estrada, your friend from high school."

He frowned and ran his hand through his hair. "Joe Estrada?"

"Let me get to the point, Diego. Tell me about the pregnant girl in San Antonio."

He looked like a deer caught in a car's headlights. "What pregnant girl?" he finally managed to say.

"It's true then."

"What's true?"

I stood up. "Damn it! Tell me the truth! Have you been seeing another girl the whole time we've been together?"

"It's not what you think, Terre." He rose and tried to grab my hand. "There was a girl in San Antonio and we did have a few laughs, but the child she's carrying is not mine."

"Do you think I'm an idiot? I should have known it was too good to be true. You're just like the rest." I felt the tears stinging in my eyes.

"I love you, Terre. Let's get past this. That girl is nobody. You're the one I love and want to spend the rest of my life with."

"No. You can't be trusted. I will not live my life like that, like my poor mother, always wondering if my husband is with other women. I will not live in that hell. I will not!" I pulled my engagement ring off my finger and threw it at him. "The wedding is off. I never want to see you again. Go to hell, Diego Gómez. Go straight to hell and take your girlfriend with you." I ran to Phoebe's car and jumped in. "Take me home," I managed to say.

"Oh, Terre," Phoebe mumbled as we backed out of the parking lot. "What have you done?"

"Something I should have done months ago."

As we drove away, I glanced over my shoulder and saw Diego still standing by the redwood picnic table, a look of incredulity on his face.

Chapter 20

Diego came by after work that first day, and when I refused to see him, Mother was beside herself.

"What happened, *mi'ja*? A lover's spat?" She paced back and forth in my bedroom, wringing her hands. I was sprawled out on the bed, my eyes bloodshot and sore from a crying jag.

"No," I managed to say between sobs, "I broke up with him for good. It's over. The wedding is off."

"Nonsense." She sat down beside me. "All couples get the wedding jitters. You'll make up and everything will be fine. You'll see." She patted my back.

I sat up and blew my nose into my handkerchief. "No, Mamá, this is not the wedding jitters. The wedding is off."

Mother frowned. "What could Diego have possibly done that you no longer want to marry him?"

I gave Mother a long, hard look. Her coppery hair was pulled up in a hairnet the way she usually wore it, and wavy tendrils framed her remarkably wrinkle-free face. Though in her mid-forties, she could have passed for someone much younger. Short and plump, she had always reminded me of a little bull ready to charge. She had certainly locked horns with Father often enough.

I debated whether or not to tell her about Diego's infidelity. The last thing I wanted to do was dredge up unhappy memories for her. I finally said, "Mamá, trust me. I just know that I've made a terrible mistake by agreeing to marry Diego. I'm not the marrying type. I should have never let this happen in the first place."

Mother pursed her lips, then rose. "Your papá will not be happy about this."

"This has nothing to do with Papá," I snapped. "It's my life. I will decide what is best for me."

Mother gave me a sour look, then stalked out of the room.

*****

At first Father didn't say anything. I think he believed, as Mother did, that Diego and I had had a lover's quarrel and that all we needed was a few days to patch things up. When a full week went by and I still refused all of Diego's phone calls and visits, Father finally confronted me. Diego had just driven away when I heard a knock on my bedroom door.

"Come in," I said.

Father lumbered in. As always, I was amazed at how Father's

134

presence could change the atmosphere of a room. He seemed to become its essence. He stopped at my desk where I was reading an old volume of *Crime and Punishment* from his library. I much preferred to read in English, but I often read Father's books to keep up my Spanish. "Terre, it's time to stop this nonsense." He crossed his arms over his large belly.

"I don't understand what you're referring to, Papá."

"This nonsense with Diego. You've made him suffer enough for whatever you think he has done to you. Enough is enough."

"I'm not doing this to make him suffer. It's over between us. I don't want to marry him."

"What did he do?"

"I'd rather not say."

"You *will* say." Father knit his thick eyebrows together.

"All right, if you insist." I rose from the desk chair and stood in front of Father, my arms crossed. "He has gotten another girl pregnant."

His eyes opened wide. "What girl?"

"A girl in San Antonio."

"Are you sure about this?"

"Yes."

"Did he tell you himself?"

"No, I first heard it from someone else, and when I confronted him, he denied it."

"Why don't you believe him?"

I gave what I suppose is called a derisive laugh and said, "Because it makes sense, all his weekend trips to San Antonio."

"Terre, why don't you give Diego the benefit of the doubt," he said in the reasonable tone he often used when talking to children. "Obviously the man cares deeply about you. He's called and come over every day for a week. Only a man in love would do that."

"Papá, I know this is difficult for you to understand. But I cannot give Diego the 'benefit of the doubt' as you call it. I cannot live my life wondering whether or not my husband has been unfaithful to me. I will not tolerate infidelity. I am not like Mamá."

Father's face turned deep crimson. "No, you are not like your mamá," he roared. "She has enough sense to know her place. You, on the other hand, are nothing more than a stubborn and unforgiving girl, destined to become an old maid. Diego is lucky to be rid of you." With that, he stormed out of my room.

*****

I couldn't bear the questioning, pitying looks and the whispering behind my back when I went to town and to church in the weeks that followed my break-up. The news of my broken engagement traveled through our community like a virus, infecting everyone. It was excruciating to know that I was the topic of conversation throughout Ruby. My heart felt battered, but even in my misery, I felt a spark of something else—anger. I was angry at myself for believing the lies. The signs had been there from the start, I will admit that now. I know I said that on that first day we met, Diego had not looked at any other girls. That was not true. He had. Oh, he had not been obvious; he didn't ogle and such. But I saw his admiring glances at pretty girls who passed by. I don't understand why I chose to block it out except to say that I was just so attracted to him that I couldn't help myself. I suppose I thought he'd change after he fell in love with me. What a laugh.

I had given up my career for Diego, and that made me angry. But I didn't want my old job back. What I wanted most was to leave Ruby, to leave the Valley, where men like Diego and my father flourished like diseased cattle on the open range. I wanted to leave Ruby and have nothing more to do with men and their treacherous ways.

What I decided to do wasn't so unexpected. It had been brewing in my mind for years and may have reached fruition earlier had not Diego come into my life. I knew of one way I could get out of Ruby, get the education I so sorely wanted, and be rid of men entirely. Through the years I had corresponded with a girl I had met at college, a young woman who had taken vows as a Sister of Divine Providence at Our Lady of the Lake. The order she had joined had as one of its primary missions the education of young women. Sister Mary Claire had earned two college degrees and was now teaching at a Catholic high school in San Antonio. From her letters, I knew she was happy with the life she had chosen.

By the middle of August I had made up my mind to become a nun and had already made arrangements for my move to the convent. My next mission was to tell my family.

*****

The gulf wind was blowing and it was a hot, humid August day when I informed my parents of my decision. My sisters were playing Chinese Checkers with Mother at the dining room table and Father was reading a book in the living room.

"I have something to tell you all," I began.

They all looked at me expectantly.

"I've decided to become a nun."

Ellie laughed out loud. "Oh, Terre, that's funny."

"This isn't a joke, Ellie." I frowned.

Father put his book on his lap, his expression thoughtful. "I cannot say that I'm surprised," he said. "I think it's the best thing."

I honestly had not expected this reaction. My father was not a great fan of the Catholic Church.

"Terre, are you sure?" Mother eyed me, concern etched on her face.

"I'm positive, Mamá. I've already contacted the convent at Our Lady of the Lake in San Antonio and I've made arrangements to leave at the end of next week so that I can start college in September. I'll be a postulant for about a year, and then I will enter the novitiate."

My parents didn't put up the fight I thought they would. I suppose they were grateful that I would no longer be around to burden them, a reminder of unfulfilled dreams.

*****

My parents and sisters saw me off at the Greyhound bus station in Edinburg. Father would be leaving in a few days himself to go to California and he was in a jovial mood. We said our goodbyes, Mother entreating me to write, Father giving his obligatory speech about calling if I needed anything. Ellie and Marta were crying, though I wasn't sure if it was because they would miss me or because they thought I was throwing my life away. Both of them had questioned me at length about my decision and seemed dubious about my assurances that I wasn't going to become a nun just because of what happened with Diego. Lupita was the only one who seemed to understand. "I think we are truly blessed that Terre is going into the religious life," she had said, defending me. "I think Terre will make a wonderful nun."

I have to admit, I didn't find her comment particularly comforting. The only nuns Lupita had ever known up to that point were a couple of prune-faced Sisters who had come down from New York one summer to help Father Carmody out with a newly implemented catechism program. They sweltered in their habits in the South Texas sun and the hotter it got, the crosser they became. I overheard one of them say, "If hell were on earth, it would be located in South Texas."

I boarded the bus taking a window seat. When the bus finally rolled forward, I waved to my family. Father stood tall and proud, his slacks pressed just so, his white guayabera shirt immaculate. Several people strolled up to greet him and Mother. It always amazed me how many people knew my parents, though Father and Mother had been *padrinos* in so many weddings that it was to be expected. I felt my heart constrict, but I never once wavered against my decision. As the bus lumbered onto the street, I recalled the trip Isa and I had made eight years before, how excited we had been. The feeling I now had was one of resignation. I tried not to think about Diego, because it still hurt too much.

Over the ensuing years, I've often wondered what kind of life I would have had had I gone through with our marriage plans, despite my misgivings. Whatever became of the girl in San Antonio, I don't know.

The child was Diego's, of that I am certain. Nevertheless, he married a Westwood girl a few months after I left. They divorced after several years, and he remarried and divorced two more times. He has five children and several grandchildren, I've been told. Ellie says that I was his true love and that if we had married, we would still be married. I hate to burst my sister's romantic bubble, but I know that Diego and I would have met the same end as he and his other wives. He had a roving eye, and I am intolerant of imperfection. I shake my head in sadness as I write this because now I can finally admit that I, too, had a flaw. In my estimation, this flaw was greater than any my father or Diego had. Father was right. I was unforgiving, and it has taken me years to see that not being able to forgive is the greatest sin of all.

I may have decided to join the convent for the wrong reasons, but becoming a nun has turned out to be the best decision I have ever made. I know now that I was called to be a nun, and I needed Diego to help me see it. I am grateful to him for that.

I turned back one last time as the bus plodded onto Highway 281. Father and Mother walked toward the green Buick, my sisters following behind. Father opened the front passenger door for Mother, and she slid onto the front seat.

That was the last time I saw my parents together.

Part III

Marta
The Youngest Daughter

1956—1959

Chapter 21

My first memory of Father is of watching him through the wooden slats of my crib. Late at night he'd turn on the lamp by the rolltop desk in his office, which I could see from where I slept in his and Mother's bedroom— the rooms were adjacent to each other, and he often kept the door between them ajar. He'd settle in a brown leather armchair by the desk and read. Sometimes, before he sat down, he'd walk over, tuck my blanket around me, and pat my head. He smelled musky from the cigarette smoke lingering on his clothes, and sour from the beer he drank every night. I'd lie there watching him, entranced by his enormous bulk. Though he was so big, I never felt threatened. In fact, his formidable presence made me feel secure.

Father often stayed up late into the night reading thick, leather-bound books. Terre says that he couldn't sleep because he had a guilty conscience, but I think he had insomnia because he had so much on his mind. When Father was in town, people came to see him frequently to ask for loans, favors, and intervention with the police and other authorities. I remember once, early in the morning, our gardener's wife came to see Father. She was hysterical, screaming and crying in Father's office. I woke up in my crib, startled and fascinated by the sight of Cipi's wife clinging to Father.

"Calm down, señora," Father said, grabbing the woman's arms and gently, but firmly, pushing her down into his chair next to the desk. "Tell me what has happened."

"It's Cipriano!" she wailed.

Father stood over her, arms crossed, thick eyebrows furrowed. He waited for her to quiet down to a whimper, then said, "I can not help you if you don't pull yourself together. Now tell me what happened to Cipriano."

At that moment, Mother walked into the office. Before she could utter a word, Father gave her a warning glance, shaking his head. He looked back at Señora Chavez. "Go on," he said.

"I woke up this morning and noticed that my husband had not slept in bed with me like he always does. I got up to look for him. I went outside when I couldn't find him in the house. He likes to drink his morning *cafecito* on the front lawn, you see. And he was there all right, but, but . . ." She began to wail again. Finally, still sobbing, she finished her tale. "My husband was hanging from the ash tree in our front yard. Ay, Don Miguel, he used his own belt, and the chair that he usually sat in to drink his coffee was turned over underneath him." Her shoulders shook violently as she sobbed into her hands.

Father waited until she quieted down a little. "Have you notified the police?"

She looked up, wiping her eyes. "No, Don Miguel. I woke up my eldest son, and together we took my husband down from the tree and carried him into the house before anyone could see what he had done. Then I came directly over here. Don Miguel, Padre Carmody will not allow him a proper Catholic burial if he finds out what Cipi has done. I'm sure he was not in his right mind when he did it. Should he be condemned forever? My Cipi was a good man. I don't know why he did it. We loved him. Please, I will be forever in your debt if you will help me. My children do not deserve this." She grabbed my father's right hand in her own, her expression pleading as tears streamed down her dark cheeks.

Father didn't say anything for a few minutes. Then with his free hand, he patted the woman's shoulder. "Don't worry. I'll take care of it." He gently pulled away from her, and after conferring privately with Mother, he left the house with Señora Chavez.

I don't know how he managed it, but somehow Father got the police to report the death as an accidental hanging, and so Cipriano was allowed a proper Catholic Mass and burial. Father even paid for our former gardener's funeral, Mother told me years later. In the weeks that followed Cipriano's death, Señora Chavez came over several times with homemade cakes and pies, and I saw Father give her money. He found her a job as a maid at a doctor's residence in south Ruby. He also gave her eldest son, Cipriano Junior, a job on his picking crew.

I was almost three when Cipi hung himself, and although I remember distinctly the sight of a wailing Señora Chavez clinging to Father, I sometimes wonder whether the conversation I remember was what I actually heard, or rather what was reiterated to me years later whenever Mother and I would talk about the sad incident. Whatever the case, such dramatic scenes were not isolated occurrences in our home, and I have vivid memories of them.

When I was six, Father went bankrupt and people stopped coming by as often as before. I think, even though he probably felt a bit of a relief, he also felt diminished by his inability to provide assistance. He continued his habit of staying up at night, but more often than not, he sat at his desk drinking. I was no longer in my crib, obviously. But I knew about his drinking because I was in charge of straightening up his office. He always kept his rolltop desk locked, but I'd often find empty bottles of beer and whiskey in the trash can by his desk in the mornings when I cleaned up.

By the time Father announced his intention to move to California when I was thirteen, I had no recollection of our family's once prosperous position in Ruby. I did, however, know that Father had already been drinking heavily for several years. I remember hoping that this "fresh new start" he talked about would include his abstinence from alcohol. How naïve I was! Father needed alcohol like babies need milk. Don't get me wrong. I'm not condoning his liquor consumption. But now I think Father drank to forget, and I suppose he had a lot of things to forget, things like the loss of two fortunes, the first because of the Revolution and the second because of a dishonest gringo farmer, things like the second class status this country conferred on him because of his ethnicity. I suppose drinking was the only way he could cope. Unfortunately, his drinking wreaked havoc on his relationship with Mother, and consequently, with us, his children.

Isa thinks that Father and Mother's relationship ended because of the bankruptcy. Terre blames his womanizing. But I know that Father's drinking is what really drove them apart. His drinking, and me.

*****

Father moved to California at the end of August, a few days after Terre left Ruby to join the convent. For the next three months we enjoyed a tension-free existence. Not that we were happy that he was gone; but when Father was around we were in a constant state of alert as if watching for an electrical storm to break loose. Mother took Father's absence in stride (as she had all his previous absences when he worked as a contractor), busying herself with her church work and so forth.

When he returned home in December, we treaded carefully around the house again, waiting to see what might happen. Initially, nothing did. Father was in good spirits when he returned to Ruby. During that visit, he even took us for a week-long visit to Monterrey to visit my grandmother. My brother, Raul, was on leave from the Air Force, and Father spent a lot of time with him. But mostly, he drove around the Valley visiting old friends and associates and spending time in cantinas. One day, I overheard Mother chiding Father, "Why didn't you just stay in California? For as much as we see you, you might as well still be there." Father's response was to storm out of the house following a well-worn path directly to the cantina down the street.

He returned home late, reeking of beer, and Mother helped him to their room, mercifully holding her tongue. She didn't often cross Father when he was drunk—his temper then was volatile. He'd never struck her, but the awful things he said and the myriad broken objects he left in his drunken wake were enough to make her keep her tongue in check.

Father left again after New Year's Day, and once again, peace reigned in our home. Mother made a visit to Soledad in February and returned home in a surly mood. She said that the house that Father had rented for us was filthy and that she had spent most of her time there cleaning.

Finally, the time of reckoning arrived. Father returned home at the end of May, 1956, to take us back to California with him. Ellie, who had graduated from high school, was as excited about the trip now as she had not been the year before. You would have thought she was going on one of those European tours that rich people take the way she was carrying on. Actually, the main reason for her excitement was that she was finally going to meet Ricky Hernández, the young man with whom she had been corresponding for the past year. He was a friend of Raul's who was in the service, and he lived in Fresno, California. He was getting out of the service in July, and had told her he was going to visit her in Soledad.

Lupita got caught up in Ellie's excitement, as she was apt to do. I was not as thrilled as my sisters. I would be starting the eighth grade in a new school in the fall, something that terrified me. Plus, there was a boy I liked who lived just a few blocks away and I would miss seeing him.

Daniel Valenzuela was in my class at Ruby Junior High and he often rode his bike by our house to get a glimpse of me. He came by mostly on the weekends, riding his rickety, paint-chipped bike slowly as he gazed at the house. I thought he was handsome, but Ellie derisively called him, "*Ese morenito*," because of his dark skin. She had noticed me peeking out the living room window one Saturday afternoon and seen him ride by, his neck strained toward our house.

"Who's that?" she inquired, her eyebrow arched as she held the chintz curtain aside and peered through the open Venetian blinds.

"Just a boy from school," I said.

"I've seen him before. He rides down our street almost every day."

"So? It's a free country." I picked up the feather duster and swatted it along Father's bookcase, which was now missing several books that Father had taken to California.

"I have to admit, he's cute," she said. "But he's awfully dark."

"So what if he's dark? You'd be dark, too, if you worked in the fields after school!"

My sister pulled the cord snapping the blinds shut. She crossed her arms and gazed at me, her eyes narrowed. "You be careful with that *morenito*, Marta. He doesn't look like the type who'll be able to keep you in style."

I threw the feather duster at her. "Shut up! You don't know him at all. He's got a lot of ambition, and what's more, he's finer and better

143

mannered than any boy you've ever brought home."

"For your sake, I hope you're right. I just can't imagine you living in one of those shacks on the outskirts of town with a bunch of bawling children at your feet. Because, let's face it, Marta, you're just like me. You want and deserve the finer things in life." She smoothed her hair, which was styled in a flip.

I looked away. Ellie was right. I did like nice things—fashionable clothes, expensive homes. Why, my favorite magazine was *Better Homes and Gardens*! I had promised myself that one day I would own a house like the ones I saw in the magazine. "He's just a friend," I said, feeling defeated.

Ellie raised her eyebrows, and as she sauntered out of the room, she said, "Well, let's just hope it stays that way."

There was nothing going on between Daniel and me, what with Mother's hawk eyes and my sisters' constant companionship. But Ellie's sobering comments made me realize that I needed to use my head when it came to boys, or God forbid, I could very well end up in some shack on the edge of some dumpy town. Even so, I knew I would miss Daniel when we moved to California. When I told him about our move, he said he'd write if I sent him my address, and I promised that I would.

*****

The day we left Ruby was one of those hot, humid days that south Texas is known for. The sun was bright and a slight breeze rustled the leaves of the ash trees on our lawn. Father had invited two other families to follow us to California. The Elizondos, Benito and Elida, and their four children, Consuelo, Rafael, Rogelio, and Anita (sixteen, fifteen, ten, and six, respectively), were waiting near their blue pickup in front of our house when we closed the door behind us. They had fashioned a tent over the bed of their truck using a canvas tarpaulin. Lorenzo and Catarina Olivares were parked behind them in a dilapidated, faded green Chevrolet. Both couples had decided to move to Soledad after Father had told them about the higher pay they could get in the fields there.

Although the government bussed *braceros* (legal temporary workers from México) to the Salinas Valley, there was so much field work that there was always plenty of work for migrants too. The Río Grande Valley, on the other hand, had too much competition, not only from the *braceros*, but also from the illegals. Field workers who lived in the Texas valley were paid poorly and that's why so many migrated to other states.

Doña Cuca and her husband, Pancho, saw us off. Father had asked them to watch over the house, which Mother had insisted he not sell. Not that he would have. I think Father was as attached to that house as Mother was, even though he had said he had no intention of ever moving

144

back to it.

Ellie, Lupita, and I hugged Doña Cuca, and all of us began to bawl. "*Dios las bendiga*," our Indian maid said, gently wiping my tears with her hand. She made the sign of the cross over us collectively. "God protect you."

We piled into the back seat of the two-year-old Buick that Father had purchased just a few days before, and watched as Mother embraced her friend. The two women hugged, and Mother, who had been trying to be stoic, began to sob, much to Father's chagrin. He gently pulled her away from Doña Cuca and helped Mother into the car. He turned around and shook Don Pancho's hand admonishing him to take care, then he kissed Doña Cuca on her cheek. He settled into the car and started up the engine. Within a few minutes, our three-vehicle caravan had pulled out onto the street, and we began our journey to California.

Chapter 22

With the exception of Father, the rest of our group had never been to any of the states west of Texas, so the three-day, fifteen-hundred mile drive through west Texas, New Mexico, Arizona, and California was an eye-opening experience. Texas seemed to go on forever. Once past San Antonio, we drove west for twelve hours to the border city of El Paso across flat sandy plains punctuated by low craggy hills, scraggly mesquite trees, and cacti.

After resting in El Paso, where we spent the night in a motel run by Mexicanos (the Elizondos slept in their pickup to save money), we drove across the sandy plains of New Mexico. The further we got from home, the more excited I got about the trip. I had decided not to think of this journey as anything more than a vacation. Also, I didn't want to be a spoilsport to Ellie and Lupita, who were in a state of euphoria about going to California. Nothing could malign their cheerful mood—not the stopped-up toilet in the restroom of our motel room, not the fact that we were crammed in the car with barely enough room to stretch our legs, not the fact that Mother kept mumbling under her breath about the heat and the dusty wind. So, I took my cue from them.

Besides, it was hard not to appreciate the scenery. Father told us that the New Mexico desert, dotted with yuccas and impressive orange mesas, was actually the northern section of the great Chihuahuan desert of México. It dawned on me later as we drove through Arizona that we had been traveling for almost two days and had seen only desert land. "Is this what California looks like, too, Papá?" I asked as we approached Phoenix.

"Like what, *mi'ja*?"

"Like a desert?"

"California does have desert land, mostly in the southern portion, but between the Sierra Madres are rich, fertile valleys. Where we will be living is the Salinas Valley, an agricultural area much like the Río Grande Valley."

After spending the night in Phoenix, we got up as the sun began to rise and drove into southern California. Our first view was of desert land surrounded by jagged mountains like those in Arizona. Tall spindly ocotillo—a cactus-like tree, and fuzzy looking cholla cacti with tubular branches emerged from flat, but boulder-strewn land. Father had told the Elizondos and Olivares to be careful to follow him closely after we passed Palm Springs because the LA metroplex was huge. There were some two million people in Los Angeles in 1956 and almost four million in the surrounding towns. I was mesmerized by the endless parade of cars that whizzed by when we arrived on the outskirts of the city. I could only imagine how Benito and Lorenzo felt driving on the four-lane freeway that had a network of overpasses, underpasses, and interchanges that were enough to make a small-town girl's head swim. And even then there was smog, a faint yellow haze that settled between the mountain valleys to the north of the city.

"Are Benito and Lorenzo still behind us?" Father peered through the rear-view mirror.

"Sí, Papa." I strained my neck looking back. The canvas tarpaulin on the Elizondo's pickup flapped in the wind and I could barely see the faded green Chevrolet lagging behind.

It was somewhere near Alhambra that we lost Lorenzo, at least that was the last time we remember seeing his green Chevrolet behind us. When we finally made it out of the LA area, we stopped on the shoulder of the freeway north of San Fernando, and Father and Señor Elizondo said that we should wait for Lorenzo and his wife at a nearby service station.

Happy to be able to stretch out and rest after the grueling ride through Los Angeles, we drank soda pops from the soda machine at the service station and strolled around the parking lot watching the cars that flew by. Since we were still in the LA area, and we thought close to Hollywood, we were hoping that we might spot a movie star in one of the many convertibles that whizzed by. When an hour had gone by with no sign of the faded Chevy or a movie star, Father said we should go on. "No telling when he'll show up," he said, shaking his head.

So we continued on our journey, and a few hours later we got off Highway 99 and drove west on a county road.

"At Paso Robles, we'll hit the new highway and before long we'll be in the Salinas Valley," Father announced as we approached the winding road where James Dean had died just nine months before.

"Isn't Paso Robles near where James Dean crashed?" I whispered to Ellie.

"I think so," she said, raising her eyebrows. "What a waste."

"How sad," Lupita murmured. "He was so young. But that's what happens when you defy the laws of gravity and drive too fast."

Ellie and I both frowned at Lupita. She was always one for stating the obvious.

From Paso Robles we drove north toward the verdant Salinas Valley.

"The Salinas River flows parallel to the towns of the valley," Father said, pointing to a winding body of water that we could see from certain areas of the highway.

The Salinas River didn't look like much. It was perhaps a few hundred yards wide, banked by tall grass, willows, and shrubbery, just about what I had expected after reading John Steinbeck's *Of Mice and Men*. I had read the book after finding out we were going to move to Soledad. It wasn't much of a novel, a book about two misfits, one a lumbering, dim-witted man, and his friend, who feels responsible for him. I still don't know what all the hoopla over the book was about. Anyway, reading it did nothing to prepare me for living in Soledad. What could two gringos, one dim-witted at that, know about what life is like for Mexicanos?

As we drove through the small towns of King City and Greenfield, my sisters and I sat up straighter in the back seat of the car and strained our necks to look out the windows. To the east and west, past acres of agricultural fields in various stages of growth, were mountain ranges. "Are those the Gabilans, Papá?" I asked pointing west at thicket covered mountains that rose like giants from the flat valley.

"The ones to the west are the Santa Lucia ranges. The ones on the east are the Gabilan," he said.

I turned to look at the Gabilans, which were smaller than the Santa Lucias and reminded me of a golden-brown woolen blanket bunched up on the floor.

"The valley is about eighty-five miles wide between the two ranges, *hija*, so since Soledad is in the center of the valley, how far are we from the ranges?"

"Oh, Papá, that's easy. It's forty-two point five. You forget that I'm going into the eighth grade."

"I haven't forgotten. I just wanted to see if you've learned anything in school." Father had always liked to quiz me, turning my questions into a lesson of some sort. "I understand that the schools in California are more challenging than the ones in Texas," he continued.

I glanced at my sisters, my eyebrows arched.

"Well, that has nothing to do with me," Ellie said. "I'm finished with all that, and good riddance."

Lupita cried out. "Oh, look! There's the town."

"Ay, that's good. My legs hurt. I need to stretch out." Mother took her compact out of her purse and began to reapply her lipstick and comb her hair.

We drove on what appeared to be the main street of Soledad; the street sign said Front Street. It was several blocks long with various businesses in white stucco buildings, some flat-roofed, like in Ruby, others with red tile. Parallel to and on the west of the business street was a

148

railroad track. "What railroad line is that, Papá? I asked.

"The Southern Pacific."

"Like in Ruby!"

"Yes, like in Ruby," he said matter-of-factly.

From Front Street, we turned right on East Street, drove a block, and then turned right again. "This street is called Monterey, like your hometown in México," I commented.

"*Sí*," Father said. "The minute I saw the name of this street, I knew I had made the right decision to move here."

"I thought you didn't believe in omens," Mother said, her tone scornful, as we passed a huge water tower with the words, "City of Soledad," printed on it.

Father's eyes narrowed, but he ignored her comment. "Here we are," he said expansively to the rest of us, stopping in front of a small clapboard house painted a mint green. The house was opposite a park lined with large trees. I noticed immediately that the street was freshly paved. This struck me as a good omen. Our street in Ruby was still nothing more than a dirt road, despite many pleas to city hall to pave it.

The Elizondos chugged up behind us in their pickup. We all clambored out of our vehicles stepping on sparse grass on the edge of the small yard, and were immediately met with gusts of wind that blew our hair in every direction.

"Is it always this windy?" I asked, holding my hair down.

Father nodded as he unlocked the trunk of the Buick. "It gets windier in late afternoon."

The day was bright and sunny, and the sky azure, but the wind marred what would otherwise have been a perfect day. I sauntered over for a closer look at the hedge of pink azaleas that stretched along the southern border of the lot.

"Aren't these beautiful?" I said, gesturing at the bushes.

"Yeah," said Ellie who had followed me.

We did a tour of the little yard, commenting on the beauty of the shrubs of blooming plumbago with powder blue flowers in front of the house, and admiring the trellis of fuschia bougainvillea set against a portion of the front wall. The vibrant colors made the mint green house look rich, and I remember thinking that we might actually be happy in that little house, a perfect example of my tendency toward optimism, no matter the reality of a situation.

The house was box-shaped with a gray shingle roof. It was considerably smaller than our house in Ruby, set on a tiny lot. Nevertheless it did have a front and back yard, and on the northwest section of the tiny front yard, a behemoth pine tree rose regally to the sky.

As he began to take our luggage from the truck, Father waved to a boy standing in the yard adjacent to ours to the north (our house was facing west). "How are you, Jaime? Did you keep an eye on my house and pickup while I was gone?"

"*Sí, señor.*"

"*Bueno.* Everything looks in order." He glanced at the blue pickup sitting in the driveway, then back at the boy. "Come here."

Jaime, who looked to be about ten, walked over to Father.

Father pulled his wallet out of his pocket and plucked out several bills, handing them to the boy. "*Gracias,* Jaime."

"No problem, Don Miguel . . . I mean, *de nada,* Don Miguel." The boy grinned sheepishly as he looked at the dollars, then stuffed them into his pocket. His two front teeth were much larger than the rest of his teeth and he reminded me of Bugs Bunny.

Father introduced us to our young next door neighbor, and then asked Jaime if he would help us with our luggage while he showed the Elizondos their new home.

"*Sí, señor,*" Jaime said cheerfully.

Mother walked Señora Elizondo to the tarpaulin-covered pickup. "I wonder if Lorenzo and Catarina will ever find their way here," she said.

"Who knows." Elida shrugged. "I hope they're all right, wherever they are. Los Angeles is no place for the likes of a simple Mexicano."

"I imagine it'll be a few days before he realizes he's even lost. Lorenzo always had a bad sense of directon," interjected Señor Elizondo with a hearty laugh as he helped his children back onto the pickup bed. "And Catarina's nagging will add another day to the trip."

"If he'd listen to her they'd get here today," Mother huffed. "But what man listens to his wife?"

Father glared at Mother, then climbed into his pickup. In a few minutes, the Elizondos' pickup pulled away from the curb following Father's International Harvester.

We followed our young neighbor into our house and were hit with the smell of ammonia and bleach as soon as we walked onto the wooden floor of the tiny living room. Father had obviously hired a woman to clean the house thoroughly before we arrived—a lucky thing for us, and him too. We glanced at Mother, who began an inspection of the room. "Well, it certainly is cleaner than last time I was here," she said, running her finger across the walnut coffee table.

The walnut table, a chintz sofa and armchair, and a small television on a stand were the only furniture in the room. No curtains draped the front window which was covered with Venetian blinds, nor were there any pictures on the wall. A family photograph sat on top of the television.

"By the way, you can call me Jimmy," Jaime said abruptly.

"But I thought your name was Jaime," I said.

"Your father calls me Jaime. He says that's my real name, my Spanish name, and that I should be proud of it. He's a very patriotic Mexican, your father is. He can call me whatever he wants. But every one else around here calls me Jimmy. Nobody goes by their Mexican name in California. Of course, some people call me *el conejo*, the rabbit," he said, flashing his two front teeth. "Mostly my uncles and some cousins. But my real friends call me Jimmy."

"O.K., Jimmy," I said, as he led us into a small hallway and then into one of two bedrooms. Ellie, Lupita, and I huddled together in the tiny bedroom that we were going to share, while Jimmy deposited two suitcases on one of the beds.

"Thank you, Jimmy," we called out as he left the room.

"No problem," he said.

Compared to the spacious bedroom that I had shared with Lupita in our house in Ruby, our new room would be like living in a closet. There was a double bed and a twin bed, each shoved against the wall, with a two-foot space between them. Mother must have noticed our expressions when she walked in because she said, "I know it's small, but it'll have to do. At least you have a roof over your heads. It could be worse. We could be living in one of the migrant camps in a tent."

That was Mother for you. Always looking at the brighter side of things.

*****

My sisters and I spent the rest of the weekend getting acquainted with our new surroundings. The first thing we became keenly aware of was the wind. Father had told us that it was windy in the Salinas Valley, but nothing could have prepared us for the late afternoon gales. At about one-thirty the wind picked up, and by five, the tops of the trees in the park across from our house were bent over at a forty-five degree angle. It was an amazing sight, reminiscent of hurricane force winds that I remembered from tropical gulf storms that often hit the Río Grande Valley.

When we mentioned the wind to Jimmy the next morning after he offered to give us a tour of the town, he said, "We have a saying here, 'If it's windy, it must be one-thirty.'"

"Why does it get so windy at one-thirty?" I asked.

"Who knows?" He shrugged. "Some kind of scientific thing. We talked about it at school, but now I forget."

Ellie, Lupita, and I followed Jimmy up Monterey Street. "How many people live in Soledad?" I asked him as we passed clapboard homes in various shades of pastel.

"About two-thousand people. How big was the town you came from?"

"About the same," I said, glancing across the street at a stretch of wood-frame buildings housing a grocery store called "José's Mercado," a restaurant called "Tía Rosa's," and a dress shop called "La Reina."

"This must be the Mexican part of town," Lupita observed.

"Of course it is," I said, exasperation in my voice. "Where else would we live?"

Lupita ignored my comment. She pursed her lips and began to walk with Ellie. "I think Marta is having her time of the month," she whispered loudly enough for me to hear. "She always gets crabby about that time."

I frowned, hoping that Jimmy, who was walking next to me, hadn't heard her. If he did, he didn't let on. In fact, he commented, "This is the Mexican side of town. Most of the gringos who have money live on the ranches outside of town, west of the railroad tracks."

As we approached the corner of Monterey and Main he changed the subject. "There's the Catholic church. Are you Catholic?"

"Yes, we are." I gazed at the white stucco walls of the church. The building had an arched entryway, and a red tile roof. Later, I found out that it was of the architectural style called Mission, a design I came to love.

We continued our tour and reached Benito Street. By now we were several blocks from home. "This is one of the government camps for the Mexican *braceros*," Jimmy said. Behind a chain link fence were several long barracks and a large building he said was the dining hall. "More than four-hundred workers live there. The harvest season starts in mid-March and ends in November, then most of them go back to México." As we strolled by two men whistled at us from the steps of the dining hall. "Those are two of the camp cooks," Jimmy said.

We haughtily ignored their cat calls.

"What a primitive place," Ellie lamented as we hurried by the camp and followed Jimmy onto Market Street. "I thought Soledad would be a little more sophisticated than Ruby."

"Men will be men, wherever they live." Lupita sighed.

We both looked at Lupita. "Since when have you become an expert on men?" Ellie demanded.

"You all think I don't know anything because I don't talk as much as you. For your information, when people talk I listen, and you'd be surprised what you can learn just by listening. You ought to try it sometime."

"Excuse me, Miss Know-It-All," Ellie said.

Lupita made a face at Ellie, then gave me a conspiratorial smile. Though I was as surprised by my sister's retort as Ellie had been, I was glad to see that she had some spunk. Lupita had always been the quietest and most timid of us girls. She was also very religious. The first thing she did when we arranged our room was set up a little altar in a corner of the bedroom. It consisted of a twelve-inch tall porcelain statue of the Virgen de Guadalupe that Tía Candelaria, Mother's sister, had given her. In front of the statue was a votive candle in a ruby-colored glass holder surrounded by plastic roses. She kept it covered with a handkerchief when Father was around because he considered such things low-class and primitive.

Though I am ashamed to admit it, Ellie and I often took advantage of my sister's timidity and Christian charity. When it was either of our turns to do the dishes or wash clothes or fix our beds, we'd coax her into doing it for us, "Lupita, I have so much homework to do. Could you please start the dishes and I'll finish up?" She'd say, "Okay," and we'd conveniently forget to help. We even began referring to her as Cinderella because of all the work she did for us. Feeling guilty, I made a mental note to quit taking advantage of my sister.

"There's the school," Elllie said after we turned onto Market Street.

The Main Street School, a flat-roofed rectangular building of red brick, sprawled over a block. "It looks new," I said.

"It was built a few years ago," Jimmy said. "It has fourth through the eighth grade. I'm going into the fifth grade, so I go to this school. Maybe we can walk to school together." He flashed his two big teeth.

Ellie nudged my shoulder and whispered. "You've already got an admirer, Marta, and we've only been here for one day."

"Oh, be quiet." I returned her nudge. To Jimmy I said, "Maybe so."

"I wonder what Gonzales High School looks like," said Lupita.

"All I know is that it's in Gonzales and we're not walking that far. I'm tired. Let's go home. Ricky is supposed to call." Ellie took off toward Main Street and started walking west, the rest of us trailing behind.

When we got home, the phone was ringing and Ellie ran to it. "Hello?" she said excitedly. Then she looked crestfallen. "It's for Papá." She handed the phone to Mother, who had walked out of the kitchen wiping her hands on her apron.

"Hello? No. This is his wife." She frowned then hung up the phone.

"Who was it, Mamá?"

"Wrong number." She walked back to the kitchen.

"It was a woman," Ellie whispered, giving me an uneasy glance.

*****

Mother, my sisters, and I were sitting on chipped metal lawn chairs in our back yard later that evening when Father joined us, beer in hand. We brushed our hair from our faces as the wind blew steadily from the northwest.

"Papá, do you know of any place I can apply for a job?" Ellie asked. "Now that I have my diploma, I could probably work in an office somewhere."

"*Mi'ja*, Soledad is a small town and such positions are hard to find. But I will ask around." He paused to take a gulp of his beer. "I thought I could get you all on at the packing shed later in the summer, doing some light work. In the meantime, why don't you just enjoy yourselves?" He smiled at Ellie, Lupita and me.

Mother said, "I don't understand why we can't work in the fields. Carrot season starts tomorrow, and you said yourself a family can make a good living from the fields. We could always use the extra money."

"Yes, for experienced pickers, which you are not. The price for a sack of carrots this year is fourteen cents. You would have to pick almost three-hundred sacks of carrots to make forty-two dollars. The four of you would be lucky to make half that amount. And it's back-breaking work." He lumbered out of his lawn chair, waving his thick finger at Mother. "I didn't raise my children to be field workers. I told you before, I will not have any of my children working in the fields. Did Ellie get a high school diploma to be a field worker? No!" He slammed into the house.

Mother rose and followed him. In a few minutes, we heard the pickup engine rev up and the truck pull out of the gravel driveway.

Mother returned and plopped back down on her lawn chair. "Some things never change." She sighed, looking up at the stars glittering on the velvet backdrop of night.

"Where did Papá go?" I asked.

She shrugged. "Where else?"

Several hours later, after we had gone to bed, Father and Mother had the first of many fights they would have that year.

"I smell perfume on you, mixed with that foul beer. Get away from me." Mother's voice carried through the paper-thin walls.

"Some women go to Pasquale's. It's not my fault their perfume lingers in the air and gets on my clothes," Father said, his voice thick.

"A woman called you on the phone this afternoon. Who was she?"

"I don't know any woman."

"You tell her never to call here again. Do you hear me? I will not have it."

"You will not have it? I am the man around here. I am the one who says what's what."

I grabbed my pillow and held it over my ears, pressing hard so that I wouldn't have to hear anymore. After a while their muffled voices became silent and I fell asleep.

Chapter 23

We heard the familiar sputter of Lorenzo's Chevy as we were cleaning the kitchen after Sunday night dinner. Dropping our dish rags on the kitchen counter, my sisters and I followed Father and Mother outside. They had been relaxing in the living room—Father with his beer and paper, and Mother with her crochet needles. The dilapidated car stopped in front of our house. I wasn't sure which looked worse, Lorenzo or the fenderless, dented Chevy. Lorenzo sported a three-day growth of beard and his wind-blown hair looked as if it had been electrified. Catarina's long hair was twisted up in a bun, and her plump face bore an expression of exasperation and relief.

"So, this is the right house," Lorenzo said tiredly as he opened the car door and stepped out of the car. "I asked at the service station where you lived and the attendant directed me here."

Father shook Lorenzo's hand, then gave him an *abrazo*. "So you finally made it." He chuckled.

"I didn't think I ever would, Don Miguel," Lorenzo said, laughing.

"*Que pasó?*" Mother asked as she directed Catarina into our house. "What happened? One minute you were following us and the next minute you were gone."

"Ay, it was awful," Catarina lamented to Mother, who motioned for her to sit on our sofa. "This car got between Benito's truck and our car. The next thing we knew we were in the wrong lane. The cars were going so fast that we couldn't get back behind Benito. Then we saw you going north and we were heading in the opposite direction! We ended up at Santa Monica, and I thought we might as well see the ocean while we were there so we drove to the Santa Monica beach. It was so beautiful."

"But that was Friday. Did you stay at the beach for three days?" Mother asked.

"*Pues*, no. We were just there a little while, then we got on the nearest highway and drove. We were almost to San Diego when we realized we were going in the wrong direction because my *viejo* here refused to ask for directions." She scowled, pointing her thumb at her husband.

"I was afraid someone would think I was an illegal," he interjected. "You know my English is not so good even though I was born in Texas. I was afraid they'd deport us."

Catarina shook her head. "So we drove around the LA area for three days, sleeping in the car at night, until somehow we reached San Fernando and found Highway 99. Ay, that LA is something else. Streets going this way and that. Cars speeding everywhere."

Mother nodded in commiseration, then invited the couple to eat, which they heartily agreed to, having sustained themselves on fruit and soda pop and packages of chips for three days. Later, after Father left the house to escort the couple to their new accommodations, Mother sneered, "See, what did I tell you? If Lorenzo had only followed his wife's advice and asked for directions, they would have gotten here much sooner. But that's men for you."

*****

The next day Father asked if we wanted to drive out to the carrot field with him. He had found picking jobs for the Elizondo and Olivares families and wanted to see how they were doing. Ellie opted to stay home. She wanted be sure to be there when Ricky called. Lupita and I, however, jumped at the chance to get out of the house where Mother was banging around trying to find places to put what few possessions we had been able to bring from Texas—dishes, clothing, linens, toiletries, her collection of favorite handmade doilies. As we left the house, she was scurrying around the living room, placing the doilies on whatever surfaces were available.

The carrot field, which was about five miles outside of Soledad in the Arroyo Seco area, was the length of a football stadium. A tractor in the distance was inching its way over several rows loosening the soil around the carrots to make them easier to pick. Scattered throughout the field were gunny sacks, some full, some empty, and several large metal cylinders. "What are those metal things, Papá?"

"They're funnels. The pickers put the smaller side of the funnel into the sack, fitting the sack over it. They clip off the carrot tops and throw the carrots into the funnel. When the funnel is full, they pull it out, and the carrots are left in the sack."

"Are the sacks heavy?"

"They're supposed to weigh around fifty pounds." He chuckled. "Some pickers put rocks in the bottom to give them the weight, but it always backfires on them because the foreman remembers those who do it and will never hire them again."

The verdant parsley-like tops of the carrots fanning in the breeze (it wasn't quite one-thirty yet), and the backdrop of the heavily thicketed Santa Lucias gave the impression of a bucolic farm scene, charming and peaceful. What we witnessed later that day as we watched the pickers at work was anything but.

We spied Lorenzo, Catarina, and the Elizondos, including their four children, taking their lunch break. About fifty other workers, mostly

156

braceros, lolled nearby eating tacos and drinking sodas. Our friends were sitting under a tree near the Elizondo's pickup. Father parked in front of the truck. He picked up his straw Stetson from the front seat of the Buick and placed it on his head as we all clambered out of the car.

"*Oyen*, how goes it?" Father said, stepping onto the road, his boots leaving deep imprints in the dirt.

Lupita and I were wearing dresses and saddle oxfords, and when we got out of the car, a gust of hot wind blew the skirts of our dresses up. We smoothed them down and followed quickly after Father. This would have been the perfect time to wear dungarees, but Father didn't approve of us wearing pants. We did, however, own dungarees and oversized shirts, a style popular then. But we only wore them when Father wasn't around.

Benito got up from the ground slowly, obviously sore. "*Buenas tardes, Don Miguel*," he answered, shaking his hand. He nodded at us, taking off his cowboy hat, "Señorita Lupita, Marta." He looked back at Father. "We've already picked about a hundred fifty sacks," he pointed to his wife and three eldest children.

"At that rate, you'll make close to three-hundred sacks by the end of the day," Father said approvingly.

"*Si Dios quiere*," his wife muttered, rubbing her back.

Their three eldest children, Consuelo, Rafael, and Rogelio, who were hungrily eating tacos, greeted us between bites. The youngest, six-year-old Anita, smiled shyly at us.

"I'm in charge of the water," she chimed, pointing to the bucket of water.

I smiled at her. "That's an important job."

"I know," she said solemnly.

"Thank you for getting us the job, Don Miguel," Benito continued.

"No problem, amigo. The farmers around here are always looking for reliable workers." He looked at Lorenzo, his expression serious. "And you, amigo? How are you today? Did you get enough sleep?"

"*Sí,* thanks to you, Don Miguel. The house you rented for us had a nice double bed with a thick mattress."

"And he dreamt about LA while he slept in it," chortled Benito.

Lorenzo grinned sheepishly.

"Leave him alone, Benito. If it had been you, we'd probably still be in LA," Elida volleyed with a smirk.

We were still laughing at Elida's response when we noticed the other workers had started trudging back to the fields.

"We'd better get back to work," Benito sighed.

"*Bueno*, if you need anything, anything at all, let me know," Father said, holding his hand out again.

"Thank you, Don Miguel."

We stayed and watched for a while. I think Father wanted us to see how difficult it was to work in the fields. But we knew. We had grown up watching field workers toil in the tomato fields in South Carolina, in the cotton fields in south Texas, not to mention in the orchards and vegetable fields around Ruby. Virtually every one we knew had been a field worker at one time or another.

The carrot pickers spent most of the time on their knees. It was a hot day; more than a hundred degrees, a dry heat that chapped lips and made faces feel taut. At one-thirty the wind picked up and we saw several wide-brimmed straw hats flapping, nearly flying off the pickers' heads, even though they were secured with straps.

Finally, Father said, "Let's go."

Lupita and I gladly piled into the car, closing the door to what could have been our fate had Mother gotten her way. It was at times like this that I was thankful for Father's stubbornness and pride.

The phone was ringing when we got home, and Ellie, who had been stretched out on the sofa nonchalantly paging through a movie magazine, suddenly came to life. She jumped up and picked up the phone, which was on the side table in the living room. "Hello?" she said expectantly. Her face lit up. "Ricky! It's so good to hear from you."

Ellie's California boyfriend had finally called.

Chapter 24

Ellie, Lupita, and I ran to the living room window when we heard the car engine whimper to a stop in front of our house. We peered through the open slats of the Venetian blinds. When I saw Ricky's red Chevrolet parked in front of our house that Saturday afternoon, a week after our arrival in Soledad, I thought of Diego, Terre's ex-fiancé. He'd had an apple red Chevrolet with tail fins outlined in shiny chrome, and my sisters and I used to love going for rides in it. Ricky's car, however, did not have tail fins. It was a standard model, the kind of car that a no-frills type would drive, a person like Ellie's *novio* would turn out to be.

Ricky sat in the car for a few minutes. He looked in the rear view mirror and ran his hand through his short dark hair, then he got out of the Chevy. When he walked around the car to the sidewalk, we were able to get a good look at him. He was of average height and slender, dressed in the khaki uniform of the U.S. Air Force. On his left cheek was a rather large mole, about the size of a dime. In his right hand, he carried a gaily wrapped gift box, in his left he held a bouquet of flowers. His shiny government issued black shoes tapped against the sidewalk pavement as he strode to the front door.

"My, look how dark he is." I glanced at Ellie, who was standing next to me.

"Not as dark as your *morenito* back in Ruby," Ellie retorted.

"I think he's cute," Lupita said. "He has a kind face."

"Get away from the window, girls." Mother walked into the room from the kitchen, pulling her apron off. The smell of *carne guisada* and beans wafted after her.

We moved away from the window and by the time Ricky knocked on the door, Ellie was sitting primly on the sofa, her hands folded on her yellow-skirted lap. She looked impossibly priggish. Lupita ran to the door, Mother following close behind.

"Hello," he said through the screen. "I'm Ricky Hernández. Eloise is expecting me."

"Hello. Come in," Lupita said shyly, holding the door open.

When he walked in, the first thing I noticed was his mole, which was oval-shaped with three hairs sticking out of it. I wondered why he hadn't shaved them off. He would have actually been a good looking man had it not been for that unsightly mole. I glanced over at Ellie to exchange a commiserating glance, but she avoided my eyes.

"Welcome, welcome, Enrique." Mother beamed. "I feel like I know you already from all of my Raulito's letters."

"It's so good to meet you, Señora Caballero," Ricky said, awkwardly thrusting the gift box at Mother. "This is for you. It's from Raul."

Mother's face lit up as she tooked the present and sat on the sofa next to Ellie. She ripped the wrapping paper off and then opened the box pulling out a green purse and a matching hat. "*Mira!* How beautiful! Raulito always had such good taste."

She looked at the mirror above the sofa and tried on the hat, a hideous-looking, helmet-like hat with green feathers and emerald rhinestones around the brim, and green netting that fell over her face.

"It's the latest fashion in England," Ricky said, noticing my sisters' and my raised eyebrows.

"It's beautiful, isn't it girls?"

"*Sí*, Mamá, just beautiful," Lupita said with a sheepish grin.

Ricky stood there holding the flowers in his hand, shifting his feet and generally looking ill at ease.

Ellie rose from the sofa, her hand out. "Hello. I'm Ellie. I'm so glad to finally meet you." She fluttered her long eyelashes, giving Ricky that piercing look that she is known for, and I knew that the poor guy was a goner.

He cleared his throat and thrust the flowers at her. "These are for you."

"How nice." She put the pink roses to her nose, all the while keeping her eyes on him.

"You do like roses, right? Raul said you did."

"Oh, yes, they're my favorite flower."

"I'll get a vase for you, Ellie," said the ever-helpful Lupita as she rushed out of the room.

Mother laid the hat back in the box. "You must be starved." She grabbed Enrique's arm and ushered him into the kitchen. "Do you like *carne guisada*?"

"Oh, yes. *Carne guisada* is one of my favorite dishes." He looked relieved to be removed from Ellie's unnerving gaze. "But shouldn't we wait for Señor Caballero?"

"Only God knows when my husband will be home, Enrique," Mother said sarcastically. "He went off this morning on some business, and he has a habit of going to the neighborhood bar afterward. It's not something I like to talk about, you understand. But I feel like you're family since you're my Raulito's friend. My husband drinks a little. He's a good man though. It's the drink that's bad. Anyway, he knows you're going to be here, so it's possible he'll be here at any time. I wouldn't count on it though."

I frowned. Drinks a little! Just how far did Mother's self-delusion go? I could tell by Ellie's pink complexion that she was also embarrassed by Mother's revelation. But Ricky would find out about Father's drinking problem sooner or later. I suppose sooner was better than later.

We followed them into the kitchen. As I watched Mother hover over Ricky, I thought again about Diego. Mother had been exactly the same way with him. Hovering. It was the woman's job, she had often said, to make sure that the man is taken care of. His job is to bring home the money, the least the woman could do is make sure his stomach is full, his clothes are clean and pressed, and he has a comfortable bed to sleep in. All that hovering didn't keep Diego around, nor did it seem very effective with Father, who never seemed satisified with anything Mother did. Of course, it was possible that Diego would still be around if Terre hadn't dumped him. I never understood why Terre had dumped Diego. He was suave and debonair, just exactly the kind of man I would have liked to marry when the time came. Plus, he'd bought her that great house in Westwood. Papá said that Terre was destined to become a nun. Too bad she didn't find that out before dragging poor Diego through the wringer.

"The picture you sent me didn't do you justice, Eloise," Ricky said between bites.

"Oh, really?" she said, making her eyes big and round.

I noticed that as he ate, he seemed to lose some of his initial reticence. He watched Ellie out of the corner of his eye. "You're much prettier in person."

"Why thank you." She smiled and ducked her head.

Mother sat down to eat with us. "Tell us about England."

Ricky paused for a moment, pursed his lips, and furrowed his eyebrows, then said as if he were going to utter something of great importance, "It's cold all the time and rains almost every day. But the countryside is beautiful. Everything is green and flowers grow everywhere."

"I hope *mi'jo* is taking care of himself. Damp climates are not good for the constitution." Mother sighed. "Ay, it's been so long since I've seen my Raulito. It's hard to think of him way over there across the ocean. When he told me he had decided to make the military his career, I was happy, but also a little sad. I won't be seeing him as often as I'd like, but there really is no other way for a *Mexicano* to make a place in this world, is there?"

"Well, in a way you're right. But for some of us, it isn't so bad. My father owns a grocery store in Fresno and I'll be working with him when I get out of the service next month." He glanced at Ellie. "Since I'm an only child, my parents depend on me."

If that statement bothered Ellie, she didn't show it. I suppose she thought that since he was a dutiful son he would therefore make a dutiful husband. Besides, she and Ricky had been writing to each other for over a year, so she already knew his plans. I couldn't help but notice, however, the warning tone in his voice when he had said, "My parents depend on me." If Ellie noticed, she kept it to herself.

*****

Ricky had arrived at noon, and when Father had not returned by four, he asked Mother if he could take us for a ride. She said yes and we happily piled into his Chevy, Ellie in the front with him, Lupita and I in the back seat. Ricky had a cousin who lived in Soledad so he had visited before and was familiar with the town.

"Have you been to the mission yet?" he asked Ellie before turning on the ignition.

"No, is it near here?"

"About four miles west. You want to go?" He included us in his question, glancing at us in the back seat.

"Oh, yes," we all said in unison.

Farms dotted several hundred acres of land between the town of Soledad and the mission. The mid-afternoon sun blazed down on the vegetation, lettuce in various stages of growth, the lacy tops of carrots, an occasional tree. The two-lane road we took wound over the verdant land in a gentle loop taking us past the carrot field we had been to earlier in the week. We reached a dirt driveway entrance and turned in. At the end of the dirt drive was a pristine stucco building with a steeple surrounded by adobe walls in varying degrees of ruin.

"It looks like the chapel has been restored. The last time I was here it was nothing but rubble," Ricky commented.

"Mission Soledad," murmured Ellie, looking at a sign near the building. "That must be how the town got its name."

"Many of the cities in California are named after missions," he said.

"We have missions in Texas, too," I said from the back seat. "Ever heard of the Alamo?"

"Who hasn't?" Enrique glanced back at me and smiled, his mole sinking into a dimple. "There's rumors that there are tunnels underneath the Soledad Mission and that treasure is hidden in them." He pulled to a stop in front of the chapel.

"What kind of treasure?" I could hardly contain my excitement. I loved stories of buried treasure and ghosts and the like.

"Gold and silver. Mostly altar pieces that the padres hid when bandits were reported to be in the area."

"But nobody has found them?"

"No, not that I know of. And no one has actually discovered any tunnels, so it's probably all just rumors."

Although the mission was not officially open, we wandered around for about half an hour. A small wing of seven rooms veered off to the west of the chapel; this wing and the chapel comprised the mission.

"I think that this mission was the only one built this far inland," said Ricky as he walked with Ellie hand in hand around the grounds, and Lupita and I tagged along. "That's why it was not as successful as the rest. Summers are blazing hot, not to mention windy, but winter is worse. Winter nights are freezing out here in the valley. You really need someone to cuddle up with." He put his arm around Ellie's waist and hugged her close to him, also giving her what I suppose was a meaningful glance.

"But you live in the Central Valley," Ellie said, her voice teasing.

"It's cold there, too," he said.

After we left the mission grounds, my imagination was fueled with visions of buried treasure. "Whoever finds the treasure, if there is a treasure, would he or she be able to keep it?" I asked as we began our drive back to town.

"Probably not," Ricky said. "I think it would belong to the state of California."

I sighed. "Oh, that figures."

Later we drove past Pasquale's and I saw Father's pickup parked in front. Lupita and I frowned at each other. A few minutes later, Ricky drove down Front Street and stopped in front of Elmo's, the town's soda fountain.

When we walked in, the noise level dropped to a quiet murmur. The only other sound came from the juke box, which was playing the Elvis Presley hit, "Don't Be Cruel." We passed several booths filled with snickering teenagers as we approached the Formica counter to order sodas. I felt self-conscious, as if I had snot hanging from my nose or my slip was showing. We got our drinks and then slid into an empty booth. I had wanted to give Ellie and Ricky some time alone, but there was no other place to sit, and truth be told, I felt more secure with them what with the palpable tension in the air.

As Ricky regaled us with the story about how he had met Raul (during latrine duty), I noticed two girls in the booth across from ours giving us dirty looks. Actually, the dark-eyed *Mexicanas*, one who looked like a plump Rita Hayworth, the other rather thin and of average looks, were frowning in response to their boyfriends' obvious interest in us, the new girls in town. I couldn't help but notice that the boys, their hair slicked back in duck tails, kept glancing at me and my sisters. Finally, the girls slid out of their booth and left in a huff, their sheepish boyfriends hastily putting coins on the table and following after them.

Little did I know at the time, but I had just made two enemies.

*****

Father was still not home by ten, so Ricky left without meeting him. Ellie seemed relieved. She knew, as we all did, that Father would be in no condition to meet anyone, much less his daughter's prospective *novio*. When the door closed and Ricky had gone, Mother jumped out of the chair where she had been crocheting and began to storm around the living room.

"I can't believe your Father didn't come home," she wailed, flailing her arms in the air. "I told him about Enrique's visit. But no, he'd rather drink himself into oblivion."

"Mamá, it's all right. Ricky's spending the night with his cousin and will be back tomorrow for another visit before he goes back to the base," Ellie said. "He can meet Father tomorrow."

"No! It's not all right."

I knew that when Father finally stumbled home, their fight would rock the walls off our little house. I wished I could be anywhere but there. "I'm going to get ready for bed." I trudged to the bedroom and changed into my seersucker pajamas before going to the bathroom. My night time toilette was a drawn-out affair of brushing teeth, setting my hair in wire curlers (a ritual I eventually gave up as hopeless in the windy city of Soledad), inspecting my face for blemishes and then splattering cold cream all over it.

Ellie walked in on me just as I was finishing up. She placed her curlers on the toilet lid and started to comb her hair with angry strokes. She kept hitting my head with her elbow in the small room.

"Can't you wait just a minute? I'm almost done." I hadn't realized until then that Ellie had really been upset that Father hadn't come home to meet her *novio*.

"Father never did anything like that to Isa." Tears formed in her eyes as she continued to run the brush through her hair.

"Do what?"

"Humiliate her."

"What are you talking about? What does Isa have to do with any of this?"

"Do you remember when Marcos came over for the first time to meet Mamá and Papá? Father took a bath, shaved, wore his best trousers and shirt, even put on cologne to meet him."

"That was different, Ellie. Marcos' parents were with him and they were already engaged."

"Still, he would never have humiliated Isa."

"Things were a lot different when Isa was home. You know that. Papá has had a hard time since then, what with his business going broke and all."

She sniffled, was quiet for a while, then said, "I suppose you're right."

I smiled and touched her arm. As I started to leave, she said, "What did you think of Ricky?"

"He's very nice."

"He's handsome, isn't he?"

I grimaced. "Well . . ."

"Of course there's the mole," she went on, "but it really doesn't detract from his over-all appearance."

"It doesn't?" I asked, astonished. When I saw the hurt look on her face, I quickly added. "Of course it doesn't." I hurried out of the bathroom to our bedroom before I said anything I'd regret.

Lupita, her waist-length hair loose down her back, was kneeling in front of her altar, her head bent in prayer. The red votive candle flickered in the dimly lit room. I walked over her legs to our bed, where I eased down gingerly, putting my wired head gently on the pillow. It was so uncomfortable sleeping in rollers, but the alternative was to wake up in the morning with my hair smashed down and bent in every direction, not a pretty sight. I moved my head to the side and glanced up at the four pictures I had tacked up on the wall by my side of the bed. The pictures were of my dream home cut from the *Better Homes and Gardens* magazine. Looking at them made me feel better, gave me something to hope for. Two of the photos were the front and back views of a sprawling ranch house on a large tree-studded property located somewhere in the Midwest. The other two were of rooms inside the house—a kitchen and living room furnished with the latest appliances and modern furniture. I often daydreamed about living in a house like that. Surely people living in such a house could be deliriously happy.

I glanced at Lupita still praying fervently for who knows what. I was sure she would end up a nun like Terre, though she told me that being pious wasn't something that was reserved only for nuns and priests.

"What are you praying for, Lupita?" I asked.

She turned to look at me. "That Mamá and Papá won't fight when he comes home."

"That's wishful thinking," I snorted.

She frowned and turned back to the virgin.

I drifted to sleep and was startled awake by my parents' loud voices.

I don't know how long I had been asleep, but the light in the room was off and I could see by the moonlight streaming in through the window that my sisters were also in bed, but as awake as I was.

"Where did you get this?" we heard through the wall.

"It's from Raulito. Put it down!"

"Raul who?" Father's voice slurred.

"Our son."

"Don't try to fool me. I know that Raul is not here. Who gave you these things?"

"It's useless talking to you when you're like this. Come to bed. We'll talk tomorrow."

"No! We'll talk tonight."

I jumped out of bed.

"What are you doing, Marta? Come back here," Ellie ordered.

Lupita crawled out of bed and grabbed my arm, pulling me toward her altar. "Let's pray, Marta."

"Are you crazy? You pray if you want to. I'm going to help Mamá."

I ran to the living room just in time to see Father ripping apart Mother's green hat. Feathers and emerald rhinestones flew in every direction. He threw the tattered hat down and picked up the purse, demolishing it with his big hands. "Papá, how could you? Raul sent those to Mother!"

I'll never forget the expression on Father's face when he looked at me. His eyes seemed out of focus and he looked at me curiously as if he didn't know who I was. It frightened me.

"Go back to bed. This is none of your concern."

"*Sí, hija.* Go back to bed," Mother implored.

I felt tears burning down my cheeks. "But it's not right. Mamá didn't do anything wrong, Papá. That hat is from your son, Raul. He sent it to her. His friend, Ricky, I mean Enrique, brought it today."

"Enrique?" Father echoed. He dropped the broken purse on the floor and scratched his head as if he recalled the name but couldn't remember from where. He made his way to the sofa and sank down on the soft cushions. His head nodded, and within seconds he was snoring.

Mother looked at me, her eyes sad. "Go to bed, *hija.*"

I shuffled back to the bedroom, still sniffling, and when I got to the door, I looked over my shoulder. Mother had picked up the hat and was holding it to her chest. She got on her knees to pick up the feathers and rhinestones strewn all over the wooden floor, then she struggled to her feet, and with a thud, sat on the one upholstered armchair in the tiny room. Clutching the tattered hat in one hand and the feathers and rhinestones in another, she just sat there, looking straight ahead. Not a tear fell from her eyes. She just sat there. Mother rarely cried, though she had reason to cry buckets by my estimation.

I'm not sure why, but it made me feel bad, my mother not crying, especially after what Father had done to her beloved hat. I cried at the drop of a hat, no pun intended. Sad movies and love songs made me cry. Sometimes just watching the sun go down made me bawl. It was embarrassing to be so emotional, but it was as natural for me to cry as for people to breathe. Why couldn't Mother cry? Or was a better question, "Why wouldn't she?"

I eased back into bed next to Lupita.

"What happened?" Ellie demanded from the other bed.

"Papá passed out on the sofa."

She grunted and pulled her covers over her. "Did he really destroy that hideous hat?"

"Yes. To pieces."

She paused, then chuckled. "Well, at least he did one thing right."

I would have laughed, too, except I had seen Mother's sad expression when she had clutched that ugly, tattered hat to her chest. I couldn't laugh. It was too heartbreaking.

Chapter 25

There was a large Tejano community in Soledad, people from the Río Grande Valley who had migrated during several harvest seasons and had decided to stay. Because of this strong Texas presence, Tejano music was popular in the town. Sometimes when my sisters and I were strolling downtown, we heard conjuntos blaring out of Mexican restaurants, music from the Beto Villa orchestra, a sort of Tejano swing band that was popular in the fifties. In some ways, it felt as if we had never left the Río Grande Valley, the ambiance of Soledad was so like the small Texas Valley cities.

Mother often got together with her Tejana friends—las Señoras Elizondo and Olivares from Ruby, and las Señoras López and Quintanilla from Mercedes. They chatted and laughed and, if the time was right, they'd listen to the one radio station in the vicinity that played Mexican music. The station aired the Spanish language music from five to seven in the evening. The ladies sat around our aqua Formica kitchen table, where our radio was perched, and to the beat of conjuntos, helped Mother make masa for fresh tortillas, and chop up tomatoes, onions, and jalapeños for salsa.

Lupita and I, on the other hand, liked to listen to rock n' roll—Elvis Presley and Buddy Holly and the Crickets. We had become more Americanized in California, though not to the extent of the many California *Mexicanos* who refused (or didn't know how) to speak Spanish. In the Río Grande Valley, Spanish was the rule, not the exception. In the Salinas Valley in the fifties, it was the other way around, particularly among second and third-generation Mexican-Americans.

When Mother visited with her fellow Tejanos, she would sigh and her expression would get wistful when talking about the Valley (to her, the Valley wasn't the Salinas Valley; it was the Río Grande Valley). She had been president of the altar Society at our parish in Ruby, and she had a network of friends and relatives with whom she visited frequently when we lived in Texas. She missed home, despite the Tejano ambiance of Soledad. In fact, we were all homesick, except for Ellie who was "in love," and in a world of her own.

Mother's longing for home and her fights with Father were setting us up for the inevitable. At the time I didn't see it, but looking back, I can see clearly where we were headed.

*****

A packing shed, which shipped carrots all over the United States and Canada, operated in Soledad during the summer harvest season with a crew of about a hundred fifty people. The hundreds of acres of carrot fields surrounding the city supplied the plant, and carrots that were not shipped out supplied the local market. The orange vegetable spilled over the bins in the produce section of every market and grocery in town.

During the season, Mother, who was a very good cook, put carrots in virtually everything she cooked. Slices of the orange vegetable were stirred in boiling beans and simmering rice. She made brown sugar glazed carrots, cheesy potato carrot casserole, carrot and rice bake, orange glazed carrots, and my all-time favorite, carrot cake. By the end of the harvest, I was thoroughly sick of carrots. By the the time cherry season started at the end of June, I was even sick of carrot cake. I went through the same thing during cherry season. Mother made several cherry cobblers over the season, but by the third pie, I had had my fill of cherries, plus I had gained a good five pounds.

Before tomato season commenced at the end of July, my sisters and I spent most of the time relaxing, going to the park across the street, the bowling alley, and the movies. Ricky, Ellie's *novio*, who had been discharged from the Air Force and had come to Soledad almost every weekend after his first visit, spent one of the weeks at his cousin's house so that he could see Ellie every day. A few days into his stay, he asked Ellie to marry him and, with Father's approval, she agreed. The wedding was to take place the following summer, but something happened that changed their plans.

*****

The tomato packing shed where Father was foreman was between Soledad and Gonzales on the west side of the freeway by the railroad tracks and across the highway from the Soledad prison. The prison was set back pretty far from the highway with tall fences and trees around it, and wasn't visible from the packing shed, but it still scared us to be so near convicted felons.

"Do the inmates ever escape?" Lupita asked when we drove past the prison on our way to work at the packing shed for the first time.

"Not recently that I know of," Father said.

"What kind of crimes did they commit?" I asked.

"It's a medium security prison, *mi'ja*. Mostly burglaries and larceny and drug offenses," he said matter-of-factly.

We pulled into the parking lot by the shed, which had a corrugated tin roof, putting the prison out of our minds as best we could. Later we found out that everyone at the packing shed was keenly aware of the proximity of the prison and the prisoners in their blue chambray shirts and blue jeans who sometimes worked outside the prison fences. The shed workers kept their anxiety in check by joking about it. "They have it better in there than we do out here," one man said, laughing. "Why would they want to escape?"

After introducing us to several of the workers, Father set us up outside the shed. We sat on some old wooden crates and secured company labels on shipping boxes that were filled with tomatoes. After we had pasted the label on a crate, a man grabbed the crate and stacked it with all the others on a platform deck to await the arrival of the truck that would take them out of the Valley and to market. The paste-on produce labels were discontinued just a few years after our stint at the packing shed, just to show how superfluous our job was. Actually, someone got the bright idea to preprint the company name on the shipping boxes. It saved money, and cost a few people their jobs.

It was a beautiful California day, though quite warm, even under the tree where Father had set us up. We spent all morning swiping the company's labels with wet sponges and slapping them on the crates.

As Father went about his business, we noticed that a woman wearing a red scarf around her head frequently spoke to Father. She touched his arm in a familiar way and made him laugh.

"I wonder if that's the woman who called that time when we first got here," Ellie snarled. "The little slut."

"Ellie! What an awful thing to say!" Lupita said.

"Don't try to take up for him."

"I'm not," she said. "But you shouldn't say such ugly things about someone you don't even know."

Ellie shrugged, refusing to comment further. However, at lunch time when Father joined us to eat the taquitos Mother had made for us, she blurted out, "Who is that woman with the red scarf on her head, Papá?

Father looked at her sharply. "Why do you want to know?"

"She seems to know you well, that's all." She looked up at him slyly.

Father's expression became thunderous. He hissed in a low voice. "You mind your own business. Do you hear me, girl? You're as bad as your sister, Terre, ever was. If you want to continue working here, keep your mouth shut." He stood up and lumbered off.

The drive home that evening was quiet. We were all tired and our necks and shoulders hurt from being slumped over crates all day. After dinner we sat in the living room groaning. I begged Lupita for a back rub, and even though she was in as much pain as I was, she obliged. Father had brought us home, eaten dinner, then gone back to the shed, which during the harvest often stayed open until midnight.

Father came home in the wee hours of the morning, drunk, as usual, and he and Mother fought, as usual. We could hear their loud, angry voices as they hurled insults at each other.

Ellie bolted upright from her bed, pressing her pillow to her ears. "I can't take this anymore," she shrilled. "I just can't take it."

Two weeks later, Ellie and Ricky eloped.

*****

I had read the novel *The Strange Case of Dr. Jekyll and Mr. Hyde* the summer before we moved to Soledad and was struck by the similarity between the two title characters of the book and my father. When my father wasn't drinking, he was intelligent and thoughtful, if a little brooding, kind and affectionate. But when he drank, he was a monster. The problem was, he drank often and he drank a lot, though oddly enough, he never drank on the job and rarely before the sun went down. So if he was an alcoholic (and I'm not sure he was), I suppose he was what psychologists now call a functional alcoholic.

Someone once told me that Father could drink more than any man he knew and not even appear drunk. But then, all of a sudden, the cumulative effect of drinking excessively would hit him and he became a bear. Father was not a happy drunk, if there is such a thing. He didn't sing boleros, like my Tío Luis did when he was drunk. No, Father got surly and mean, and he took whatever was bothering him out on Mother. He never hit her. But sometimes I think that would have been preferable to all the ugly things he said to her.

Nighttime was hell for our family, and my sisters and I often woke up tired and sluggish in the mornings, not to mention tense. Then we would go to the kitchen and there my parents would be, Mother making breakfast, Father sipping his *café con leche* and reading the paper as if nothing had happened, as if he hadn't called her those horrible names, and she hadn't accused him of all manner of atrocity.

Ellie had escaped. She couldn't take it any more. But she had left Lupita and me, and I was angry at her. How could she have left us? Mother and Father had gotten into a terrible fight when they found out about the elopement, blaming each other for Ellie's running away. They were right to blame each other. They were both to blame, though I'm sure they would never see it that way. Ellie had left a note under her pillow that we found the day after her elopement. In it she had written that she loved Ricky and wanted to be with him, but more than that, she couldn't take the fighting any more. That started another argument.

The week following Ellie's elopement was emotionally draining. I didn't think things could get any worse.

I was wrong.

*****

About one-hundred fifty people worked in the packing shed during the tomato season— packers, sorters, checkers, stackers, truckers—everyone

171

had their special job. The packers especially took pride in their work. They made more money than the other shed workers because they were paid piecemeal, that is, by the box. Some of the best could pack up to two-hundred boxes of tomatoes a day, and they were looked upon with admiration and respect.

Saturday was a special day at the shed. We got paid at the end of the day, and anticipation fairly crackled in the air. Most of the women in the shed wore their hair in curlers with scarves wrapped around them so that they could be ready for the Saturday night dance sponsored in town by the Lion's Club. We weren't allowed to go to the dances after Ellie eloped (I guess Father thought elopements were contagious or something) but we enjoyed listening to the women's stories on Monday about what had happened at the dance the Saturday before, who danced with who and such. There was a camaraderie at the shed among the workers, but because we were the foreman's daughters, Lupita and I were treated somewhat more formally than we would have liked. But at least everyone was kind.

The tomato packing shed stayed open for four months until the beginning of November, but Lupita and I worked there only until school started in September. Even though I was happy to quit the packing shed, I was frightened at the prospect of going to a new school because no one my own age, with the exception of Jimmy (who really wasn't my age), had been friendly with me all summer. Girls my age actually turned up their noses at me, and I didn't know why.

Chapter 26

I wore a new pair of black and white oxfords and white crew socks with my shin-length dress and knew immediately when Father dropped me off in front of the Main Street School that I had made a mistake of grand proportions. The older girls (the seventh and eighth graders) were wearing flats with no socks, and their dresses were shorter than mine, closer to knee-length, and definitely more stylish.

As I self-consciously walked up the sidewalk to the front entrance, several girls leaning against the wall snickered at me. I recognized two of them as the girls I had seen at Elmo's the week after I had arrived in Soledad. The pudgy one who looked like Rita Hayworth—almond shaped eyes and long wavy hair—actually sneered as I walked by her. Her friend, a girl of medium height with a mild acne problem, muttered, "*Tejana fea*" (ugly Texan).

I have never felt as bad as I did that day. Had it not been for Julia, I would have run home after school and begged Mother to send me back to Texas. Julia saw me wandering around at lunchtime. No one wanted me to sit with them—every time I walked to an empty chair, someone told me it was taken. I stood for a long time with my lunch bag in my hand trying to keep the tears that were forming in my eyes from spilling out, and trying to figure out what to do when she walked over to me and introduced herself.

"Hello," she said. "I'm Julia Segura. Would you like to sit with me and my friends?"

I smiled with relief. Julia had thick curly hair--the type of hair that is hard to control--pulled back with a red headband. She also had the kindest eyes and widest smile I had ever seen.

"Thank you," I answered eagerly as I followed her past a group of girls who had refused to let me sit with them. One of them muttered, "Tejana lover."

Julia stopped. She walked over to the girl. "I'm a people lover, although I might make an exception where you're concerned."

The girl frowned and her friends giggled self-consciously. My new friend grabbed my arm and led me to the table she was sharing with two other girls.

I sat next to her. "I'm Marta." I smiled at her friends. "Thank you for letting me sit with you."

The girls smiled back shyly.

"I'm Clara." She grinned, revealing a rather large space between her front teeth.

"I'm Hope," said the one wearing tortoise-shell cat-eye glasses.

I smiled, first at Clara, then at Hope. "Pleased to meet you."

"I hope you don't mind sitting with seventh graders," Julia commented as she opened her paper bag lunch.

"Are you kidding?"

"No, I'm not kidding. We're in seventh grade."

"That's not what I meant. I meant, I don't care what grade you're in. It was awfully nice of you to invite me to eat with you."

"Don't let them bother you," Julia said, waving her hand in a gesture of dismissal at the eighth grade girls. "They're just jealous."

"Jealous? What of?

"Of you."

"Why?"

"Have you looked at yourself in the mirror lately?"

"This morning," I said, perplexed.

"What did you see?"

I thought for a moment. "An ugly haircut. I went to the beauty salon on Saturday and the hairdresser cut my hair shorter than I normally wear it. I usually wear it to my shoulders, but she cut it way higher." I grimaced touching a strand of my hair.

"You have the most beautiful hair I have ever seen." Clara sighed. "It looks natural, too."

"Yes, it is natural. My mother has red hair."

"You also have a beautiful complexion. You could give Suzy Parker a run for her money."

I laughed. "You're crazy." Suzy Parker was a famous red-headed model. Her picture had graced every glamour magazine published in the fifties.

"No, we're not. Sylvia and Roberta are green with envy."

"Is that why they're being so mean to me?" I glanced at the girls who now had names. "Which one is Sylvia?"

"The shorter one," Julia said. "Don't let them bother you. They'll come around. You seem like a regular girl. Do you honestly not know how beautiful you are?"

I felt my face burn. "I'm not any more beautiful than any of you," I said and meant it. "I mean I don't feel beautiful. I feel like a regular girl, like you said."

"We're going to have to do something about your name," Julia said abruptly.

"What's wrong with my name?"

"Marta," she said, rolling the r, "It sounds too Mexican." She looked at her friends. "What do you think?"

"What about Martha? That's a good American name. Like Martha Washington, the president's wife. What could be more American than that?" Hope said.

"Martha it is," Julia announced.

And so I became Martha, which struck me as pretty funny. I started to laugh, and my new friends laughed along with me.

"Oh, and one more thing, Martha," Julia said after the laughter had died down.

"What's that?"

"Those oxfords and socks have got to go."

I burst out laughing again, and so did they.

I actually started to feel at home in Soledad.

*****

Julia, Clara, Hope, and I became fast friends, but Julia became my best friend. It turned out that her father and my father were friends, and so her parents invited my family to their house for barbeques and parties. I also spent the night at her house, which put me in the awkward position of having to reciprocate, something I was loath to do considering Father and Mother's proclivity to fight at night after his drinking bouts. Nevertheless, I did invite her to spend the night several times, and only once did Mother and Father embarrass me when she was there. That night Julia pretended to be asleep (she had to have been pretending because the fight my parents had would have awakened the dead). The next morning she didn't say one word about what had happened. When I started to apologize, she put her finger to her mouth and shushed me. "Do you think your father is the only one in this town who drinks? It's not your fault, and we don't have to talk about it, unless you really want to." I shook my head, wiping the tears from my eyes. I certainly did not want to discuss it, not then, not ever. Julia touched my arm in a gesture of empathy, then began talking about something else. I knew that I could depend on her discretion.

Julia was a singer and a gifted musician. She often played her guitar at parties on the weekends, belting out Mexican boleros. She was fond of Tex-Mex music, songs by Beto Villa, Ruben Vela and Paulino Bernal. She invited me to the parties she played at, and it was mostly because of her that people began to warm up to me, especially the boys.

There were quite a few boys from the school who hung around the park across the street on the weekends, and Jimmy told me that he had never seen them around before Lupita and I moved into the neighborhood. Even though they were nice, and a few exceptionally good looking, I was still nursing a crush on Daniel. We had been corresponding since

175

the first few weeks after I moved to Soledad. I went to the post office every day hoping for a letter, and by October, I had received three, in answer to the three I had sent him.

During one of my trips to the post office on a Saturday afternoon Julia drove by with her older brother in his old, beat-up Ford and asked me if I wanted to go see something funny. I got in their car, and Larry, her brother, took us up Front Street and then onto the highway.

"Look." She pointed at a woman sitting on a chair, a suitcase at her feet. The woman's thumb was up as if she were trying to hitch a ride.

"Are we going to pick her up?" I asked from the back seat as the car slowed down.

Julia laughed. "Sure."

I wondered what was so funny until we got closer to the woman. Then I burst out laughing. Some jokester had dressed up a life-size dummy like a woman with a dress and wig, and had put a skeleton mask on its face. From far away, it looked like a real person, and I imagine at night, it was even more convincing.

"Who do you think did that?"

"Probably Alex Quintanilla. He's the town prankster. Every year he does something like this at Halloween. He owns the market on Front Street. Remember, Larry, the year he put a dummy by Pasquale's and the drunks came out and started talking to it." She turned to look at me. "That year, he made her look like a real woman, no mask, and those drunks thought she was the real thing. It was pretty funny."

I laughed, but I didn't think it was funny. Father often went to Pasquale's to drink. I hated to think of him talking to a dummy like that and having people laugh at him, although I really couldn't imagine anyone laughing at my father. He just wasn't the type of man you laughed at.

On Halloween, four days later, Julia came over. We were too old to dress up in costumes, so we sat in lawn chairs in the front yard with my sister and passed out candies to the little kids coming by. Father was at the packing shed, and Mother was chatting with Jimmy's mother, Señora Menchaca.

As my mother and our neighbor conversed, Julia got quiet and I could tell she was thinking about something. Later, after the last of the trick-or-treaters had gone by, my mother and Lupita had disappeared into the house, and darkness had descended on the neighborhood, she whispered excitedly, "I've got a great idea for a Halloween prank."

"What is it?" I asked, infected by her excitement.

"Let's exchange all the potted plants from Mrs. Menchaca's front porch with the ones from the house next door to hers."

"That would be funny, wouldn't it? I wonder how long it would take her to figure out that the wrong plants were on her porch?" I said, warming to the idea.

Julia's face brightened. "Let's do it!" She stood up. "It's getting late. I have to go home now. Can you sneak out of the house at midnight and meet me out here?"

"Sure."

"Okay, I'll see you then." She grinned before running home.

*****

I have to admit, I'm not what you call a daring soul, but compared to Lupita, I was Amelia Earhart. Therefore, I tried to be as quiet as possible when I got out of bed. But despite my care, Lupita woke up.

"What are you doing, Marta?" she asked groggily.

"Nothing," I whispered, "Go back to bed."

She sat up. "You'd better tell me right now what you're doing or I'm going to wake Mother up."

Ever since Ellie had eloped right from under our noses, Lupita had gotten a little paranoid. I quickly related Julia's plan.

"You're going to do what?" she sputtered.

"Quiet, Lupita," I whispered as I slipped my jacket on over my flannel pajamas. "Come on, it's not like we're going to damage anything. It's just a harmless prank. Don't be a spoilsport. Don't you ever feel like doing something different? Something exciting?"

She was quiet for a minute, then she jumped out of bed. "I hope we don't get thrown in jail," she muttered as she grabbed her own jacket from the closet and put it on over her flannel nightgown.

"You're going to help?"

"Why not? Like you said, it's a harmless prank," she whispered as she followed me out of the room.

Julia was hiding in the bushes when we slipped out the front door. "Hey! I'm over here." She sprang out from the darkness of the bushes. She paused when she saw Lupita, giving me a quizzical look.

"It's okay. She's going to help."

Julia smiled. "That's good because I just finished counting the pots. Mrs. Menchaca has fifteen and some are pretty big. The lady next door has eight and they're all big."

"Let's take turns watching for the patrol car," she added. "Thanks for helping, Lulu."

Lupita frowned. I couldn't help laughing. I remembered what she had said when she came home after the first day of school. "Do I look like a Lulu to you?" she demanded.

"No," I said, laughing.

"Well, believe it or not, that's what all my classmates are calling

177

me. I told them over and over again that my name was Lupita and they kept calling me Lulu." She put her hands on her hips.

"You're looking at Martha," I said haughtily, pronouncing it MAH THA.

"Martha?" She grimaced.

"Like Martha Washingon."

"Well, don't expect me to call you that, and if you start calling me Lulu, I'll, I'll whack you on the head," she had said, whirling around and stomping to our bedroom.

Lupita took the first watch as Julia and I began exchanging pots, a more difficult job than we had anticipated, given their weight. The police car came down the street once and we hid in the shade of some bushes. It took about thirty minutes for the job to be complete. The three of us stood in front of Mrs. Menchaca's house admiring our handiwork. Her pots had had beautiful flowers growing in most of them. The pots now gracing her porch were mostly dried sticks and spindly plants. "I wish I could be here when Mrs. Menchaca comes out to water," Julia giggled, stopping when she heard a car coming down the street.

We peered out from the bushes as the pickup rumbled to a stop in our driveway. Father lumbered out of the truck, slamming his door. I could feel my face get hot with embarrassment as I watched him stumble to the front door and into the house. I felt deflated.

Julia touched my arm. "I'll see you tomorrow at school. I need to get home. Bye." She gave me a sympathetic glance, then hurried to the alley which connected our streets.

"Bye Julia," Lupita and I whispered.

"Let's wait a while before we go in."

Lupita nodded.

We waited in the cold night, listening for sounds of crashes and shouting, but when several minutes had gone by and nothing happened, we decided to go back in. We opened the front door slowly. Father had fallen asleep on the sofa, and was snoring loudly. We inched our way to our rooms, removed our jackets and jumped in our beds, relieved that we had been spared another drunken scene, and that we hadn't been caught.

*****

Julia walked home with me from school the next day and when we got home, Mother was standing outside with Mrs. Menchaca.

"Can you believe this, girls?" Mrs. Menchaca said, "Somebody moved all my pots and put them on Mrs. Ybañez's front porch and then put all her plants on my front porch. I thought it might have been Jimmy and some of his friends. But he swears that he didn't do it."

"Who else could it have been?" I asked nonchalantly.

"Who knows? But it's going to take a lot of work putting things back. There's some really heavy pots."

"Yes, I know." Julia sighed.

I looked at her askance.

"I mean, yes, it looks like some of those pots are very heavy," she added quickly.

Mother glanced at us, her eyes narrowed.

Just then the high school bus stopped at the end of the street and Lupita got off. Her smiled quickly faded when she saw all of us congregated in front of Mrs. Menchaca's yard. "What's going on?" she asked.

"Somebody exchanged Mrs. Menchaca's pots with the lady's next door. A Halloween prank, I guess," I said.

"My, how strange," Lupita said, her eyes sparkling. "But I suppose as a Halloween prank it's not too bad or anything. Just a nuisance. Right? I heard someone splashed red paint on three cars on Soledad Street last night and two fires were set on some ranches."

"Is that right?" Mrs. Menchaca said. "It's terrible what kids are doing nowadays."

"Yes, terrible," Lupita said solemnly, casting her long eyelashes downward.

"We'll help put your pots back," I offered.

"No, no, that's not necessary. Young ladies such as yourselves have no business doing such heavy work. Jimmy is bringing over some of his friends to help do that."

The three of us glanced at each other uneasily, feeling Mother's penetrating stare. Finally, Julia said goodbye, giving me a long look before she ran down the alley.

When we got into the house, Mother surprised Lupita and me by chuckling, "You should have seen the look on Elvira's face when she came to the door this morning. 'Beatriz,' she said, her eyes all bugged out. 'Something very odd has happened. All my potted plants are gone and someone else's have been put in their place.' '*De veras*?' I said. So I went outside and sure enough, all the pots on her porch were not the same ones that had been there the day before. Do you know what I thought?"

"No, what did you think, Mamá?" I asked sort of gulping, still clutching my schoolbooks to my breast.

"I thought, whoever did this prank has a good imagination. It's a prank that is not harmful, but is effective. But I also thought that the kids who did this prank must have a lot of time on their hands to be doing such things. Maybe they need to be given more yard work since they seem to like to work outside."

Lupita and I hung our heads.

"On the other hand, if the kids who did this thing were to use their imaginations in school, they might get better grades. I don't think these kids are bad kids, do you?"

"No, Mamá, I don't think so," I said.

"Neither do I. But I think they should learn to occupy their time more productively."

"You're right," I said nodding. "Absolutely right." I grabbed Lupita's arm and pulled her to our room.

Lupita, master of the obvious, said, "She knows. I don't know how she knows, but she knows."

No catty retort escaped my lips. This time, I just nodded.

For the next few days, we behaved like the perfect young ladies Mrs. Menchaca thought we were. We were diligent in our schoolwork and industrious in our housework. We didn't want Mother to change her mind about our little prank, or heaven forbid, give us yard work.

Mother had surprised us by the calmness of her response. She was a highly volatile individual, set off by the smallest things—an unwashed dish by the sink could set her off on a tirade of gargantuan proportions.

We finally realized that Mother had actually thought our prank was funny. She told Father about it (not of our involvement, of course), and though he was not the type to encourage such useless, youthful antics (I sometimes wondered if Father had emerged from the womb fully grown), even he appreciated the humor in it.

It felt good to have been able to give Mother and Father some diversion from their constant battling. The truce wouldn't last long, of course.

Chapter 27

The tomato packing shed closed in mid-November for the winter and the population in the labor camps dwindled to just a few families. Father, who didn't like to be idle, drove his pickup to the Central Valley where pickers were still harvesting fresh produce. He bought in bulk and then came back to sell his purchases to small markets and groceries in the area. When he wasn't traveling he spent much of his spare time at the neighborhood bar.

On one of the rare occasions that Father was home, the prison siren went off. It was three days before Christmas.

"*Ay, Dios mío!*" Mother ran into the living room from the kitchen where she'd just put on a pot of beans. "What's that horrible noise?"

"It sounds like the prison siren." Father rose from the upholstered chair. He set his newspaper on the seat and walked to the front door.

I dropped the *Better Homes and Gardens* magazine I was perusing and Lupita rose from the coffee table where she was writing a letter to Terre, and we followed Father outside, Mother at our heels.

Several of our neighbors had assembled in their yards looking up at the sky as if they could actually see the sound of the siren.

"It's been a while since a prisoner escaped," Jimmy's mother commented as she tramped across the lawn toward us.

"Is that what that noise means?" Mother gasped, wrapping her arms around herself. It was quite chilly and, in our haste, we had neglected to grab our jackets.

"Don't worry, Beatriz, they'll catch him, or them. They always do," she said.

Father joined some of the neighborhood men a few houses down the street. I remembered how he'd put our fears about living so close to a prison to rest when we first moved to Soledad. Prison escapes were rare he had said, and besides, Soledad didn't house hard-core criminals, so we had nothing to fear. We had often seen prisoners on work detail outside the security fences clearing fields. We'd become accustomed to the sight of guards in their army green uniforms and caps leveling their rifles at the blue-clad prisoners. In the seven months we had lived in Soledad, we had so adjusted to our prison neighbors that we barely gave them a second thought, until today.

"There's nothing to be afraid of," Señora Menchaca said noticing mother's stricken expression. "They'll catch him before he gets too far. I doubt if he'll even make it a mile."

181

In that case, Jimmy's mother was correct. The prisoner, a thirty-two year old convicted robber, was picked up after only three hours on the loose. A Soledad police officer and prison correctional officer had made the arrest.

When Ellie and Ricky came to Soledad to spend Christmas with us (Father and Mother had forgiven them for eloping), the prison escape was the main topic of conversation at our house. When Isa called, all the way from Japan, where she and Marcos had been transferred, Mother told her how awful the siren sounded and how terrible it was to live so close to a prison.

Father grabbed the phone from Mother, scowling at her. But when he spoke to Isa, his face softened and his voice became tender. "How's Marquitos, *mi'ja*? And Teresita?" he crooned. Isa had had a baby girl in March of that year and had named her after Terre.

I knew that Father had always favored Isa, but it had never bothered me the way it did the others. I'm not sure why, except that perhaps I favored Isa, too. She had always been so good to me when she was at home. My other sisters treated me like a sister. But Isa, well, Isa treated me like a friend.

"How are you, Martita? How's school?" she asked when it was my turn to talk to her.

"It's okay," I said. "Sylvia and Roberta still won't give me the time of day. I don't know why they enjoy being so mean to me." I had written to her of my school troubles.

"They're just insecure. Don't lose any sleep over them."

"I don't, Isa," I lied. I hate to admit it, but it really bothered me that these two girls didn't like me. I was one of those people who wanted everybody to like them. I was the insecure one.

Raul and Terre (now Sister Michael Frances) also called, and when Father spoke to Terre, his expression was not as tender as it had been with Isa. Terre had always been a thorn in Father's side. After her phone call, Father brought out the whiskey, and Mother started in on him. Our quiet Christmas had ended.

*****

The holidays passed and school started again, and at the end of January, another prison break occurred, and this time, my family was directly involved.

The siren went off on a Wednesday afternoon when I was getting out of school. I could sense both the excitement and terror in the air as parents grabbed their younger children, the fourth and fifth graders, and hurried home. At ten o'clock that night when Lupita and I went to bed, the prisoners were still at large.

All evening Mother was jumpy. She had spent most of the night muttering against Father, who had not come home from the bar to, in her words, protect us. When he did come home later that night, we heard her confront him at the door. "Did they catch the prisoners yet?"

"No," he said, his voice booming and slightly slurred. "Don't worry. They're either long gone from the area or hiding in the hills. You've got nothing to worry about, *mi vida*."

Father must have tried to kiss Mother because she said, "Leave me alone. You know I can't stand the smell of that foul beer."

I plugged my ears with my pillow, not wanting to hear what was coming next.

The next day, the prisoners still had not been caught and their escape was the talk of the school. There were two of them, men in their early twenties, convicted of first degree robbery. It was rumored that they had climbed the twelve-foot high fence in the recreation yard. The boys were making bets on whether or not they would be caught. The girls, well, we were wondering if they were handsome, as ridiculous as that sounds.

Julia came home from school with me that Thursday and stayed for dinner. Father did not come home, so we ate without him. That always put Mother in a sour mood because it meant that she had to keep everything warm on the stove until he did finally show up. A knock on the front door startled us.

"I'll get it," I offered moving my chair back.

"No, I'll get it, *mi'ja*. Stay with Julia." Mother wiped her mouth on the cloth napkin as she rose.

A few minutes later, Mother came back into the kitchen, her face a pasty white, like the masa for flour tortillas. "Call the police, Lupita, this instant!"

"Why? What's wrong?" she asked.

"The prisoners are in our front yard."

Lupita, Julia, and I looked at each other and burst out laughing.

Mother scowled. "What's the matter with you? They asked me to call the police. They said they're tired of being on the run."

"They asked you to call the police?" Julia and I said in unison looking at each other.

"Lupita, call the police and tell them to come here this minute before the prisoners change their minds," she wailed.

We stopped laughing, and a perplexed Lupita rushed to the living room while Julia and I pushed our chairs back to follow her.

"Don't go out there, girls." Mother grabbed our arms as we went by. "Ay, I knew something like this would happen. Where's your father when we need him? Out drinking as usual. Ay, my head is starting to ache."

"We just want to look out the window, Mamá." I gently pulled away from her.

Julia and I peered through the open slats of the Venetian blinds and saw two bedraggled men hunched on our lawn, their blue shirt-tails out, their clothes soaked and streaked with dirt and mud. They were tired, wet, cold, and probably hungry. When the police car arrived a few minutes later, the convicts stood up with their hands in the air. They were whisked away with no incident, and another policeman stayed behind to talk to us. He extolled our calmness and bravery, particularly Mother's. After he left, she went to bed with one of her migraines.

When Father came home and rushed to his and Mother's bedroom not more than five minutes later (news travels fast in a small town, and Pasquale's is just a few blocks away), Mother's headache luckily prevented her from giving him the full force of her venom. We heard her lash out at him for a few minutes, but she quickly quieted down and we heard her mutter, "Ay, my head is killing me."

The next day at school, everyone wanted to hear about what had happened. Julia and I became minor celebrities. Even Sylvia and Roberta condescended to talk to me.

"Were you scared?" Sylvia asked.

"Actually, we were more surprised than anything," I said.

"What did they look like?"

"Pretty rough," I said. "They hadn't shaved and looked pretty bad from sleeping out in the cold."

"But were they handsome?" Sylvia demanded.

Julia and I looked at each other. Finally I said, "Very. One of them resembled James Dean. Right, Julia?"

Julia looked at me aghast, but quickly recovered. "Right, very handsome. Those pictures on the news didn't do them justice."

After that, Sylvia and Roberta began to nod at me in the hallways between classes, and once they even smiled.

*****

When the prison siren went off yet again the next month as we were eating breakfast, Mother scowled, put her hands on her hips and said, "What kind of a prison is that anyway? I thought prisons were supposed to keep prisoners in? That place is like a hotel where people come and go as they please!"

Lupita and I smiled at each other. Mother was right. It did seem that three break-outs in as many months was excessive.

"I heard that one of the last prisoners to escape had only a six-month sentence to serve." I looked at Father, who was sipping his *café con leche*. "Why would he risk adding to his sentence by escaping? It seems pretty stupid to me."

"*Sí, hi'ja*, it does seem stupid. But then, you have never lost your freedom." He looked out the kitchen window above the sink, his thick eyebrows furrowed together. "During the Revolution, my father was incarcerated twice. The first time he was thrown in the state penitentiary in Monterrey. The second time he was held by the Villistas at the Governor's Palace. My mother had to pay huge ransoms, several thousand pesos, to get him out. He told me that being behind bars was the worst thing that had ever happened to him. He said that he would have done anything to get out. And he was only kept in jail for a few days."

"But he wasn't in prison because he had done something wrong," I ventured.

"His crime was that he was rich, and in México in those days being rich was a grave offense. The revolutionaries didn't care that my father had worked by the sweat of his brow to become rich, that he employed hundreds of people and paid them good wages. No, they only cared about getting the money the easy way, by stealing it. They were thieves and crooks and murderers."

Lupita and I glanced at each other uneasily. Father rarely talked about his childhood in México. As he spoke and his voice became harsh, I realized why. He had bitter memories about what the Revolution had done to his family. Even so, he was the most patriotic Mexican I had ever known, and this perplexed me. "Then why don't you become an American citizen if you hate México so much?" I asked, my voice tentative.

"I don't hate México, *mi'ja*," he looked at me with his chocolate eyes, no trace of malice. "I love my country as I love my own mother, but I hate what happened there. There is a saying in México, 'One bright man and a thousand fools, that is a Revolution.' There were some brilliant and honorable men who were leaders in the Revolution. Unfortunately, the vast majority of their followers were illiterate, uneducated bullies, bent on revenge. No good could come of that." He rose from the table. "As for the escaped prisoners, hopefully, they'll have enough sense not to come to this house." He glanced at Mother, his expression serious. "She'll tongue lash them to death."

Lupita and I laughed.

Mother didn't.

The prisoners, two *Mexicanos* this time, were captured in Santa Clara two weeks after their escape—Father said that *Mexicanos* were more resourceful than gringos and that's why these prisoners managed to remain at large for a much longer time. When they were caught, however, the men were in possession of marijuana and heroin, so several years were added to their six-month sentences (which they had initially incurred for theft). So, they may have been more resourceful than the gringos, but they sure didn't seem any brighter.

When I mentioned this to Father, his response was, "I wouldn't be surprised if the police planted the drugs on the men. Gringos can't stand it when a *Mexicano* gets the better of them."

Father's world was black and white, tit for tat, and as I have found, it is hard to live in a world like that.

Chapter 28

The harvest season of 1957 began with spinach in mid-March, followed by lettuce a few weeks later. Contractors trucked *braceros* in from México, and the labor camps began to bustle with men. Julia worked in the fields along with her parents and siblings, mostly on the weekends, and it was from her that I learned about the conditions under which the seasonal laborers had to work. Julia (who would one day work alongside César Chavez), did not like the contractors who brought the *braceros* into the Valley. She said that they were getting rich off the poor Méxicans who had to pay for their travel expenses to and from México, and to and from the fields. They even had to pay room and board (the contractors took the money out of their pay). She also complained that the contractors took no care for their safety.

"Just half a block from my house," she told me one night when I was visiting her, "a labor bus carrying *braceros* to work exploded."

"How did it happen?"

"The contractor put gas tanks in the back with the workers. The tanks were old and leaking. They exploded and killed most of the men in the bus. It was horrible. I heard the explosion and ran out to see what had happened. Many of the *braceros* burned to death."

I felt uneasy when Julia talked about the labor contractors, most of whom were Mexican American. My own father had been a contractor for many years, and I know he had made a lot of money working for the *bracero* program at one time. "You know, my father was a labor contractor, and he still sometimes gets jobs for migrants."

"Your father is the exception," Julia said. "My father said he never met a more honorable man than Don Miguel. Besides, I don't notice you living in a big mansion or anything. It's obvious he didn't get rich off of those less fortunate."

Father had once been a millionaire; at least that's what Mother had told me. I could not reconcile the view that Julia had of contractors with what I knew of my own father. But I did know this—if Father had been ruthless, as Julia had said the California contractors were, then he would not have sold all his land in Ruby to pay his workers. I even remember him saying, "It's good to be rich, but not at the cost of your soul."

Julia was passionate about doing something to improve working conditions for the field workers, and I admired her. Although I agreed that something needed to be done to help them, I didn't feel the fervent calling that she did. Perhaps it was because I had never worked in the fields. I don't know. But even then, I knew that rabble-rousing wasn't my style.

When the harvest began, Julia worked only on Saturdays and Sunday afternoons until school ended in May. Many other families, however, allowed their children to work before and after school. I knew this because several of my classmates would come to school and fall asleep at their desks. They would get up at four in the morning to be out in the fields at five and work until school started. Then, right after school they would go back out to the fields and sometimes work until midnight. I felt sorry for those kids. I realized how fortunate I was that Father believed in education.

At the end of the school year, carrot season started again. It was a never-ending cycle of low-paying field work, and I felt bad for Julia who spent so much time out in the fields. When tomato season started early that year, in mid-July, Father took Lupita and me along as he had the previous summer to work as labelers. His and Mother's fighting had escalated over the previous months—the more he drank, the more they fought, the more they fought, the more he drank. The final straw came one hot summer day in July when Mother made a surprise visit to the packing shed.

*****

Lupita and I sat at our usual spots under a tree sponging and swiping, sponging and swiping. We recognized the Buick as it swung into the gravel parking lot, but could barely see Mother, who was under five feet tall, behind the wheel. She stopped the car with a jerk—she didn't drive much—then opened the door and climbed out of the car, holding a rather large picnic basket.

Surprised, I walked over to her. "What are you doing here, Mamá?"

"I made a pot of menudo and brought some for you, Lupita, and your father." She moved the red and white checkered cloth. "Look, I even have some chopped onions and limes, and I made some fresh corn tortillas. Where's your Father, *hija*?"

I thought it was a nice gesture on Mother's part, bringing us such a great lunch. But I also thought it odd. Mother had never done such a thing before. As far as I knew, she had never set foot on the packing shed property.

"He's in the shed. I'll go get him," I offered.

"No, no, I'll go," she said.

She made her way across the dirt parking area to the wooden platform, her short auburn hair glistening in the sunlight. She was wearing one of her best dresses, a green dress with a white collar, and three-quarter length sleeves with white cuffs. She was even wearing pumps. What was she up to?

Not more than five minutes after she had disappeared into the packing shed, Mother emerged with Father, whose expression was ominous. His bushy eyebrows were furrowed together and his lips were pursed. He seemed to be propelling Mother toward the car with his right hand, which had a tight grip on her elbow. When they reached the car, he opened the front door, grabbed the basket from Mother's arm and flung it onto the front seat.

Lupita and I ran over to them. "Papá, what are you doing? What's wrong?" I asked. I glanced into the car. He had hurled the basket with such force that the greasy, rust-colored menudo broke out of its plastic container and was now dripping down the passenger window. The sliced limes and chopped onion pieces were strewn all over the green vinyl seat.

"I will not be spied on," Father growled, pushing Mother into the car.

"*Desagradecido*! Ingrate!" Mother shouted. "You must have a guilty conscience to think something like that!"

"I don't have anything to feel guilty about," he shot back.

Many of the workers, now on their lunch break, had gathered on the loading dock and were looking at us. "Papá! Mamá! Stop it! People are watching," I implored.

"Let them watch!" Mother cried. "It's about time people see him for what he is—a liar, a drunk, and an adulterer!"

The expression on Father's face turned even more menacing and he raised his hand as if to slap her.

"No!" I screamed, startling them both. "Stop it!"

Father moved away from the car. He looked at Lupita and me. "Take her home," he said gruffly. "Both of you. And don't come back."

Lupita and I were both sobbing by then, and I wanted the earth to swallow me up. I would have welcomed an earthquake at that moment.

Father strode back to the packing shed. "Everyone back to work," he said loudly. The workers dispersed as he lumbered up the steps to the loading dock and into the shed.

Lupita and I cleaned the front seat and window as best we could, all the while sobbing and sniffling.

Mother had not uttered a word, but she was breathing heavily and her face was flushed.

"Come on, Mamacita. Let's go home," I said, using the diminutive form for Mother, something I rarely did. I helped her onto the cleaned front passenger seat, and then slid in the back.

Lupita drove south on the highway, passing the prison.

"I can't take the fighting any more, Mamá." I paused, then continued, "I'm going back to Texas."

"Me too," Lupita said between sniffles.

Mother didn't say anything for a while, then she said in a low, trembling voice, "He doesn't love me anymore."

Lupita glanced back at me. We had often talked about that very thing. I wondered why Mother was questioning it now. Why not all the other times he was mean to her?

I said, "Of course he loves you, Mamá. It's just that . . . well, Father has a drinking problem."

"He wasn't drunk today."

I didn't respond. She was right. Father hadn't been drunk. He never drank at work. So what had precipitated his strange behavior? "Who knows what's going on with Papá. All I know is that I can't take it anymore. All the fighting and screaming. It's been going on for too long. I'll never be able to show my face at the packing shed again. It's too humiliating." I buried my head in my hands and wept.

When we got home, Lupita and I ran to our rooms. I began thrashing about looking for my suitcase. "I'm getting outta here today." I found my suitcase in the back of the closet and began throwing clothes in it.

Lupita sat on the edge of her bed, dumbstruck.

"Well? What are you going to do? Stay here and watch them kill each other?"

She got up slowly, bent over and pulled her suitcase out from under the bed. "What about Mamá?" she said in a small voice.

"She can do whatever she wants, but I'm leaving," I said with more bravado than I felt.

Mother walked into our room just then. I could tell by her pained expression that she was torn between leaving and staying. She glanced at our suitcases. "You're both underage. You can't go to Texas without me," she said.

"Then come with us, Mamá. Don't make us stay here one more night!" I sat on the bed and started to cry again.

"Has it really been that terrible?"

"How can you even ask that?" I said.

She sat down next to Lupita and put her arm around my sister's shoulder, giving her a hug. A few minutes later, she rose, her lips set in a determined line. "Take only what you can fit in your suitcases. We'll send for the rest of our things later."

I now feel bad that we didn't even say good-bye to Father. He may have been a bad husband, but he was a good father, and he didn't deserve that. But our love for our Father gave way to something more expedient.

We had to get out quickly for Mother's sake, and the best way was to make a clean break. She left a note that said, "We went back to Texas," and suitcases in hand, we trudged to the Greyhound Bus Depot on Front Street to catch the late afternoon bus to LA.

*****

We got to the bus depot about an hour early, so Lupita and I went to the drugstore to buy some books to read on the bus. I purchased *Peyton Place*, and predictably, Lupita got *A Nun's Story*, both popular books at the time. We sat on the bench in front of the depot watching cars and trucks go back and forth on the street. I thought about Julia out in some vegetable field in this hot weather. I was leaving without saying good-bye to her and that made me feel even worse than I already felt. She had been such a good friend to me. I hoped she would forgive me. I would write to her and tell her what happened. She would understand. Still, I felt as if I was leaving things unfinished. I felt tears stinging my eyes, and I wiped them away.

Finally, we boarded the bus and I sat with Mother on the first leg of the journey. Mother immediately took out her needles and began to crochet a doily. About an hour away from Soledad, she stopped, putting the needles on her lap. "She had brown hair, Marta. When I saw her, I knew that your Father didn't love me anymore." A tear rolled down her cheek.

"Mamá, what are you talking about?"

"That woman in the packing shed. She had brown hair."

"What does that have to do with anything?"

"Your Father's girlfriends all had red hair, like mine. I never liked that he had other women, you understand, but it made it less painful. It always made me feel as if he thought he was with me. But this new woman, she has brown hair. Her hair is brown." Tears fell in rivulets down her cheeks.

I didn't reply. What could I say? It dawned on me that the reason Mother consented to our leaving was because of some strange notion about a woman with brown hair. Well, if that's what it took to get her out of there, thank God for the brown-haired woman.

*****

I don't think Mother knew that she would never see Father again when she left Soledad that day. I know it didn't occur to me. But that's what happened. Father was angry when he found out we had gone back to Texas without his knowledge, much less his consent. I don't think he even once considered the part he played in our departure. All he knew was that his wife had left him, and no matter what he had done to deserve it, that was unforgivable. He never held it against Lupita or me. Mother was the target of his anger, as she always had been. When she went back to Soledad a few years later to visit, he refused to see her.

I feel so bad about having forced Mother to leave. I often wonder if I hadn't insisted on leaving, if Mother would have stayed with Father, the brown-haired woman notwithstanding. They never divorced. It was never even brought up to my knowledge. I always thought it was because they were Catholic. But now I'm not so sure.

My parents' marriage broke down because of Father's drinking; but I also know that they separated because of me. This has been a hard burden to carry all these years, especially when I consider how acutely Mother grieved when Father died. She cried for days, and on several occasions, she looked at me through tear-stained eyes and said, "If I could have seen him one last time, just one last time before he died."

My guilt was profound.

Epilogue

Isabel

Mother, Marta, and Lupita arrived back in Ruby in late July, 1957. The girls offered to work the rest of the summer in the fields to help Mother with money, but to their surprise, Mother, who had been trying to get us out in the fields since Father's bankruptcy, said no. "We did not raise you to be field workers," she told them, echoing Father's remonstration.

She, however, found work in one of Ruby's tomato packing sheds as a sorter. On the off season, she began to sell Natural Glow beauty products, and within two years, had earned the pink Cadillac for high sellers. Watching her drive that Cadillac around the dusty town of Ruby was a sight to see. She did so well as a cosmetics saleswoman that she never went back to the packing shed. Without Father to hinder her, she became an American citizen in 1959. And Mother, who had been plagued with severe headaches all her married life, never had another migraine again after she and my sisters returned to Ruby. I always knew that Mother had an entrepreneurial spirit; she could have been a great asset to Father had he been able to throw off the shackles of his upbringing.

Lupita did not follow in Terre's footsteps as we all thought she would. She fell in love with a grocery store clerk, Martín Loredo, whom she met at a church prayer meeting. After she graduated from high school, they married and had five children in quick succession. Although Lupita did not become a nun, she found work at the Catholic church in Ruby running the children's catechism program. She eventually became a lay minister and a Guadalupana (a member of a Catholic organization that venerates the Virgen de Guadalupe). We teasingly call her Sister Lulu. Marta married Daniel, the *morenito*, in 1962, and he turned out to be a better catch than Ellie had predicted. He and Marta moved to California and lived with Father for a while. From Father, Daniel learned the produce business. He and Marta eventually returned to Texas where he opened a chain of grocery stores. Daniel is now one of the wealthiest men in the Río Grande Valley, and the house he bought for Marta and their children could rival any pictured in *Better Homes and Gardens*.

Terre got her Ph.D. in education, and is the principal at an all-girl Catholic high school in San Antonio, a job she loves, and for which she is well suited—there being few men around. Ellie was a homemaker for many years, but after Ricky died, she became a translater for the

Immigration Service—also a job well suited considering she was always so vocal—and she still lives in California. I have made homemaking my career, and Marcos and I settled in San Antonio after he retired. And as for Raulito, my brother, he eventually went to college on the GI Bill and got his degree, and a commission as an U.S. Air Force officer just a few years before Father died. I know that Father was extremely proud—not only of Raul, but of all of us.

*****

Father died on Valentine's Day, 1971. I have always thought it was ironic that he died on the day for lovers, considering his ill-fated love life. Ellie, who lived in Fresno, was closest to Papá, so she and Ricky identified and claimed his body. They made arrangements for his flight to Texas because Mother insisted that he be buried in Ruby.

Mother hadn't seen Father in fourteen years, and we didn't want her to see him then, particularly after what the mortician told me and Terre.

"Mrs. Benavides, Sister Michael, may I speak with you privately?" The tall, somber-looking man gently pulled us away from Mother and the others in the viewing room. "As you can see, the casket is closed. In my humble opinion, I think it is best that we keep it that way. It is my understanding that your sister, Mrs. Hernández, has seen the body. Perhaps she can explain."

We motioned for Ellie. "Mr. Gutiérrez says that we should have a closed casket," I said.

Ellie nodded. "I agree."

"Is it that bad?" Terre asked.

She nodded again, tears running down her face.

Mother walked over to our group, a handkerchief clutched in her hand. "What's going on?"

"We think that it's best if you don't see him like this, Mamá," I said.

"I want to see him."

"I don't think that's a good idea, Mamá," Terre said.

"I don't care what you think. He is my husband, and I have the say in this matter." She looked at the mortician. "Open the casket."

We knew better than to fight her.

I put my arm around her and we walked slowly to the ebony casket, Terre, Ellie, Lupita, and Raul following close behind. Daniel was behind them, holding up Marta. The mortician grabbed the gold-plated handle and lifted the top portion up. Father had always been a big man, but nothing could have prepared me for what I saw in that casket. His face, in fact, his entire body was terribly bloated; he didn't look at all like Papá. I heard my sisters' collective gasp and then wrenching cries. Raul blew his nose in his handkerchief. Tears flooded my eyes and through the blur, I glanced at Mother. Her eyes were red and swollen; her features contorted in pain. Tears streamed down her cheeks. She reached out and touched this man's face, this man who didn't look like the Father I had loved so desperately. In a tremulous voice that I could barely hear, she whispered, "I forgive you, *mi amor*. I forgive you. Rest in peace." She made the sign of the cross on his forehead, pulled her hand back slowly, and wept.

*****

Mother did consent to a closed casket for the service after she saw Father. But Tío Gabriel wanted to see him, and in deference to their close relationship as first cousins, Mother had the casket opened just for him. I have never seen a man cry like my Tío Gabriel did that day, and his grief deeply moved me.

Several hundred people came to Father's funeral. It is a testament to the kind of man he was that so many people paid their respects—people he hadn't seen in over fifteen years, those who had migrated with him to Mississippi, people he had helped, people he and mother had sponsored in baptism, confirmation, and marriage. There were also several friends from California. They came in droves to offer their condolences, and they were a great comfort to my family.

*****

Now, all these years later, when I think of Father, I remember how he used to hold me in his arms when I was a little girl, uttering soothing words to me in the beautiful Spanish he spoke so well. Not the ugly Tex-Mex that is spoken so frequently now, but in that beautiful, musical language of our Spanish ancestors. He called me, "Isabelita, *hija de mi corazón*," as he stroked my hair.

I picture him with one foot in México and one foot in the United States, as if he were standing on a map of the two countries. He could not declare for one, because he could not revoke the other. I remember him saying, "Denouncing México would be like denouncing my own mother." He was a man without a country.

Though he did admire many things about the United States, particularly the fact that a man could better himself if he worked hard enough, he brought with him the mores and customs of a country in conflict with the American way of life. His marriage to Mother, someone from a different social class, was his way of acknowledging he would no longer be subject to the rules of Méxican society. But I believe that his upbringing, even after all the years he lived in the United States, proved too strong.

Why did my parents separate after thirty years of marriage? Was it

195

the bankruptcy or the womanizing or the drinking, or a combination of all three things? Or were those things symptoms of something else? Was Marta the one who pulled the final brick that toppled their marriage?

I know she was not.

Marta needs to put her heart and mind to rest. My little sister did not cause my parents' marriage to end. That marriage was doomed almost from the start. In fact, I'm surprised my parents stayed together as long as they did, considering everything.

I have now been married to Marcos for more than fifty years, and I can say for a fact that marriage is a living thing, not an institution, like so many of this generation refer to it. This living entity must be nurtured in a loving environment or it will fail to thrive. It will die.

Ellie told us that Father was living in migrant housing on the outskirts of Soledad when he died, a little room with a single bed, a nightstand, a chair, and a light bulb dangling from the ceiling. It breaks my heart to think of him there, all alone, when he could have been in the bosom of a family that loved him. She said that on his nightstand were three things: a photo album of all the family pictures we had ever sent him, a framed picture of Mother when they first got married, and a book written in Spanish. The title of the book was *Una Vez, Yo Fui Rico*, roughly translated as *Once Upon a Time, I Was Rich.*

Father was rich. Mother was his gold mine. He just couldn't see it.